LABOUR RELATIONS AND THE NEW UNIONISM IN CONTEMPORARY BRAZIL

ST ANTONY'S SERIES
General Editor: Eugene Rogan (1997–), Fellow of St Antony's College, Oxford

Recent titles include:

Mark Brzezinski
THE STRUGGLE FOR CONSTITUTIONALISM IN POLAND

Peter Carey (editor)
BURMA

Stephanie Po-yin Chung
CHINESE BUSINESS GROUPS IN HONG KONG AND POLITICAL
CHANGE IN SOUTH CHINA, 1900–25

Ralf Dahrendorf
AFTER 1989

Alex Danchev
ON SPECIALNESS

Roland Dannreuther
THE SOVIET UNION AND THE PLO

Noreena Hertz
RUSSIAN BUSINESS RELATIONSHIPS IN THE WAKE OF REFORM

Iftikhar H. Malik
STATE AND CIVIL SOCIETY IN PAKISTAN

Steven McGuire
AIRBUS INDUSTRIE

Yossi Shain and Aharon Klieman (editors)
DEMOCRACY

William J. Tompson
KHRUSHCHEV

Marguerite Wells
JAPANESE HUMOUR

Yongjin Zhang and Rouben Azizian (editors)
ETHNIC CHALLENGES BEYOND BORDERS

St Antony's Series
Series Standing Order ISBN 0–333–71109–2
(*outside North America only*)

You can receive future titles in this series as they are published by placing a standing order. Please contact your bookseller or, in case of difficulty, write to us at the address below with your name and address, the title of the series and the ISBN quoted above.

Customer Services Department, Macmillan Distribution Ltd
Houndmills, Basingstoke, Hampshire RG21 6XS, England

Labour Relations and the New Unionism in Contemporary Brazil

Maurício Rands Barros
Professor of Labour Law
Federal University of Pernambuco
Brazil

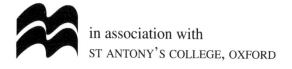

in association with
ST ANTONY'S COLLEGE, OXFORD

First published in Great Britain 1999 by
MACMILLAN PRESS LTD
Houndmills, Basingstoke, Hampshire RG21 6XS and London
Companies and representatives throughout the world

A catalogue record for this book is available from the British Library.

ISBN 0–333–73616–8

 First published in the United States of America 1999 by
ST. MARTIN'S PRESS, INC.,
Scholarly and Reference Division,
175 Fifth Avenue, New York, N.Y. 10010

ISBN 0–312–21846–X

Library of Congress Cataloging-in-Publication Data
Barros, Maurício Rands, 1961–
Labour relations and the new unionism in contemporary Brazil /
Maurício Rands Barros.
p.   cm. — (St. Antony's series)
Includes bibliographical references and index.
ISBN 0–312–21846–X (cloth)
1. Industrial relations—Brazil—Recife.   2. Trade-unions—Brazil–
–Recife.   3. Political participation—Brazil—Recife.   4. Central
Unica dos Trabalhadores (Brazil)   I. Title.   II. Series.
HD8290.R43B37   1999
331'.0981'34—dc21
98–44284
CIP

This book is printed on paper suitable for recycling and made from fully managed and
sustained forest sources.

10   9   8   7   6   5   4   3   2   1
08   07   06   05   04   03   02   01   00   99

Printed and bound in Great Britain by
Antony Rowe Ltd, Chippenham, Wiltshire

To Patrícia, Tatiana, Diego, Rands and Célia

Contents

List of Tables and Figures

Tables

Figures

Preface

This book links the development of the Brazilian system of labour relations to the expansion of the all too limited citizenship of the workers, with an emphasis on the contribution of the 'new unionism' which emerged in the late 1970s. It analyses the complex interplay of the old elements of the state corporatist framework introduced in the 1930s with those of pluralist proposals advanced by the main employeee and employers' organisations. Following the trajectory of the 'new unionism', we identify the process of gradual implementation of its alternative to the current hybrid corporatism. Such an alternative, summed up in the phrase 'collective labour contract', entails different organisational arrangements and practices which have consequences for the attitudes of both the leadership and the rank-and-file towards work-related and wider socio-political matters alike. In order to ascertain the effect of the alternative model on the attitudes of the rank-and-file, rather than merely on the union officials, a survey was carried out with urban workers of Recife. Since attitude changes were scrutinised with a view to assessing the contribution of the 'new unionism' to the expansion of workers' citizenship, a scale was constructed to measure attitude differences which might stem from workers' exposure to different types of unionism. We show that the ongoing process of transition from 'regulated citizenship' towards 'conquered citizenship' is in debt to the 'new unionism' alternative model in a threefold sense: it has been able to enlarge the country's agenda by asserting labour as an important player in alliance with other popular sectors; it has helped to change the corporatist system of labour relations by enhancing the autonomy of the relevant actors; and finally, not least, it has gradually forged critical and participatory attitudes which shape a political culture more suitable to the extension of the workers' citizenship.

MAURÍCIO RANDS BARROS

Acknowledgements

A book cannot be credited to sign just one author without failing to do justice to a number of people who helped him or her to develop and express ideas. Knowledge is fundamentally a collective endeavour, by its very nature. Whatever contribution a piece of scientific work may afford, the weight of the common efforts of scholars, colleagues and friends is not negligible. Authorship is therefore acceptable only on the condition that the 'collective author' is properly recognised.

Even if unfair omissions are unavoidable in any such attempts, among the many people and organisations to whom I feel indebted I will stress my gratitude to the following.

Hermínio Martins, under whose supervision I wrote the thesis from which this book originated, was much more than a supervisor. His extraordinary erudition and lucidity guided this work and helped me to grasp some of the most important attributes of a true intellectual. Our long-lasting tutorials were moments of joy, intellectual challenge and much learning. For all he has taught me and his careful dealing with this work, my gratitude to him is enormous.

Alexandre Rands Barros helped me with the conception and development of the statistical test employed in the analysis of the survey. But in addition to his generosity and expertise, his encouragement was crucial in making me believe that the task of making this research would be achieved at all.

Patrícia Ferreira, my beloved and eternal 'girl-friend', has always made life really worth being lived. Without her love and willing support I would not have been able to write the book. She also helped in the research by integrating the team of interviewers who carried out the survey and collecting other data.

Analice Amazonas and Almeri Bezerra de Mello played a crucial part in encouraging me to pursue my postgraduate studies in Oxford. Their warm friendship made life more amenable in Oxford and in Recife.

Jorge Ventura de Morais shared with me his vast knowledge through enlightening discussions on the Brazilian new unionism. His thesis and other essays also provided many insights for my own work.

An immense gratitude goes also to Alcides Spíndola who helped me in many different ways during my periods in Oxford. I am likewise extremely indebted to all my colleagues and friends of 'RR Advogados Associados' who had to shoulder a heavier burden of work during my absences. My friend Ricardo Estêvão de Oliveira receives my thanks in the name of the group.

In Oxford, many other friends made me feel at home. They are remembered through my dear David and Márcia Saitovitch whose warmth, assistance and all-night chats are unforgettable.

Nigel Knight deserves many thanks for helping the orthographic and grammatical review of the drafts.

I would also like to thank the researchers who helped me in the survey of the urban workers in Recife. The effort and diligence of André Gustavo de Vasconcelos, Fernando Antônio da Silva, Maria Lindomar da Silva and Patrícia Ferreira were deeply appreciated.

The financial support of the 'Conselho Nacional de Desenvolvimento Científico e Tecnológico – CNPq' was vital in making this study feasible. Its programme of supporting Brazilian students' post-graduation studies deserves our full commendation.

Thanks also to my parents for nourishing me with their love and support.

I wish to express my gratitude to all the people who contributed to the field research by volunteering to give oral testimonies, transmitting their ideas and helping with data collection.

My final thanks are devoted to the workers and militants whose struggles keep alive the dream of a 'full citizenship for all'.

MAURÍCIO RANDS BARROS

List of Abbreviations

ABRH   Brazilian Association of Human Resources
AFL-CIO   American Federation of Labour – Congress of Industrial Organisations
ANAMATRA   National Association of the Judges of the Labour Court ('Associação Nacional dos Magistrados Trabalhistas')
ARENA   Alliance for National Renovation ('Aliança Renovadora Nacional')
BNDES   National Social Development Bank ('Banco Nacional do Desenvolvimen to Social')
CEAS   Social Action and Studies Centre ('Centro de Estudos e Ação Social')
CGIL   Confederazione Generale Italiana dei Lavoratori
CGT   Central General Central of Workers ('Central Geral dos Trabalhadores')
CGT   Confederação General Confederation of Workers ('Confederação Geral dos Trabalhadores')
CIPA   International Commission for Accident Prevention ('Comissão Interna de Prevenção de Acidentes')
CISL   Confederazione Italiana Sindacati Lavoratori
CLT   Consolidation of the Labour Laws ('Consolidação das Leis do Trabalho')
CNA   National Confederation of Agriculture ('Confederação Nacional da Agricultura')
CNC   National Confederation of Commerce ('Confederação Nacional do Comércio')
CNI   National Confederation of Industry ('Confederação Nacional das Indústrias')
CNS   National Council of Rubber Tappers ('Conselho Nacional dos Seringueiros')
CNT   National Confederation of Transport ('Confederação Nacional dos Transportes')
CNTC   National Confederation of Workers in Commerce ('Confederação Nacional dos Trabalhadores no Comércio')
CNTI   National Confederation of Industrial Workers ('Confederação Nacional dos Trabalhadores nas Indústrias')

CNTM National Confederation of Dock Workers ('Confederação Nacional dos Trabalhadores Marítimos')

CONCLAT National Conference of the Working Class ('Conferência Nacional das Classes Trabalhadoras'), later on, National Co-ordination of the Working Class ('Cordenação Nacional das Classes Trabalhadoras')

CONTAG National Confederation of Rural Workers ('Confederação Nacional dos Trabalhadores na Agriculture')

CONTEC National Confederation of Bank Workers ('Confederação Nacional dos Trabalhadores nos Estabelecimentos de Crédito')

CUT United Workers Central ('Central Única dos Trabalhadores')

DESEP Social Economic Studies Department ('Departamento de Estudos Sócio Econômicos')

DIAP Inter-Union Department of Parliamentary Advisory ('Departamento Intersindical de Assessoria Parlamentar')

DIEESE Inter-Union Department for Statistics and Socio-Economic Studies ('Departamento Intersindical de Estudos Estatísticos e Sócio-econômicos')

DRT Regional Labour Office ('Delegacia Regional do Trabalho')

ENCLAT State Meeting of the Working Classes ('Encontro Estadual das Classes Trabalhadoras')

ENTOES National Meeting of the Workers Opposing the Union Structure ('Encontro Nacional dos Trabalhadores em Oposição à Estrutura Sindical')

EPA 1975 Employment Protection Act

EP(C)1978 Employmento Protection (Consolidation) Act

FEBRABAN Brazilian Federation of Banks ('Federação Brasileira dos Bancos')

FENABAN National Federation of Banks ('Federação Nacional dos Bancos')

FETAPE Rural Workers' Federation of Pernambuco ('Federação dos Trabalhadores Rurais de Pernambuco')

FGTS Fund for Compensation for the Time of Service ('Fundo de Garantia do Tempo de Serviço')

FIEPE Industrial Federation of Pernambuco ('Federação das Indústrias de Pernambuco)

FIESPE Federation of Industries of the State of São Paulo ('Federação das Indústrias do Estado de São Paulo')

FOSP   Worker Federation of São Paulo ('Federação Operária de São Paulo')

FS   Union Power ('Força Sindical')

IAPB   Bank Employees Pensions Institute ('Instituto de Aposentadorias e Pensões dos Bancários')

IAPC   Commerce Employees Pensions Institute ('Instituto de Aposentadorias e Pensões dos Comerciários')

IAPI   Industrial Workers Pensions Institute ('Instituto de Aposentadorias e Pensões dos Industriários')

IBGE   Brazilian Foundation of Geography and Statistics ('Fundação Instituto Brasileiro de Geografia e Estatística')

IDESP   Development and Socio-Political Studies Institute ('Instituto de Desenvolvimento e Estudos Sócio-Políticos')

ILO   International Labour Organisation (Office)

LAFEPE   Pharmaceutical Laboratory of Pernambuco ('Laboratório Farmacêutico de Pernambuco')

MDB   Democratic Brazilian Movement ('Movimento Democrático Brasileiro')

MG   Minas Gerais State ('Estado de Minas Gerais')

MR-8   Revolutionary Movement October 8th ('Movimento Revolucionário 08 de Outubro')

MT   Labour Ministry ('Ministério do Trabalho')

MT   Mato Grosso State ('Estado de Mato Grosso')

OAB   Brazilian Lawyers Association ('Ordem dos Advogados do Brasil')

OWW   Organisation Within the Workplace

PCB   Brazilian Communist Party ('Partido Comunista Brasileiro')

PC   do B Communist Party of Brazil ('Partido Comunista do Brasil')

PCBR   Revolutionary Brazilian Communist Party

PDS   Social Democratic Party ('Partido Democrático Social')

PDT   Democratic Labour Party ('Partido Democrático Trabalhista')

PE   Pernambuco State ('Estado de Pernambuco')

PIS-PASEP   Social Integration Programme ('Programa de Integração Social')

PMDB   Party of the Brazilian Democratic Movement ('Partido do Movimento Democrático Brasileiro')

PNBE   National Thought of the Entrepreneurial Grassroots ('Pensamento Nacional das Bases Epresariais')

PSDB   Party of the Brazilian Social Democracy ('Partido Social Democrático Brasileiro')

PSTU   United Socialist Workers' Party ('Partido Socialista dos Trabalhadores Unificados')

PT   Workers' Party ('Partido dos Trabalhadores')

RFFESA Federal Railway Company ('Rede Ferroviária Federal S.A.)

SINDPD   Data Processing Workers' Union ('Sindicato dos Trabalhadores em Processamento de Dados')

SINFAVEA   Employers' National Union of Motorcar Industry ('Sindicato National dos Fabricantes de Veículos Automotores')

SINTRAFARMA   Pharmaceutical Industry Workers' Union ('Sindicato dos Trabalhadores na Indústria Farmacêutica')

SINTTEL   Telecommunications Workers' Union ('Sindicato dos Trabalhadores Telefônicos')

SNI   National Service of Information ('Serviço Nacional de Informações')

SP   São Paulo State ('Estado de São Paulo')

TELPE   Telecommunications of Pernambuco Company ('Companhia Telefônica de Pernambuco')

TRT   Regional Labour Court ('Tribunal Regional do Trabalho')

TST   Superior Labour Court ('Tribunal Superior do Trabalho')

TURL(C)A   1992 Trade Union Labour Relations Consolidation Act

UIL   Unione Italiana del Lavoro

UNE   Student National Union ('União Nacional dos Estudantes')

USI   Independent United Nations ('União Sindical Independente')

1 Introduction

1 PRESENTATION

This book is about Brazilian workers. It identifies their return to the public arena from 1978 onwards as a turning point in their quest for full citizenship in a country where the majority of the people are still pre-civic. When, throughout the 1980s, the labour movement was fading elsewhere, the Brazilian workers rose up against a democratisation engineered through a pact between the elites and forced the agenda to induce a higher priority for the social question. Their mobilisation, epitomised in the advent of the so-called 'new unionism',[1] paved the way to a new conception of labour relations and succeeded in addressing issues far beyond the limits of capital–labour relations. They resisted iniquitous working conditions and the steady process of wage deterioration in a decade hit by economic stagnation and soaring inflation. In this journey they cemented a broad alliance with the rest of the Brazilian people, having incorporated demands for health care, education, housing, improvement of social services, land reform and against the high cost of living. Very often these demands were summarised in the 'quest for citizenship'. They also proved capable of forging new conceptions of labour relations challenging the corporatist framework bequeathed by Getúlio Vargas in the 1930s. Such a distinctive approach led the new unionism to build up an alternative model of unionism and labour relations, entailing varied structures and practices that have shaped distinctive workers' attitudes towards citizenship. As we shall seek to demonstrate, a novel political culture, proper to an active citizen, has been gradually emerging out of their struggle and alternative conceptions.

2   REPLACING CORPORATISM: THE NEW UNIONISM AND WORKERS' CITIZENSHIP

The experience of the new unionism brought to light the inappropriateness of the Brazilian system of industrial relations inherited from the 1930s. Tensions between the institutions of state corporatism – the framework still prevalent – and the proposals and practices concerned with a more pluralist mould soon became apparent. As will be discussed in Chapter 2, state corporatism represents a tradition of organisation of interest groups in which the state structures and regulates such groups. Industrial relations are centred in the State, little ground being left for the autonomy of the parties and direct settlement of conflicts. In Brazil, even a specific judiciary apparatus was conceived – the Labour Court – in order to settle both collective and individual disputes between labour and capital.

The alternative conceptions and practices that gradually developed among the ranks of the new unionism represented a rupture with long-standing traditions of the country's system of labour relations. The new unionism challenged the corporative patterns of intervention of the State both in union organisation and in conflict settlement by advocating that, instead, it should provide enabling collective rights supportive of union action and collective negotiation, such as the right to strike, the prohibition of retaliation for workers' participation in unions and industrial actions, union autonomy and so on. Such a reaction to the core tenets of state corporatism seems to grow out of workers' perception of the constraints it poses for the legitimacy, freedom and strength of the union movement. The repressive intervention of the State, which was particularly exacerbated during the military regime of 1964–85, led to the rejection of the model and to the claim for enlarged areas of autonomous organisation and direct bargaining backed by rank-and-file militancy.

Whilst addressing the unprecedented conjuncture of the re-democratisation initiated in the late 1970s, the alternative conceptions may be traced back to old traditions of the labour movement which flourished in the first half of the century. There are contrasting emphases in the interpretations of the labour movement at that period, specially in respect of the issue of the original reaction of workers and left-wing militants to the incorporation of the labour movement into the corporative framework. Some authors tend to stress either the repression of the reluctant anarcho-syndicalism or the dubious position – and even adherence to the basic statist conception of unionism – of the left-wing leadership, particularly that of the Communist Party (PCB), which is believed to stem from a 'populist approach' (Weffort, 1973; Simão, 1981; Araújo, 1993). Other analysts are more inclined to underscore worker opposition to the objectives of the government. Gomes (1988), for example, has argued that the Communists and other left-wing militants tried to retain a combative outlook for the union movement in the 1930s and 1940s though making use of some benefits of the official structure.[2] She recalls that initially both some independent and some left-wing activists penetrated the official unions with the aim of turning them into authentic bodies of representation of the working class, though without much success. In the same stream, albeit departing from somewhat distinct approaches, the work of French (1992) and Wolfe (1993)[3] has provided further evidence of workers' efforts in certain critical conjunctures (early 1930s, 1946–7 and 1950–54) to create factory commissions and other grassroots informal organisations, which in essence meant a rejection of the 'social-peace promoter' or 'social benefit-purveyor' type of unions to the point of refusing to join certain official unions as voluntary due-paying members. It may therefore be argued that the survival of practices of factory commissions and of some traditions of anarcho-syndicalism prevalent up to the 1930s provided seeds for the 1970s' move of the new unionism towards rank-and-file structural organisation within the workplace and the wholesale rejection of the prevalent industrial relations framework.

These alternative conceptions evolved both at practical and theoretical levels. The debate over the changing system of industrial relations in Brazil gains a further component when it is associated with the broader issue of the so-called social question. The awesome social problems of the nation were brought into public discourse with the re-democratisation initiated in the late 1970s. Influential sectors of Brazilian society began to demand changes in the working conditions and the standards of living of the poor. Such a concern with the terms of insertion of labour in the wider society was embraced both by the social agents and by theorists. Workers in Brazil, it is commonly asserted, have to struggle to improve their conditions of participation in society if they are to assert their citizenship. In the light of such claims, the controversies over the changing system of labour relations might be linked to the quest for extending workers' citizenship. The problem underlying this study may, therefore, be addressed in terms of an examination of the different patterns of labour relations and their influence in the process of asserting workers' citizenship. Such distinctive patterns or models of labour relations are materialised in different types of unionism. The experience of the years from 1978 onwards showed that new unionism has led the way in the building up of an alternative to the old corporatist arrangements. Hence, we need to address the question of how far the new unionism model of labour relations has contributed to extend the citizenship of workers and how it influences such a process.

The challenge to corporatism was launched through a number of proposals that shaped an alternative conception of unionism and labour relations in contradistinction to the state corporatist model. Such an alternative encompasses the following chief characteristics, which likewise may be interpreted as the key elements of the new unionism:

• Mobilisation of the rank and file and search for increasing union democracy;
• overhauling of the union structure through articulation of different organisational levels and forgoing the union tax and the statutory monopoly of representation;
• emphasis on direct procedures to settle conflicts between capital and labour;
• demand for a shift in the role of the State, from intervention in conflict settlement and union organisation towards a role of support for union action and collective negotiation.

We have seen that our problem deals with the terms in which workers participate in society; or, putting it another way, with the citizenship of workers. Since citizenship is a construct with a long and complex elaboration in social thought, for the purpose of the following argument we understand it as the terms in which individuals are considered as full members of societies (Marshall [1950] 1964), in other words, the set of rights, duties, and principles to which individuals are bound as participants in the life of the community.

As already apparent, this book studies the contribution of the new unionism towards changing labour relations and extending citizenship to workers. As 'engines of political progress' (Ranis, 1992: 7), unions have had a distributive impact counteracting the inequalities of market societies, an impact which can be identified as an incentive to extension of citizenship operating at two broad levels. Firstly, they may expand rights by forcing employers and the State to concede entitlements hitherto denied to the lower classes. Secondly, unions often presuppose collective action and forge new attitudes and political cultures which may be functional to assert the citizenship of workers.

Yet unions are not entirely alike in their social function and historical roles. Depending on their structural characteristics, they have different effects on the citizenship of workers, or at least, they contribute to its development to varying degrees. In the following chapters we shall look at the varying impact of both the 'new unions' and the more traditional sectors of the Brazilian labour movement on the workers' citizenship. But what we are labelling 'workers' citizenship' cannot be investigated and measured if one considers merely the entitlements and provisions enjoyed by workers. Basic elements of full citizenship such as adequate education, health, transport, housing and even industrial rights, have long been denied to the poor by an exclusionary pattern of development. In the face of such a reality, it is reasonable to assume that most Brazilian workers are not yet full citizens. Hence, in a context of widespread and acute material deprivation, if one is interested in assessing the chances for developing citizenship, it seems more fitting to look at the attitudes capable of shaping a political culture conducive to the struggle for citizenship.

Accordingly, we will focus on a specific sub-set of political culture – the one roughly considered to consist of participatory and critical attitudes proper to an active citizen. The attention to this modality of culture contrasts with a number of studies which deal with nation-wide political cultures (Almond and Verba, 1965; Richardson, 1974; Inglehart, 1990) in that it recognises the *contradictions* existing among different social groups which prevent the emergence of a uniform political culture at broader levels.[4] The following study will therefore employ the notion of a specific variant of political culture – the 'active citizenship' one – which we believe evolves in the particular setting of workers exposed to the alternative model of the CUT unionism. Such a potential development is further envisaged as fostering broad processes of social changes described as the building up or assertion of workers' citizenship. This last observation also suggests a subsequent distinction about the uses of the concept of political culture. It may be deployed to explain outcomes such as democratic stability of certain national polities (the main concern of Almond and Verba's seminal *The Civic Culture*) but also to explain different kinds of socio-political change as exemplified by some work on communications, bureaucracies and political development carried out by Almond and Coleman (1960), and Pye and Verba (1965), and the more recent studies by Inglehart on the culture of post-modernism (1990) and Putnam (1993) on the culture of civic engagement. While hypothesising that the engendering of a certain political culture is conducive to a process of socio-political change which may assert the citizenship of the Brazilian workers, this study fits in with the latter line of research projects. But, since the basic hypothesis investigated in this book concerns the relationship between the new unionism model of labour relations and the advancement of Brazilian workers' citizenship, a brief consideration of the theory of citizenship is required in order to establish the suitable links with the research context. This is the objective of the following section.

3 LIMITS AND POSSIBILITIES OF CITIZENSHIP IN BRAZIL

The turbulent world-wide evolution of citizenship has unfolded upon the basis of sharp battles for both the enrichment of its substance and for inclusion in the rank of membership. An account of the struggles for expansion of citizenship cannot overlook the role played by the endeavour of the underprivileged to improve their life chances and subsequently their conditions of participation in community. Some authors argue that such a process involves other social conflicts besides that among classes (e.g., Dahrendorf, 1988; Turner, 1992). But in any case it is generally agreed that the class conflict and the labour battle for universal suffrage, 'industrial citizenship' and social rights are undeniably significant. From the foregoing remarks, obviously, it does not follow that the extension of citizenship is merely a mechanical response to the protest against denial of rights, as Bendix observes (1974). On special occasions, the State anticipates pressures from below amid processes that are more complex, even if the underlying presence of social conflicts cannot be ruled out.

For all these reasons, the present study is closely concerned with the role of social conflict in the evolution of citizenship and especially with the role played by the labour movement. Whilst other arenas of social conflict have played a part in the history of citizenship, in this section the particular case of Brazil will be dealt with in the light of the vicissitudes of both labour and the State. Such a choice is grounded on the actual role played by these two agents in the uneven process of construction of Brazilian citizenship.

In the 1930s, programmes for strengthening the State and promoting its role in industrialisation were couched in terms of organicist and corporative doctrines. What were to become the ideological foundations of the Vargas regime were laid down by the so-called 'instrumental authoritarians' – among them Alberto Torres (1865–1917), Azevedo Amaral (whose main work was published in 1938) and Oliveira Vianna (1883–1951) – who argued that major hindrances to the sustained and co-ordinated developmental effort by the central power lay in the hitherto prevalent decentralisation and the oligarchic structure of the country.[5] Regarding the urban labour movement, the solution was its forced incorporation through a state-imposed framework designed to encapsulate workers' unions.

Such a move towards a bigger relative autonomy of the State was conceived against a background of an untamed urban labour movement which hitherto had grown independently of the State although steadily harassed by the police. The corporatist framework designed to keep labour under control aimed at forming interest groups from above within a set of measures reshaping the State attitude towards labour. The State moved to sponsor, support and control unions, the creation of which became solely dependent on its writ. This process of incorporation from above implied the endowing of urban labour with a number of benefits and incentives through the corporatist framework. Such incentives are analysed by Collier and Collier (1991) as inducements, under the argument that they consist of the bestowing of some 'advantages' – such as chartering occupational categories, state-provided revenues and social programmes – in an exchange for acceptance of state control. In November 1930 the Vargas government created the Ministry of Labour which proceeded to issue a stream of corporatist measures in the field of labour law which were eventually collected in the 'Consolidation of the Labour Laws – CLT' enacted in 1943. From March 1932 ('Lei de Sindicalização') onwards unions, in order to operate legally, had to be recognised by the State and were established as bodies mandated to replace antagonistic labour relations by co-operation and integration in the pursuit of 'national goals'. Unions were designed to be prevalently social service institutions handing out benefits of health care, education, leisure and social security to workers.

Social welfare was therefore a primary concern of the Vargas administration. A number of decrees were issued dealing with accidents at work, retirement schemes, pensions and maternity benefits. All these 'inducements' functioned as a network directly linked to some occupational categories (in the urban sector) and their official unions. The social security system accordingly was built up on those occupational categories whose members contributed and were entitled to benefits which varied from one category to the other. Separate institutes were organised for each branch of activity of the beneficiaries. For industrial workers it was the IAPI, for those in commerce, the IAPC, for those in banking, the IAPB, and so on. In addition to such services, trade unions were compelled by law to maintain their own welfare structure, complementary to the official one.

A complex edifice of this kind means simply that the recognition of certain citizenship entitlements was bestowed upon specific occupational categories framed by the State itself. Peasants, non-unionised workers, the labour force in the informal sector and other social groups altogether remained outside of this process of selective handing down of citizenship from above. This shift in the State attitude entailed an initiative directed towards prevention of and response to labour demands through the extension of certain rights of citizenship. Yet such an extension was implemented at the price of what analysts such as Vianna (1986) interpret as the 'political expropriation of the urban workers and the unionism' in that unions were turned into a sort of 'parastatal' institution lacking autonomy and freedom to pursue the workers' political goals.

Noting the singularity of such a process of state conferring of social rights on specific occupational categories, Santos (1979) has defined it as 'regulated citizenship'. In fact, Santos has distinguished four phases in the history of citizenship in relation to social policy. The first phase lasted from the abolition of slavery in 1888 to the 1930 revolution. It involved 'repressive laissez-faire' (Santos, 1979) whereby urban workers were allowed to organise without official authorisation, yet were systematically harassed by the police. 'Outside the order of the market there existed just the order of coercion.' (Santos, 1979) The second phase (1931–45) was marked by the incorporation of the labour movement and the selective bestowing of limited social rights on the members of the state-chartered occupational category. The third period envisaged by Santos corresponds to the populist democracy (1946–64) which he defines as 'semi-competitive'. The process of industrialisation both deepens and gives rise to the emergent conflicts allowed by the limited democratic order. Although workers mobilised mainly within the official apparatus, they started addressing some issues which went beyond the state assumptions. The movement for structural reforms in the socio-economic system of the early 1960s ('reformas de base') and the creation of unofficial employees' top organisations are only the more visible examples of the conflicts that potentially transcended the assumptions of the order of 'regulated citizenship'. As Santos recalls (1979), new urban groups and rural workers initiated movements independently of state recognition. As long as the social conflict eluded the State institutions and received no adequate answer, the result was the radicalisation of demands and attitudes which ultimately led to the institutional rupture of the military intervention of 1964. The order of 'regulated citizenship' proved inadequate for the conflicts, demands, and responses produced in a phase of 'limited democracy' (Santos, 1979). A fourth period was inaugurated with the military take-over. Political rights were substantially restricted though the size of the electorate grew substantially during the period and from 1974 onwards some form of relatively free elective participation took place. Although there existed some programmes (such as 'Planasa' and 'Pronan') targeted on universalisation of certain social goods and values, in general the notion of citizenship without a public and universal connotation persisted. The major part of the population continued on in its pre-civic condition, deprived of essential basic rights. This enduring exclusion ultimately derived from the priority the military gave to growth rather than equity.[6]

Therefore, the key interpretive concept of the author is that of 'regulated citizenship: '[a] concept whose roots lay upon a system of occupational stratification defined by law, rather than upon a code of political values. Citizens are all the members of the community who are located in one of the occupational categories recognised by law.' Instead of universal recognition of citizenship rights to all the members of the community, what happened in Brazil was the gradual extension of entitlements by the State through the expansion of the number of occupational categories and the set of rights attached to them. 'Who holds a job, enjoys benefits' ('quem tem ofício, tem benefício'), as Gomes summarises it (1988). Since one needed to belong to an occupation defined in the regulated area to enjoy the rights of membership, occupational category stratification paradoxically brought inequality into a concept originally conceived in terms of basic equalities. As Weffort notes, 'regulated citizenship' in Brazil, resting on differences of occupation, reflects existing inequalities, and reinforces them (1981: 143).[7] This type of citizenship was crystallised in the second phase singled out by Santos (1931–45), withstood the democratic period (1945–64), was reinforced during the period of military rule, and has been challenged ever since the transition to democracy.

We may claim that a new phase in the history of citizenship in Brazil began with the transition to democracy: this phase is shaped by a still unresolved conflict between 'regulated citizenship' and what we see as the ideals of 'conquered citizenship'. The revival of the labour movement with claims for the overcoming of the corporative framework of labour relations is the major example. Initially arising in the ABC industrial belt of São Paulo (Santo André, São Bernardo and São Caetano), the renovated labour movement – which became the new unionism – spread rapidly throughout the country to assume demands which transcended mere economic limits. The following articulation of labour with the civil society democratic movement and also with peasants and other sectors of the poor launched the basis for the superseding of the order of 'regulated citizenship'. Manifold organised interests and NGOs (nongovernmental organisations) exerted pressures on the Constituent Assembly during the period of constitutional debate with the result that the final text registered more inputs 'from below' than that of any previous Brazilian Constitution. The final text thus incorporated many kinds of social rights such as medical and health care rights, gender equality, racial equality, rights of Indian communities as well as other rights of protection for diffuse interests, not least environmental rights. Although interest groups played a major part in the process of articulation of social rights in the 1988 Constitution, the role of organised labour, notably the new unionism grouped under the CUT, remains vital for the prospects of the expansion of citizenship beyond the narrow limits hitherto prevailing in the country.

The recurrence of the demand for redemption of the so-called social debt, a concern expressed by different protagonists such as the president of the Constituent Assembly, deputy Ulysses Guimarães, and the union leaders quoted at the outset, testifies that the quest for expanding citizenship is definitely on the country's agenda. The identification of such a general claim allows a better grasp of the failure of the path hitherto prevalent. In a country with a huge informal sector and a heterogeneous economy which combines traditional with very modern production, it is certainly inadequate to limit citizenship within the narrow borders of the 'regulated' model. The shortfall in citizenship must not be attributed solely to the level of development of the country. Admittedly, this is a factor to take into account, and it is even an ultimate limit to any claim for expanding entitlements and provisions. Yet the Brazilian unequal distribution of income would not necessarily be expected on the basis of the GDP per capita or the level of economic development, as cross-national comparisons with like-situated economies both in Latin America and East Asia make clear. The period of the so-called economic miracle (1968–75) affords a clear example. The country grew at an average annual rate of 11 per cent of the GDP without any corresponding upgrade in the level of inclusion of the popular sectors. On the contrary, the exclusionary modernisation adopted by the military in the period contributed to an increase in the number of 'pre-civic' Brazilians. The evaluation of the 'regulated citizenship' model cannot be other than negative in respect of the assertion of the universal character of citizenship. In such a context, the claim for a more active practice of citizenship develops over a general assessment of the inadequacy of previous experiences.

4 CITIZENSHIP, CONFLICT AND THE LABOUR QUESTION

The theme of citizenship lends itself to quite disparate construals of its meaning and scope. The breadth and controversial nature of the concept have much to do with its identification with full membership of a given community. From this point onwards it is rare to find agreements on what it means to be a member, who should be considered as a member and what principles govern such a status.

One of the key issues that must be addressed in any overall account of the extension of citizenship as a major historical process is the role of class conflict, not least the struggles of the underprivileged. Some scholars go so far as to assert that 'it is more valid to say that class conflict has been a medium of the extension of citizenship rights than to say that the extension of citizenship rights has blunted class divisions' (Giddens, 1982: 174).[8] Whether we concur with this or not, we must grant that this is a concern frequently present to some degree in a variety of approaches to the phenomenon. Moreover, a careful account of the historical careers and contexts of citizenship in different countries cannot neglect such a link. True, some advanced industrial societies may have entered a stage in which the central role of the class struggle if it ever obtained has been attenuated, as a number of major commentators have suggested (Dahrendorf, 1988; Hobsbawm, 1995; Tilly, 1995). But such a game is far from fully played. Both at the workshop level and in broader spheres, the tensions stemming from an inherently conflictive relationship are still present.

The close historical, structural and cultural links between labour and citizenship which we have sought to bring out in the foregoing discussion and throughout the present work have been neglected in a great deal of the recent scholarship in citizenship theory.[9] Notwithstanding this theoretical neglection, one must concede that the issue has not been entirely absent from the literature. Indeed, Dahrendorf (1968: 184) has acknowledged that 'an entire chapter could be written describing the labour movement's contribution to the establishment of citizenship rights in Germany'. The same ties are noticed by Bendix in his analysis of the role of the right to combine in the sequence of extension of citizenship to the lower classes: '[the] practical achievements of trade unions have a far-reaching effect upon the status of workers as citizens' (1969: 104).

Of course, how far this relationship between labour movements and the expansion of citizenship holds depends on the historical circumstances of specific societies. Different patterns of labour relations will mediate the interactions between the labour question and citizenship in distinctive ways owing to the existence of a variety of models of labour relations which may either hinder or facilitate the expansion of citizenship. Authors like Barbalet have observed that the rights of trade unionism, understood as an element of the idea of citizenship, contribute to make feasible in relation to workers the Marshallian notion of citizenship as a sharing of a civilisation which is a common possession of all (1988). We argue that the array of possible arrangements for the rights of trade unionism is not indifferent to the likely outcome in terms of the kind of involvement of workers in their respective community, that is, in their conditions of citizenship. In sum, the analysis just outlined indicates that the theoretical discussion of citizenship points to the contribution of the labour issue to the assertion of citizenship.

Accordingly, this book investigates the hypothesis that the Brazilian new unionism's alternative organisational arrangements, practices and proposals, as they developed from 1978 onwards, have fostered the expansion of workers' citizenship. Since these alternative conceptions arose against the current of the traditional practices linked to the resilient corporative model of labour relations, we shall compare the distinct effects of two basic types of unionism: the new unionism and the more traditional sectors of the country's labour movement. The claim that the new unionism develops workers' citizenship, of course, has been too easily put forward by previous studies and by the union militants themselves. But such claims have very often been confined to the rhetorical level. Instead, this study aims to check if the empirical evidence supports the hypothesis that the new unionism's alternative model has had a noticeable impact on workers' citizenship. Since, however, the concept of citizenship is not an easily measurable construct, the investigation will concentrate further on the effect of the new unionism's practices on the workers' attitudes. With such a goal the study relies upon a scale specifically designed to measure their attitudes. We have argued that the attitudes which shape a distinct political culture are a crucial factor in the attainment of the rights constitutive of citizenship, and further, that the specific political culture which we label the 'culture of active citizenship' is the most suitable for the workers to attain citizenship.

5 THE STRUCTURE OF THE BOOK

This Introduction (Chapter 1) has already advanced the central hypothesis which is the object of the current study. It is concerned with the impact of 'new unions" alternative conceptions about unionism and labour relations on workers' citizenship. It has identified certain links between the theory of citizenship and the role played by labour and labour relations in the process of its extensions towards subordinate social strata. An analysis of the evolution of citizenship in Brazil was also undertaken in order to locate the background of contemporary developments. Chapter 2 describes the Brazilian system of labour relations and the revival of the labour movement in the late 1970s with the goal of providing a background to the course of labour relations in the country as well as to the strategies adopted by the new unionism to challenge the received arrangements. Attention is also paid to the recent debate on the alternatives to the current corporatist framework, widely recognised as unsuitable for the country's stage of development. Chapter 3 discusses in detail the alternative conceptions of the new unionism in an attempt to highlight how those proposals seek to enhance workers' participation and democratise both the union life and the labour relations system at large. Chapter 4 provides a general account of unionism in the state of Pernambuco, in the Northeast region of Brazil, with the purpose of presenting the setting where a specific comparison between the two types of unionism – the 'new unions' and the 'traditional unions' – was carried out. In order to compare those effects on the development of a political culture of active citizenship a number of urban unions were selected and their members surveyed. The scale conceived as the instrument of measuring the attitudes of 'active citizenship' of the survey-population, the employed methodology and the theoretical basis warranting such a procedure, are together discussed in Chapter 5. The research findings are comprehensively presented and analysed in Chapter 6, which also discusses the extent to which the new unionism has lived up to the claim of developing the political culture of 'active citizenship'. Finally, the Conclusion (Chapter 7) offers an assessment of the contribution of the 'new unions' to the building of the workers' citizenship in terms of either improving labour conditions or in terms of the more indirect attainments bound up with the development of the alternative political culture measured in the survey, and suggests additional lines of enquiry which would either develop the argumentation of the present work or test further its hypotheses.

2 The Brazilian System of Labour Relations and the Revival of the Labour Movement

1 THE CORPORATIST MODEL

As part of its strategy to pursue developmental goals, the entire period of Vargas's leadership, including the initial phase before the 'Estado Novo' (1937–45), rested upon state corporatism. For the purposes of this book we shall leave aside other types of corporatism and focus on the statist variant, historically by far the most important, at least in the Brazilian context. Reference to corporatism therefore will mean state corporatism. As a model, corporatism refers to a specific structure of organisation of interest groups by the State. In Mericle's words (1977: 303), the term describes 'a system of interest-group representation in which the State plays a major role in structuring, supporting, and regulating interest groups with the object of controlling their internal affairs and the relations among them'.[1]

The regime led by Vargas aimed at forming interest-groups from above, that is, by the State, and also at controlling the labour force then emerging as a result of industrial development.[2] Soon afterwards it adopted a set of measures to change the State's attitude towards the labour issue. Creation of trade unions became dependent on the State's permit. The latter began to sponsor, support and control unions, and thereby the whole system of labour relations. Little ground was left for the parties' autonomy and direct relationships between employers and workers.

17

1.1   The Consolidation of Labour Laws (CLT)

In 1943, all the scattered labour laws hitherto existing were brought together in the 'Consolidation of Labour Laws' (CLT). This encompasses dispositions dealing with practically all aspects of labour relations, ranging from individual workers' rights such as vacations, minimum wages, working time and health and safety, to trade-union organisation, labour courts and the Ministry of Labour, Industry and Commerce. The CLT assembled all this legislation in a systematic manner, proudly announced as one of the most advanced labour law systems of that time. The enactment of certain statutory workers' rights along with the incorporation of the unions and the conflict into the state apparatus has been characterised as a strategy of 'inducements' and 'constraints' by Collier and Collier (1991) or as 'combination of co-optation and repression' by Wolfe (1993: 61).

1.2   State Recognition and Monopoly of Representation

Employers and employees were organised in two co-ordinate occupational categories, previously defined by Article 577 of the 'CLT' through a parallel framing.[3] To each employer's activity corresponded two types of parallel unions: one for workers, another for employers. A special tripartite commission was created to deal with the framing of categories ('Comissão de Enquadramento Sindical'). By such a mechanism the State chartered interest groups.

The legal personality of the trade union was bestowed by the Ministry of Labour according to the indication of the mentioned commission. Only one union was allowed to be constituted upon one 'basis of representation', which normally covered one or more municipalities (the rough equivalent of the American county). In so doing, the State created the monopoly of state-recognised unions. In practice, creation of parallel or independent unions became virtually impossible.

In addition to this first level of organisation – the union's – two others were designed. The federation, usually covering the area of one state of the Brazilian federation, gathered five or more unions. The third one, the confederation, was expected to represent the interests of the categories which integrate one branch of the economy (transport, industry, commerce or agriculture, for instance). To be recognised, a confederation had to muster three or more federations. It is worth stressing that no horizontal structure was permitted. The possibility of constructing a general central confederation representing all the working class was outlawed, given the assumptions that the general interests have to be provided by the State.

Once officially recognised, a union had its life fully under control. Elections were regulated by the Ministry of Labour, which approved the candidates wishing to run for offices. In the same way, the statutes approved by the Ministry of Labour explicitly prohibited the spread of doctrines deemed incompatible with the institutions and the interests of the nation. Equally, partisan activity was strictly forbidden.

1.3 The Union Tax

Financial support was provided by the state-imposed trade union tax, through compulsory payroll deduction applied to all members of the category, irrespective of voluntary affiliation to the union. Accordingly, all workers under an employment relationship were obliged once a year to pay one working day's wage or salary to the union structure.

The impact on unions' life of such revenues provided by the State is quite profound.[4] Before the 1988 Constitution, the expenditure of resources derived from the union tax was tightly controlled by the State through enforcement of article 592 of 'CLT'. Unions were obliged to spend them only on welfare and social activities. Expenditure on militant goals was forbidden. Even those revenues whose use was not prescribed by the State (voluntary monthly dues of the members, for instance) were very often channelled to maintain the huge welfare apparatus built up as a consequence of the constraints imposed on the tax revenues. The device succeeded in shaping union activity, restricting it to providing services and facilities for membership. The mandatory union contribution, or union tax, is responsible for the major part of the total incomes of unions. In the case of federations and confederations, they account for almost the whole of the revenues.

1.4   The Labour Court Control

The settlement of collective conflict by the labour court is another pillar of the Brazilian corporatist system. Although collective bargaining is formally accepted, the existence of the labour court with power to dictate compulsory settlement inhibits the direct initiative of the parties inasmuch as the negotiation can be interrupted and the dispute sent to the court either unilaterally by one party or by the labour court itself in cases of strikes. Consequently, this prerogative of the labour court, named 'normative power', avoids the self-settlement based upon the correlation of forces of the agents of the system in that, it has been argued, both unions and employers would have to rely on their bargaining power to settle their differences if the courts were not allowed to rule on such matters. Compulsory arbitration in Brazil has had two related effects on both the behaviour of the parties and the overall level of protection of working standards. Firstly, the paternalist role of institutions is reinforcēd because an occupational category can attain rights and benefits prescinding mobilisation and representativeness merely by taking advantage of administrative means. Efforts tend to concentrate in the skills and instruments necessary to act before the courts. Even the rank-and-file tends to feel less impelled to mobilise in the expectation that the labour court will protect their rights. Secondly, the possible influence of achievements reached by strong occupational categories in the whole labour market is neutralised. Those categories cannot exert all the pressure they could because the court intervenes as soon as industrial action starts. Consequently, they get less than they would possibly achieve under direct bargaining with employers. The wage rates negotiated by those strong categories would influence the ongoing 'accepted' levels of the wage rates in the broader labour market. This 'beneficial' effect is just prevented by the stifling of the bargaining power of strategic categories through compulsory arbitration.

In addition to dealing with collective conflicts, the labour court is assigned the function of solving individual grievances. Because the corporatist framework transfers to the State the responsibility for settling all sorts of labour conflicts, there exist virtually no other ways to tackle grievances inside companies. The obvious consequence is that workers' individual complaints are poorly dealt with. On one side, lacking job security since 1967,[5] they face a great risk of becoming unemployed whenever they dare to start a claim.[6] As a result of absence of job security and other factors inherent to corporatism, the Brazilian labour courts have become the 'justice of the unemployed', in that workers are only able to sue employers after the termination of their employment contract. Most employers deliberately withhold the payment of compensation to which workers are entitled on dismissal because they expect to obtain financial advantage thereby from the delay of the court decision (which can take up to seven years). Moreover, employees are often unable to wait for court rulings and prefer to settle with the employer for much less than they could reasonably obtain if the case reached completion in the courts. Data provided by the statistical service of the 'Tribunal Superior do Trabalho', the highest-ranking of the labour court, gives us an idea of the significance of conciliation as a percentage of the cases concluded at the first level (the so-called 'juntas de conciliaçao e julgamento'). From the total of 1,726,677 cases decided in 1994, no less than 759,832 were conciliated. Since those conciliations are often settled through significant 'concessions' on the part of the employee, it is fairly safe to assume that at least 44 per cent of the court solutions were reached at the expense of the workers' full rights. This is an example of the perverted effect of an institution whose original rationale was just the opposite. The poor results of the labour court are a consequence of both its overburdening and the structural characteristics of a system designed to channel almost all the labour disputes to the State. Not surprisingly, some analysts such as Camargo[7] (1995) have underscored such a perverse effect of the labour court which is seen as a major factor stimulating the high turnover inflicted to the workforce (one-third of jobs change their holder every year).

Table 2.1   Overall movement of the Brazilian Labour Court

Years	Cases started	Cases solved
1960–69	3,333,214	3,055,783
1970–79	4,827,884	4,498,883
1980–89	9,091,374	8,423,171
1990–94	8,911,179	8,113,855
1993	1,882,388	1,816,164
1994	2,099,377	2,116,329

Source: Statistical Service of 'Tribunal Superior do Trabalho', Brasília, 1995.

Table 2.1 gives us an idea about the intensive and distorted use of the labour courts in the country.

The structural impossibility of responding to demands in good time is apparent. If one takes the numbers of cases received and solved in each period, one can easily see that the backlog of undecided cases is steadily increasing. In the 1960s, this backlog amounted to 277,431 pending cases; in the 1970s, to 329,001; in the 1980s, to 668,203; in the five years to 1994, to 797,324. Apart from the rising number of pending cases in itself, one should remember that after 1988 many of these cases started grouping several workers because of a new procedural right bestowed on unions enabling them to advance one single case on behalf of workers' groups under similar circumstances.[8]

The spectacular growth of the number of cases submitted to the labour court is especially striking from the 1980s onwards. Compared with that for the previous decade, the number of started cases almost doubled in the 1980s. Such a jump coincides with the liberation of repressed demands which did not surface until democratisation provided a less authoritarian atmosphere. It is also probably linked to the emergence of the new unionism which often used the union-sponsored legal initiatives as a way of addressing workers' demands. The growth in the number of cases taken to the courts showed another sharp increase from the late 1980s onwards. From then on, the figure for the cases started in the five years to 1994 is virtually equivalent to that for the entire decade of the 1980s. In the years 1993 and 1994 alone, the number of new cases taken to the labour courts mounted to around *2 million* each year. Apart from the structural reasons connected with labour turnover and the employers' calculus as they were just outlined, the role of unions in explaining such an expansion is also relevant in that they impelled millions of workers to take their employers to the courts in pursuit of overdue wages in connection with the stabilisation programmes enacted in that period. Unions often sponsored large groups of workers, often the whole labour force under their representation, to demand wage readjustments required by the government manipulation of official figures for inflation rates on the occasion of the launching of the stabilisation programmes and the consequent change of the legally enforced income policies. Those legal initiatives became well known as 'the cases of the economic plans' ('1987 Bresser Plan', '1989 Summer Plan' and '1990 Collor Plan').

Such a growth has led the State to enlarge the already huge apparatus, particularly after the 1988 Constitution. This comprises (1,097) 'juntas de conciliaçao e julgamento' (1st level) throughout the country, twenty-four regional tribunals (2nd level) and one 'Tribunal Superior do Trabalho' (the highest level) made up of five groups of judges (interview no. 16, with the president of the National Association of the Judges in the Labour Court – 'Anamatra' – judge Ivanildo da Cunha Andrade). In spite of this immense structure, which employs 2,200 career judges admitted through public contest and another 2,348 'classist judges'[9] (Brandão, 1994), the institution has been unable to cope with the steadily swelling demand. In short, the critical situation reached by the Brazilian labour courts means that workers have experienced increasing difficulties in trying to make employers abide by the labour law.

2 THE LONG SURVIVAL OF THE MODEL

The corporatist model in Brazil has a long-term record of control over the urban-industrial working-class. Political regimes as different as Vargas's 'Estado Novo', the populist democracy of the period 1946–64, the military authoritarian state and the democratic governments from 1985

onwards have benefited from such a structure. Such a 'pro-
digious longevity', as Camargo puts it, is epitomised in the
half-century-long CLT which has endured three constitu-
tions.[10] Whilst the repressive features were loosened under
populists looking towards unions as a source of support,
the same instruments were employed by the military in
order to exclude labour and depoliticise the whole society.
Merely by strengthening the application of the law, the
military succeeded in establishing strict control over union
activity, considered a potential threat to the national interest.

Obviously, a model with such a strong staying power deeply
marked Brazilian unions. Unions created by corporatism
are regarded by Boito Jr. (1991a) as pervaded by populist
ideology, which draws on the image of the 'protector state',
that is, the expectation that the state intervenes on behalf
of the popular sectors regardless of either the actual correlation of forces in society or their autonomous organisation.
The impact of populism at the level of workers' organisation
has generated one particular variant of such an ideology,
the 'ideology of union legalism', which stresses the role of
the State and labour legislation in supposedly ensuring the
protection of workers against powerful employers. The unions
displayed passivity, lack of organisation at the rank-and-file
level, and absence of organic links between the workers
and the union officers, whose actions are very limited both
in scope and nature. Benefits for workers are expected to be
gained by state provisions awarded after union claims through
official channels rather than as a result of shifts in the
correlation of forces due to workers' organisation. It should
be noted that Boito's analysis of the populist ideology of
'union legalism' bears affinity with the 'culture of gift, bestowal
or favour' which we mentioned in the account of the extension of citizenship to the workers in the previous chapter.

3   THE COMPROMISE TREATMENT OF THE 1988 CONSTITUTION

Although there was a rhetorical consensus about the need
for diminishing state intervention in the labour relations
system during the Constituent Assembly process, the nature

of the changes was controversial. The strength of the former model was still relevant. For hegemonic interests, it had successfully endured the difficult period of democratic transition. Labour conflict had proved to be controllable through the existing apparatus even though Sarney's government had made less use of available mechanisms. On the other hand, large sectors of the labour movement were still attached to the old framework and had no interest in dispensing with inducements such as monopoly of representation and the power to secure benefits for workers through compulsory arbitration by the labour courts, in that their overestimated legitimacy was thus presumed by state institutions with no further probing.

Concerning union organisation, the 1988 Constitution, in its Article 8, 'caput' and first paragraph, asserted the principle of union freedom through prohibition of the State's interference in union organisation. But such a provision proved somewhat dubious. On the one hand, unions started enjoying the right to approve their own statutes in the sovereign general assembly and the Ministry of Labour lost its former powers to monitor union administration, to cancel its recognition or to suppressing union leaders' mandates. At the same time, in another paragraph of the same article, the monopoly of representation was guaranteed, as the creation of more than one union per category within the same geographical area was prohibited. Moreover, completing such a monopoly of representation, the 1988 Constitution ensured the representation of all the members of the category by the union and not only of the members affiliated to it (Article 8, II and III). The type of vertical organisation inherent to corporatism was reproduced as a result of the imposition of a contribution to the 'confederation system' in addition to the union tax to be paid by workers (Article 8, IV). What those constitutional provisions implied was merely the elimination of state interference as far as the control previously exerted by the Ministry of Labour over the creation and functioning of unions. Expressed otherwise, only certain effects of a structure which remained fundamentally based on the role of the State were displaced.

This was in effect a compromise solution between contradictory trends faced by the Constituent Assembly. The democratic transition process had created an awareness of the need for modifying the system. But a powerful combination of interests had been formed between those who were conscious of the implications of the corporatist heritage for controlling the work force and those traditional beneficiaries of the official union apparatus. The ratification of the monopoly of representation and the confederation vertical structure was to coexist with pluralism at the central level. This was a hybrid solution which provides a relative autonomy to unions coexisting with the pillars of the old corporatism. As Souza observes (1992a), pluralism and its inherent competitiveness were confined to the central level, with all the other levels conforming to the uniqueness norm, which constitutes a substantially incoherent and unstable outcome.

The 1988 Constitution maintained the union tax revenues. The persistence of the monopoly of representation combined with the union tax has meant that representation of unions is still awarded by the State. It does not derive from workers' membership constructed from below. Rather, it simply consists of a concession by the State following the same pattern as the previous model. Notwithstanding the maintenance of such pillars of corporatism, some analysts have assessed the changes brought about by the 1988 Constitution in a more positive way than that presented in this work. Mangabeira (1993) and Almeida (1988), for example, have highlighted the strengthening of the union autonomy before the State resulting from both the lifting of the former controls of the Ministry of Labour over union internal affairs and the recognition of the right to strike. Such an evaluation, however, appears to underestimate the comprehensive effects of a system which reinforced a model of unionism shaped by the State in a different context with the chief purpose of controlling workers' autonomy and mitigating the expression of the conflict between capital and labour. The resources provided by the State through the union tax, the imposition of the official structure of federations and confederations, the 'classist judge', the compulsory arbitration of the labour courts are but some examples of the heavy weight of the old pattern. The bestowing of the freedom on workers to create and run their unions is overshadowed by those elements. Even the right to strike enshrined into the Constitutional Charter in practice is curbed by the potential intervention of the labour court and the subsequent illegality of the stoppage in the event the workers continue on strike.

Regarding the settlement of collective disputes, the constitutional solution was equally contradictory. On the one hand, there was an identifiable move toward strengthening negotiation. The right to strike, as seen, was asserted. In addition, unofficial arbitration chosen by the parties was contemplated by the Constitution for the first time, even if it was not put into practice due to the prevalent features of the model which induce reproduction of the rooted attitudes. On the other hand, if deadlock arises between the parties, the compulsory arbitration of the labour court is maintained. Furthermore, labour court jurisdiction was expanded both in the individual and collective competence. The employment relationship in the public sector enterprises ('empresas públicas'), for instance, which was formerly assigned to the 'federal jurisdiction', came under the jurisdiction of the labour courts in the new arrangements. Similarly, collective conflicts in public sector enterprises, once not liable to compulsory arbitration, became subject to the normative power of the labour court. Those contradictory trends inhibited negotiation even though the right to strike was established. In fact, the weight of the resort to compulsory settlement by the labour court and the constraints on the organisational structure of the unions were both to prevail over the slight flirting with voluntary procedures.

4 THE REVIVAL OF THE LABOUR MOVEMENT

4.1 The Emergence of the New Unionism

After a period in which union activity was almost reduced to welfare programmes, workers' mobilisation erupted yet again in the late 1970s. Both the hard working conditions and low wages prevalent even in the strongest sectors of industry contributed to this phenomenon. The relative relaxation of the dictatorship also created conditions for the manifestation of the workers' discontent. Strikes broke out in the ABC industrial belt of São Paulo (Santo André, São Bernardo, and São Caetano) led by metalworkers who had become by far the largest component of the industrial labour force in the country.

In 1978, their example was followed by over twenty occupational categories involving more than 500,000 workers throughout the country (Keck, 1989: 263). In 1979, another wave of strikes provoked the government's intervention in the São Bernardo's Metalworkers Union and the crack-down of the police on the strikers, imprisoning around 200 workers. In October of that year, during the strike of the metalworkers of São Paulo and Guarulhos, the police killed the worker Santo Dias da Silva. In 1980, again the metalworkers of ABC and fifteen other cities had to suffer the sharp intervention of the State. The Regional Labour Court of the state of São Paulo declared that the movement was illegal, the Minister of Labour purged the union leadership, and the police arrested eleven leaders, among them the already famous Luís Ignácio Lula da Silva. Subsequently, the Federal Military Court ('auditoria militar') tried and charged them with violation of the national security law.[11]

Those events attracted public attention to workers and aroused the sympathy of civil society as exemplified by the support offered by organisations such as the Catholic Church and the Brazilian Lawyers Association (OAB).[12] Huge mobilisations of rank-and-file had to cope with the strong reaction of the State and employers. Following the example of the metalworkers of the ABC, other occupational categories throughout the country also came to the fore demanding better wages, direct bargaining and the end of state intervention in union life. In October 1979 the rural workers of Pernambuco represented by the 'Federation of Rural Workers of Pernambuco' managed to secure an unprecedented wage increase and related benefits after a strike that involved 23 rural workers unions and around 200,000 members and non-members of the unions in a sector whose employers had traditionally kept labour under tight control without ruling out even violent means (Alves, 1994: 434). Other workers' mobilisations in the state of Pernambuco, the setting of this study, are described in detail in Chapter 4 as evidence of the rapid spread of the new unionism in other sectors besides the industrial belt of Sao Paulo.

The emergent unionism displayed a significant rupture with the patterns of the populist official union of the corporatist tradition. It rejected the intervention of the Ministry of Labour in both labour relations and union life; resisted the normative power of the labour court whose awards were easily perceived as directed towards stifling mobilisation; drove existing union bureaucracies towards militancy and democracy, and insisted on direct bargaining backed by shop-floor representation. As Comin summarises (1994), despite certain nuances inside its currents, the new unionism presented some basic unifying elements:

• criticism of both state intervention in labour relations and the existing, legally imposed, bureaucratic organisation of the unions;
• preference for grassroots mobilisation instead of involving official institutions and negotiations behind closed doors;
• rejection of both capitalism and the then existing 'real socialism' at the broader programmatic level.

The shift towards the rank-and-file in the Brazilian labour movement, although for different reasons provided by a unique socio-political context, was to parallel some recent tendencies of the labour movement elsewhere. As Heery and Kelly recall (1994), in the 1970s the British unionism witnessed a shift of activity and power towards workplace organisations, shop stewards and lay activists. The rationale for such a 'participatory unionism' was the claim that these latter spheres were closer to rank-and-file feelings and grievances. Those, too, were concerns central to the Brazilian new unionism militants.

4.2   Forging New Conceptions

Demands of the rank-and-file faced two major obstacles: first, repression by the State and employers as a permanent threat; second, most unions were under the control of government appointees who had replaced the former purged leadership. Given these constraints, the new unionism tended to emphasise organisation on the shop floor as both the only outlet for workers' initiative and the only way to accumulate forces to resist repression. It was also a natural development of trends which had already emerged in the advanced sectors towards organisation and demands at the enterprise level which were pointed out by Moisés as early as 1982. The leadership that emerges from those struggles since the beginning perceives the organisation of the workers within the factory as both the best strategy to pursue in order to fulfil workers' aspirations and a value in itself.

For Moisés (1982), the trajectory of the movement which erupted in 1978/79 was determined by the challenge of combining the grassroots mobilisation with institutional action at the official union plane. This challenge could be met in so far as the the official unions gradually lost their bureaucratic subordination to the State. The break in the 'silence' of labour brought about two approaches concerning the participation of the rank-and-file. The first one, named 'Union Opposition', gathered militants opposing both the whole union structure and the leadership of the unions in which they acted. Having its strength in São Paulo's metalworkers, and those of Osasco and other cities around São Paulo, its prevalent concern was the organisation of the factory commissions as the strategy to build another union framework. 'Union Opposition' stressed the autonomy of the factory commissions vis-à-vis the union and envisaged it as the base body of a whole framework to be reconstructed from bottom up. Although the 'Union Opposition' was made up of different tendencies, the majority of its militants was linked to the Catholic Church. As Rodrigues recalls (1991), this presence of the Catholic Church provided the new unionism with legitimacy and material support. This would prove to be an important factor in the subsquent development of the new unionism.

The second current within the emerging unionism was composed of the independent or 'authentic' union leaders who had succeeded in seizing control of the official unions of their occupational categories. Mainly located in the metalworkers' unions of the ABC region, the independent unionists were also concerned about organisation within the workplace. But they were equally aware of the need to seek the unity of the working class. So they tended to emphasise the articulation of the grassroots mobilisation with the official union in order to transform it from the inside. Accordingly, they regarded factory commissions as necessarily articulated with the union, and, therefore, as requiring less autonomy than in the Union Opposition's conception. They were inclined as well to pose the shop steward's recognition by the employers as another mechanism to bring together the union and the rank-and-file. As will be analysed in Section 7, the 'authentic' unionists' strategy of transforming the official union framework from inside prevailed in the end.

Apart from the variation of strategies noted above, the new unionism from its birth criticised the corporatist framework and the related conceptions. Restrictions on direct collective bargaining with employers, the prohibition of strikes, the monopoly of representation and its bureaucratisation effects, the union tax, altogether were perceived as obstacles to the free constitution of a unionism capable of expressing workers' claims. In addition, those general guidelines stressed working-class independence in contrast with the former ideology of the unionism of the populist period (1946–64), which often used the official union structure to cement broader political alliances to combat oligarchies and foreign interests (the national-development goals).

The corporatist framework was challenged in practice by the formation of organisations at the workplace and the emphasis on direct collective bargaining backed by industrial action. As early as in 1980, those union sectors, both the opposition groups acting within their categories and the unions whose control had been gained by the so-called militant unionists, met in the National Meeting of The Workers Opposing Union Structures – ENTOES. The seeds for the maturing of the new conceptions and spreading country-wide had been sown.

5   EVOLUTION: CONCLAT, CUT, CGTs AND FORÇA SINDICAL

5.1   CONCLAT and the Birth of the CUT

While labour resurgence continued to expand workplace organisation, the building of national-level co-ordination was widely acknowledged to be crucial for strengthening the movement. In August 1981, in Praia Grande, São Paulo, the first National Conference of the Working Class – CONCLAT – was held with the purpose of unifying national workers' demands and discussing the creation of a unitary and general national-level organisation. In a time when repression of union activities was still a policy under government consideration, the attendance of 5,247 delegates from 1,126 unions, confederations, federations and associations was a great achievement. Autonomy from the State, land reform and political democratisation of the country were also agreed as goals of the labour movement, alongside wage demands. An important deliberation of that conference was the setting up of a provisional commission entrusted with preparing the congress to be held in the following year with the specific task of founding a national entity of the workers, then named 'Central Unica dos Trabalhadores' – CUT. This congress was postponed under the pretext that the 1982 gubernatorial elections would have a divisive impact on the labour movement owing to the parallel partisan activity of many militants.

By this time two obstacles stood out preventing the pursued unity. Not only had the differences of political identifications already surfaced (in 1980 the Workers' Party – PT – had been founded with considerable participation by union leaders identified with the new unionism), but also distinctive conceptions about union organisation and the labour relations system itself had become clearer. In fact, two broad tendencies could be identified. The first, the new unionism, emphasised mobilisation and confrontation. It opposed the existing model of labour relations, stressed the autonomy of the working class, and, although participating in the general struggles of democratic forces against the regime, tended to underline the specific workers' claims within the democratic programme. The second, named 'Unidade Sindical', did not represent a complete rupture with the unionism of the period before 1964. It was another conception of fighting for the strengthening of workers' position in the public arena. For its supporters, at that moment, the predominant task was the unified action of all the opposition forces against military rule. Its strategy benefited from the corporatist apparatus, in practice denouncing only the more repressive effects of such a structure. Permeated by the conceptions of the unionism of the period before the military's takeover, 'Unidade Sindical' grouped together both the more moderate sectors of the official unions' old guard (the so-called 'pelegos')[13] and the unionists close to the communist parties (PCB, PC do B and MR-8). Despite nuances in political conceptions, both sectors were held together by the relative acceptance of some of the basic pillars of corporatism and the less confrontational approach to the democratic transition, a stance which was to surface throughout the process of elaboration of the 1988 Constitution (Martinez-Lara, 1994). Rather than seeking to transform the existing labour relations by independent pressure from below, they managed to employ the union hierarchical apparatus to strengthen the workers' position toward the State and the democratic opposition forces.

Such divergent approaches led to the split of the movement in 1983, when the sectors grouped in 'Unidade Sindical' proposed once more to postpone the congress designed to found the 'Central Única dos Trabalhadores'. However, in spite of the non-participation of the other sectors, the new unionism branch of the movement decided to maintain the scheduled congress. Consequently, in August 1983, in São Bernardo, 5,054 delegates representing 911 union entities voted to found the CUT. On that occasion, they chose a national co-ordination body with the mandate of organising the framework of the nascent national entity (CUT, 1991a). The decision to call the congress without the entities aligned in the bloc 'Unidade Sindical' then represented a risky leap in the dark. From one angle, the split was a rupture with the consensual objective of building up a unified national labour movement as a means to strengthening its position in the public arena. From another, the material resources of the official structure lay unevenly under majority control of the unions, federations and confederations gathered in the 'Unidade Sindical'. A decade later, when asked about the most difficult moment of his career as a union leader, Jair Meneguelli, the first president of the CUT created in that congress, had no doubt in recalling the uncertainties of that decisive moment for the future of the Brazilian movement:

> I think the most difficult moment was the foundation of the 'central'. It was a difficult moment because the expectation, our will, was to create a 'central' capable of gathering together all the Brazilian unions. This proved not possible and then, it was very difficult because we had, I mean, previously things were marching to the setting up of a huge congress and all of a sudden one part decided to give up, and we, suddenly, with nothing in hand, we held not even the secretariat of organisation of that meeting, the Conclat that had been convened in Praia Grande, we had absolutely nothing. Then we had to arrange things by ourselves, you know, under a terrible fear of making mistakes, a fear that things would go wrong, and we carried on the congress. On the opening day, early in the morning, we were there in the space 'Vera Cruz' in São Bernardo, where the congress was being staged, and we were trembling, trembling, trembling with fear that the congress was not a success. We were not sure whether the delegates would come down as they had promised because there were many difficulties of transporting the workers from Amazonas, Rio Grande do Norte, Acre and Rio Grande do Sul to São Paulo. We were surely apprehensive. And, then, after 8 p.m. we started feeling another fear, asking God that no more delegates came over because we could not afford to accommodate all of them. Eh! approximately 5,200 delegates from all over the country arrived. This was a very difficult moment, of apprehension and fulfilment![14]

5.2   CGT

The sectors who had opposed the creation of the CUT by the 'independent or authentic' militants convened a conference in Praia Grande in November 1983 and launched the National Co-ordination of the Working Class – CONCLAT. Representatives of 1,258 entities and 4,254 delegates took part in the event and agreed to create an organisation with a provisional nature. Deciding against setting up a definitive central organisation, they intended to demonstrate their willingness to continue to seek the unity of the whole movement. This provisional character of the 'co-ordination' also rested on the assessment that the CUT constituted by the new unionism would be short-lived, so rendering feasible the reunification of the movement. The conference appointed the president of the CONTAG, José Francisco da Silva, as its first president.[15]

The attendance figures at the two national conferences cast light on both the fairly even strength of the two blocs of the labour movement and their distinct patterns of representation. On the one hand, the conference called by new unionism was attended by one national confederation, 5 federations, 355 urban unions, 310 rural unions, 134 pre-union associations, 99 civil servants associations and a minority of unspecified other entities. On the other, the conference of 'Unidade Sindical' assembled 5 national confederations, 66 federations, 4 national unions, 440 urban unions, 645 rural unions, 43 pre-union associations, 29 state civil servant associations and a handful of unspecified associations. This picture makes clear the prevalence in 'Unidade Sindical' of the unions of the official structure, particularly the upper-level confederations and federations. By contrast, among the attendees of the conference held by the new unionism there was a strong presence of unofficial and non-recognised entities (Comin, 1994: 367).

Given its outlook, the 'Unidade Sindical' branch of the labour movement was not as concerned with rank-and-file organisation, direct bargaining and confrontational strategies as the CUT. Later on, such differences in practical behaviour led to an increasing relative growth of the CUT to the detriment of the CONCLAT's. In fact, by 1986 the strength of the CUT was very prominent, as testified by its substantial presence in the more organised sectors of the working class and in the more powerful unions, not to speak of its solid roots at plant level. In response to that situation,

CONCLAT's leaders called a second national conference to be held in Praia Grande, São Paulo on 21, 22 and 23 March 1986 with the purpose of forming a central organisation and replacing the existing co-ordination. So the 'Central Geral dos Trabalhadores' (CGT) was created by 5,546 delegates from 1,341 unions, federations, confederations and associations. Among the principles of the approved programme was the rejection of ILO Convention 87, acceptance of the uniqueness awarded by law (monopoly of representation) and the strengthening of the normative power of the labour court. Regarding the union tax, various remarks were made. While the programme advocated the retention of this corporatist institution, it also demanded the devolution by the Ministry of Labour of the percentage of 20 per cent of the union tax established by law to finance the Ministry's activities (through the 'Conta Especial Emprego e Salário' defined in Article 589 of CLT). The reunification of the whole labour movement was kept among its principles (Article 3 of the CGT's statutes).[16]

The CGT went on assembling all the less antagonistic sectors of the labour movement up to its second national congress held between 27 April and 1 May 1989 in Praia Grande, São Paulo. This Congress, gathering 984 union organisations and 3,500 delegates, culminated in the split between the followers of the old leader Joaquim dos Santos Andrade and, opposing them, the militants linked to the emerging leader Antônio Rogério Magri. In fact the split may be attributed to a mere power dispute between factions. The union militants affiliated to MR-8, perceiving that the Magri group had the majority of the delegates, succeeded in persuading the then president of the entity, Joaquim dos Santos Andrade, to walk out of the congress. Their idea was to make the congress illegal as its president had not conducted the proceedings. Another version stresses the resort to fraud and physical violence by Magri's followers to the point of virtually impeding the group led by 'Joaquinzão' from taking further part in the congress (CGT, 1989; Antunes, 1991: 59; interview no. 24 with the president of the CGT in Pernambuco, José Carlos Andrade).

Following the walking out by one of its chief factions, two CGTs were created. The 282 entities led by Joaquim dos Santos Andrade and the MR-8 activists abandoned that congress claiming to represent the former CGT. Arguing that its denomination should be kept as the 'Central Geral dos Trabalhadores', the label chosen in the foundational congress held in 1986, they set up another one on September 30th and October 1st and elected 'Joaquinzão' to the presidency of what they claim to be the 'true CGT.[17]

The other section, having the majority of the delegates of the 1989 Congress under the leadership of Antônio Rogério Magri, carried on the congress's tasks and also claimed to continue the CGT, now under the label 'Confederação Geral dos Trabalhadores'. They maintained that this denomination had been agreed by all the CGT's fractions in a national meeting held in September 1988 convened to prepare the Second National Congress of 1989. Thus, for them, the official name of the CGT had changed into 'Confederação Geral dos Trabalhadores' since that national meeting of 1988. It was merely a matter of continuation. The reasons for altering the denomination in 1988 from 'Central' to 'Confederation' pay tribute to emblematic, deeply rooted traditions of the labour movement in the country. The term 'confederation' was the one accepted by law as the top organisation of the union structure. By that time the constitution of a nationally inclusive organisation of workers was forbidden. Only top organisations of the official union structure were allowed. By naming their inclusive top entity as a 'confederation', those unionists aimed at becoming the only national peak body permitted to be legalised. Their expectation at the time was that the Constituent National Assembly would maintain the prohibition of the creation of any top organisation other than the 'confederations' (interview no. 24, with José Carlos Andrade).

In the wake of those events, the Brazilian union chart ended up with a confused look where two national organisations are designated by the label CGT. The CGT created by 'Joaquinzão' and the MR-8 militants, named the 'Central Geral dos Trabalhadores', claimed to assemble 692 entities, in 1991, and 811 in May 1995 (Rodrigues, 1990a: 121–2; *Folha São Paulo*, 01.05.95). In 1995 its president was Antônio Neto, a unionist connected to the MR-8. The fraction led by Magri persisted with the same CGT label, but as an abbreviation for 'Confederação Geral dos Trabal-hadores'. In 1991, it claimed to represent 1,100 organisations. In May 1995, its total of affiliated unions had shrunk to 528 (Martins, 1991: 152; *Folha de São Paulo*, 01.05.95), having as its president in 1995 the former leader of the telecom workers of the small state of Rio Grande do Norte, Francisco Canindé Pegado.

5.3   Força Sindical – Polarising with the CUT

The CGTs' evolution proved to be highly contradictory due to the heterogeneity of their ranks. Some ideological groups aligned themselves with the pelegos. From the non-ideological sectors, an important tendency arose under the main leader-ship of Luís Antônio Medeiros, the president of the biggest worker union in Latin America – the Metalworkers' Union of São Paulo – who had succeeded Joaquim dos Santos Andrade. Another prestigious leader of the rising current was the president of the urban workers, Antônio Rogério Magri. More dynamic and largely financed by some sectors of American unionism, initially this current undermined the leadership of 'Joaquinzão' and eventually split the CGT when Magri took over the presidency in 1989.

Subsequently, as a result of the apparent loss of appeal and ineffectiveness of the CGTs, they moved toward the founding of a novel central organisation, called 'Força Sindical', henceforth named FS. Thus, when one of its exponents was the head of the Ministry of Labour,[18] what was initially a tendency turned into a national 'central' organisation. The foundational congress reassembled in São Paulo, on 8, 9 and 10 March 1991, with the participation of 1,800 unionists from 792 entities. Luiz Antônio Medeiros was declared its first president.[19]

Determined to combat the growing influence of the CUT, FS claimed to practise a 'unionism of results'. Instead of what its formulators alleged to be the 'ideological' union-ism of the CUT, emphasis was put on the pragmatic ob-taining of benefits for workers. Particularly after 1987, initially inside the CGT, afterwards through the new 'central', the current which became known as 'unionism of results' con-centrated on distancing itself from the policies pursued by the CUT and on an increasing availability to dialogue with the government. The three attempts made by the Sarney government at a 'tripartite' negotiation with the principal social actors were characterised by the reticence of the CUT and an intensive engagement on the part of Medeiros and its current in search of assertion as a moderate and reliable interlocutor. The 'unionism of results' seemed keen to negotiate even when the government refused to discuss basic economic policies and proposed relatively secondary matters to the round table. This attitude provoked the criticism that the former tended to lay excessive emphasis on the so-called agreements at the top.

The self-proclaimed pragmatism of FS entails that worker demands are dealt with on the basis of a so-called 'economicist' approach. In this light, it alleges complete independence from politics (hinting at a contrast with the CUT's links with PT), albeit this claim could be questioned by recalling the well-known intimacy of Luís Antônio Medeiros and Antônio Rogério Magri with President Collor in the early 1990s. In practice, Medeiros has been involved in virtually every political election since his ascent in the second half of the 1980s, as in his support to right-wing candidacies such as those of the entrepreneur Antônio Ermírio de Morais to the São Paulo state governership in 1986, of Paulo Maluf (the former candidate of the military in the indirect presidential election won by Tancredo Neves in 1984) to the mayorship of São Paulo, and of Collor in 1989. He himself ran for the governorship of São Paulo, earning a poor fourth place in 1994.

FS then emerges as an alternative to the militant and politically-linked CUT. But it also claims to depart from the more traditional old guard of the Brazilian labour movement, which it regards as still dependent on the inducements provided by the corporatist framework and on a statist and clientelistic approach. In fact, the managerial style developed by Medeiros in the running of the Metalworkers' Union of São Paulo went beyond the mere delivering of welfare provisions to members. He held elections for shop stewards in some enterprises, tried to increase membership and put the union in the command of a number of strikes. While those initiatives were scarcely matched by other unions affiliated to FS,[20] some analysts have interpreted them as marks of departure from the old bureaucratic unions of the pelegos (Comin, 1994: 381).

FS presents itself as the only 'central' in tune with the necessary reforms of both the state and the economy as they have been defined by the agenda adopted by most of the Latin American countries in the 1990s. In its formulators' words, FS claims to be 'modern, democratic, independent, non-partisan, pluralistic and Latin American' (Rodrigues and Cardoso, 1993: 20). To distance itself from the CUT, since its birth FS has attempted to demonstrate a disposition to dialogue with both the government and the business community and an acceptance of most of the agenda defined by the latter. Through such a stance, Medeiros and his followers claimed to address workers' needs more efficaciously and to provide them with concrete results. Hence, their claim to practise a 'unionism of results'.

By the end of the 1980s, the media and the entrepreneurs were not parsimonious in their hailing of a 'new type' of unionism characterised by disposition to dialogue, independence from ideologies and ability to address the 'true' interests of production and of the workers themselves. Notwithstanding such a warm reception, FS had to face a union scenario where there were few 'vacuums' to be filled, given both the widespread insertion of the CUT in practically all the sectors of the organised labour force and the presence of the CGTs. As the survey undertaken by Rodrigues and Cardoso (1993) in their foundation congress in 1991 reveals, the entity concentrated on just a handful of states and economic sectors. Some important unions such as the Metalworkers of São Paulo, Volta Redonda, São Caetano, Guarulhos and Osasco have been affiliated to the central. But they are concentrated in one single industrial sector of one single region of the country. Indeed, as it emerges from Figure 2.1 and Table 2.2, FS concentrates on the states of São Paulo (45 per cent of the delegates to the inaugural congress), Minas Gerais (13 per cent) and Paraná (12 per cent), and basically on the metallurgy industry, food industry and service sectors.

As for the system of labour relations, FS claims to favour the overcoming of the corporatist framework through the

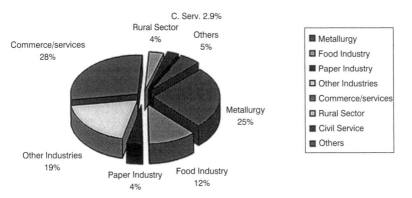

Figure 2.1   FS: representation by type of unions of the delegates to the foundation congress, 1991

Table 2.2   FS: representation in the first congress and directorate, by states and regions

States and regions	No. of delegates	Directorate (%)
São Paulo	547	52.4
Rio e Espírito Santo	92	13.8
Paraná	143	9.2
Minas Gerais	155	6.2
Rio G. do Sul e S. Catarina	57	7.7
Northeast Region	107	7.7
North Region	39	1.5
Centre-West Region	64	1.5

Source: Rodriguez and Cardoso, 1993: 28–9.

introduction of an alternative based on the 'collective labour contract' as it was initially proposed by the CUT. As will be seen in the next chapter, although most of the FS-connected unions have not taken further practical steps towards superseding the corporatist framework, it has gradually stressed its commitment towards a new arrangement for the country. But apart from the already noted question of its narrow insertion into a small range of economic sectors, FS had to attract the existing official unions not already committed to the CUT. Hence, most of its affiliated unions are not so different in kind from the accommodated old guard of the Brazilian unionism. Besides this relative 'traditionalism' of the FS unions at the base, the internal life of the entity has been marked by the absence of organic structures connecting the national directive body to the affiliated unions, internal procedures and regular widespread publications. All these factors combine to produce a picture where the rhetorical proposals put forward by the national direction are weakly matched by the practice of its affiliated unions. Such a gap is apparent from the recent publication sponsored by FS (1993), whereby a team of scholars led by the economist Antonio Kandir elaborated a set of proposals supposed to summarise the platform of the entity. Such a huge work, addressing virtually all the current issues in discussion in the country, has not been followed by any attempt at its diffusion among the grassroots, let alone by the adoption of practices in tune with its directives.[21]

The actual behaviour of the Força Sindical leadership and affiliated unions have led some authors to conclude that, although it has approximated to the CUT's position on the need to change the system of labour relations, in fact it has failed both to advance a comprehensive alternative project and to introduce distinctive practices (Oliveira, 1994: 507, 514). Regarding the internal life of the 'central', it has been suggested that the president still concentrates too much power in his hands (Comin, 1994: 390). Early in 1995 internal disatisfaction with Medeiros's leadership style had already surfaced. Enilson Simões, known as 'Alemão', Lúcio Bellantani and José Avelino Pereira, prominent members of the national executive body, the former being the FS general secretary, expressed publicly their discontent and disillusionment with FS type of unionism. Bellantani was not prepared to accept that 'decisions are taken by a small part of the FS direction' and 'Alemão', in turn, declared that he did not feel 'committed to this model of unionism any longer' (Folha de São Paulo, 01.05.95, 1–6) and that he held 'ethical and political differences with Medeiros' (interview no. 9). Besides these national leaders of FS, the important Metalworkers' Union of Guarulhos and some leaders of the Metalworkers' Union of Osasco have also considered leaving the 'central' in order to create a fresh one. These criticisms coincided with the denunciations by a former Medeiros aide, Wagner Cinchetto, according to whom Medeiros held a parallel financial scheme to collect contributions from employers which have raised around US$2 million since 1990 (*Folha de São Paulo*, issues of 09.04.95 and 01.05.95).

5.4 Union Pluralism at the Top

The existence of a single union for the same area at the lower levels of the Brazilian union structure has paradoxically cohabited with pluralism at the top level. Not yet mentioned is the creation in July 1985 of the 'União Sindical Independente – USI', an attempt to group together some traditional unions, particularly from the commerce sector. This 'central' was very conservative, having served as a mouthpiece for the old pelegos who had not succeeded in adapting to the new phase of union competitiveness. By the end of the first half of the 1990s it had virtually disappeared, many of its affiliates having migrated towards other top organisations, as was the case of one of the unions in our sample, the Commerce Employees of Recife, later becoming one of the strongholds of Força Sindical in the state of Pernambuco. By May 1995, its president, Antônio Pereira Magaldi claimed to rely on the adherence of 26 federations and 2 confederations, quoting the federations of commerce employees in the states of Rio de Janeiro, Pernambuco and Bahia as the most influential affiliated bodies. This data suggest that rather than a 'central', USI is a loose articulation of some official federations with merely bureaucratic existence.

Another national articulation worth mentioning is the 'Corrente Sindical Classista'. Constituted in 1987 as a dissident group of the CGT by unionists close to the Communist Party of Brazil ('PC do B'),[22] it served as an articulation of unions disagreeing with the path of the CGT and with the prevalence of the methods of the 'unionism of results'. Having being expelled from the CGT in 1988 due to attrition with the current led by Medeiros and Magri, the 'Current Sindical Classista' subsequently decided – in its second congress held in March 1990 in Rio de Janeiro – to dissolve and affiliate its 584 unions in the CUT.[23]

Finally, there is the 'Central Sindical de Trabalhadores Independentes – CSTI' launched in March 1994 as another national articulation of unions either dissatisfied with existing confederations or seeking fresh political space. This is another another loose group based on the drivers' unions of São José do Rio Preto (SP), Uberlândia (MG) and Cárceres (MT) which could scarcely be regarded as a national top organisation. Nevertheless, it has claimed that it brought together 623 unions by May 1995 (*Folha de São Paulo*, 01.05.95).

With the virtual irrelevance of the USI and CSTI, besides the fading of the CGTs' strength, it is safe to assert that, at the top level, the significant central organisations which shape and will shape the development of the labour relations system are the CUT and Força Sindical. Nevertheless, the CGTs still enjoy a relative presence in the hierarchy of the old corporatist apparatus. They have been able to resist changes which have been urged by other organisations through lobbying against the complete legislative elimination of the corporative union structure. Table 2.3 offers a summary of the national top organisations around May 1995 providing information on date of foundation, main affiliated unions, number of affiliates and international allegiances.

6   THE 1990s: A NEW CYCLE

6.1   Hard Times for Labour

The first direct presidential elections held in the country after two decades of general-presidents appointed by the military is deemed to have inaugurated a phase of consolidation of democracy. The two candidates in the second ballot represented different sectors and projects. On the one hand, Fernando Collor ran on a platform of modernisation, advancing a neo-liberal stabilisation programme. Claiming to represent a major break with traditional politics and launching a strong appeal to rescue the excluded sectors – the shirtless ('descamisados') – he was in fact supported by the establishment, industrialists and the political forces that had sustained the military regime. On the other

Table 2.3   Workers' national top organisations, May 1995

Central	Date of foundation	Main unions	Number of unions	International affiliation
CUT	August 83	Metalworkers ABC; Bank Employees of SP; Teachers Assoc. (SP).	2,256	Intern. Confed. of Free Union Organisations
Força Sindical	March 1991	Metalworkers (SP); Commerce Emp. (SP); Textile Industry (SP).	978	ICFUO
CGT – Confederação	April 1986	Railway Workers (SP); Railway Workers of Sorocaba; Railway Workers of Mogi.	528	ICFUO
CGT – Central	March 1986	Data Processing Employees of SP; Building Workers of Campo Grande (MT); Drivers of Espírito Santo.	811	World Union Federation (WUF)
Central Sindical de Trabalhadores Independentes – CSTI	March 1994	Drivers of São José do Rio Preto (SP), Uberlândia (MG), and Cárceres (MT).	623	Latin American Workers Confederation (CLAT)
União Sindical Independente – USI	July 1985	Federations of Commerce Employees of Rio de Janeiro, Pernambuco and Bahia	26 federations/ 2 confederations	Not affiliated

Source: *Folha de São Paulo*, 01.05.95, pp. 1–6, on the basis of data provided by the 'centrals'.

hand, Lula presented himself as the candidate of the popular sectors and the other democratic forces which had fought the democratic struggle in the past years.

Although his adversary had mustered the support of more than 31 million voters, the modernisation programme proposed by Collor was clearly legitimated by the democratic process. The set of measures included the following: privatisation, internal administrative reform with a drastic reduction of civil servants, who were made redundant,[24] the freezing of wages and prices, and the confiscation of savings accounts deposits. All these initiatives posed a heavy strain on the labour movement, with the further aggravation of the recession into which the country was driven by governmental economic policies.

Despite some attempts by the CUT and to a lesser extent by the CGTs to mobilise the workers against the recessive stabilisation programmes in June 1990 ('Brasil Novo' Plan) and May 1991 ('Collor II Plan'), the conjuncture pushed the labour movement to a defensive position. The number of strikes fell considerably in relation to the last year of the Sarney government. Research carried out by scholars from Unicamp shows that the number of strikes in those years went down from 3,943 in 1989, to 2,357 in 1990, 1,399 in 1991 and 568 in 1992 (Noronha, 1994). In fact, it has been suggested that this decline was a relative one, for the other indicators of industrial action such as *number of strikers* and *non-worked days* remained similar to 1989, with the exception of 1992. According to Noronha's interpretation (1994), the labour movement pursued a strategy of strikes per category or sector rather than merely per factory. For 1992, he suggests that the political uncertainties of the process of impeachment of President Collor (lasting from May to September) shifted the labour movement towards a more cautious stance (1994). Arguably, too, most unionists were concentrated in the broad massive demonstrations which drove millions of people into the streets. Be that as it may, the fact remains that the Collor government inaugurated a new phase for the labour movement, where the confrontational strategies of the 1980s were no longer easily feasible, and the challenges of the restructuring of the economy brought fresh constraints.

Faced with recession and a decisive anti-labour government, the labour movement, particularly the new unionism, entered a phase where the conditions that had enabled the explosion of militancy of the 1980s were no longer in place. The political spaces had been occupied, the government divergence about which strategies to pursue came to light dramatically in its fourth congress held in Minas Gerais in 1991. Two broad tendencies embraced different projects. On one side, the so-called 'Cut pela Base' advocated that the 'central' should continue to act as an 'articulator' of the popular movement rather than institutionalising itself and participating in the institutions as a formal representative of workers. Mobilisation of rank-and-file should be the sole concern of the CUT, which had nothing to do in tripartite negotiations with government and employers. Workers' demands were to be met merely by direct actions. On the other, the majority current, the so-called 'Articulação', maintained that the end of the cycle of growth experienced in the 1980s demanded that the CUT act as the representative of workers in all the available channels in combination with continued emphasis on organisation of the rank-and-file. As Comin puts it, it became apparent that there were two great challenges confronting the 'central': the need to produce qualitative alterations in both its own organisational structures and in the affiliated unions, and the assertion of its negotiating role as representative of workers (Comin, 1994: 391). Having prevailed in the 1991 congress by a slight majority, the elected leadership of the CUT gradually impelled the movement towards more proactive ('propositivas') stances. In the words of Jairo Cabral, the president of the CUT branch in the state of Pernambuco in the period 1988–93, and a member of the National Executive Body from 1994 onwards, 'the CUT moved from the initial merely antagonistic phase, passed to a rhetorical phase of being "propositive", and finally to being propositive in practice' (interview no. 19). By the expression 'propositive' the new unionism militants meant taking part in negotiations with government and employers, either through formal or informal channels, not only in order to push forward slogans but to articulate well-worked-out alternative policies in all areas of interest to workers and other popular sectors such as in housing, land reform, social security and pensions, fiscal reform, etc.

Correspondingly, the CUT began to take part in certain public bodies whose management the 1988 Constitution had reserved to tripartite representation, the first and foremost being the so-called 'Fundo de Garantia do Tempo de Serviço'.[25] Following that initiative, the 'central' entered into the directive council of the following entities: Fund for Supporting the Worker ('Fundo de Amparo ao Trabalhador – FAT'),[26] Fund for Social Development ('Fundo de Desenvolvimento Social – FDS'),[27] National Council for

Health and Social Security ('Conselho Nacional de Saúde, Previdência e Seguridade Social'), National Council for the Children ('Conselho Nacional do Menor e do Adolescente'), and National Council for Social Work ('Conselho Nacional de Assistência Social').

6.2   The 'Forum on the Collective Labour Contract' and the Impulse of Minister Barelli

As Minister of Labour (October 1992–March 1994), Walter Barelli showed a consistent determination to foster discussion of the alternatives to state corporatist labour relations. Having long served as a director of DIEESE, a statistical institute sponsored by the labour movement, Barelli identified with the approach developed by the new unionism as an alternative to the current system. His view was thus expressed in an article published in 1993 (pp. 28–9):

> To establish the collective labour contract we must modify the principles and fundamentals of the current system, attempting to put forward a system capable of fulfilling the following requirements: a) enhancing workers' protection; b) providing a safe and rapid answer to economic transformation, in order to ease negotiations about adaptation and flexibility; c) devolving union freedom and autonomy, boosting collective bargaining and ensuring the right to strike.

In conformity with such a view, one of his first initiatives was the urging of all the parties to formulate their proposals to change the labour relations system. The impulse towards the discussions led some of the main parties (CUT, FIESP, PNBE and CGT) to sign a document resulting from the 'Forum Capital–Labour' of the Institute of Advanced Studies of the University of São Paulo in mid-1993. Under the label 'Modernisation of Capital–Labour Relations' that document presented the first consensual points such as the diminution of state intervention in the labour conflict, and the end of both the union tax and the monopoly of representation. Some controversial points were also noted such as the FIESP's resistance to the combination of statutory legal rights with the regime of the collective labour contract. Unions' rights within the enterprise were also resisted by employers (*Folha de São Paulo*, 09.08.93).

The next step was the 'Forum on the Collective Labour Contract and Labour Relations' called by the Ministry of Labour for the second semester of 1993. All the main actors of the system took part in the three-month discussions, starting on September 22nd with the participation of representatives of 33 entities from state institutions, business, worker unions and other sectors of the civil society (*Folha de São Paulo*, 04.09.93). Besides the national representatives attending the main meetings in Rio de Janeiro, the local branches of the Ministry of Labour reproduced the forum at state levels in order to allow the regional parties to follow the national meetings and advance the local proposals. The final document of the 'Forum', announced in the final session held on 10 December 1993, outlined the following consensual views (Ministério do Trabalho, 1994):

- Critical assessment of the current corporatist system, its extensive and outdated legislation, state tutelage and negation of the conflict between workers and employers;
- Under that system, it becomes difficult to reach concerted solutions to labour conflicts through democratic means;
- The existing model needs a thorough overhaul in order to become participatory and transparent and to adopt the major goal of asserting citizenship;
- The urged changes must rest upon the following values: valorisation of employment, improvement of working conditions and payment, professional formation and qualification, and protection of unfair dismissals.
- The transformation of the model is feasible through the fulfilment of the following conditions and measures: enactment of supportive or auxiliary legislation to make union action and collective bargaining feasible at all; direct bargaining without compulsory intervention of the State; guarantee of the possibility of negotiating alternative ways of applying the labour law without the repeal of its provisions; possibility of arbitration of the collective labour conflict by the courts only through consensual initiative of the parties, forbidding the appeal to higher levels;

possibility of judgement by the labour courts in the collective conflicts just in disputes about interpretation of contractual clauses or legal provisions; validity of the clauses of the collective contract until revision by the new contract; extension of the jurisdiction of the labour court in interpretation of collective contracts to the public sector; adoption of the principles of union freedom and the right of worker representation within the workplace; provisions to force employers to comply with the collective agreement provisions, including the strengthening of the Ministry of Labour inspection power.

- Preservation of a period of transition before the introduction of the modern and democratic model.

In contrast with the old attitude of sending a bill to the Congress with a proposal solely elaborated by the government, Minister Barelli refused to present a bill without consulting the relevant parties, with a view to reaching a democratic consensus. In this sense, the conclusions of the 'Forum' represent a landmark in the history of the Brazilian labour relations. First, because in broad terms the corporatist framework was acknowledged to be outdated and in need of overhauling. Second, because it brought all the actors to negotiate their distinct approaches to the reform. But the consensual points described above in fact hide strong divergences when the proposals are examined in close detail and underlying principles. The analysis of the debates and proposals put forward in the 'Forum', accordingly, allows a classification of the proposals in three basic groups as follows: the global reform proposal, the proposals concerned exclusively with direct bargaining, and the proposals for partial modification of the model.

6.2.1   *The Global Reform Proposal*
First developed by the CUT under the label 'collective labour contract' this approach is addressed to the complete replacement of the current model in all its aspects, namely, the role of the state, union organisation, structure of collective bargaining, the solution of the labour conflict, the role of the labour court and the statutory labour law. Its proponents stress the view that the system of labour relations should

be oriented towards the participation of workers in the management of day-to-day capital–labour relations and the democratic resolution of the conflict. Since the expression 'collective labour contract' has recently been employed in different approaches as loosely denoting any alternative to corporatism, the CUT has preferred to designate its proposal as 'the democratic system of labour relations'. Recognising the extreme diversity of the different regions and economic sectors whose particularities are to be addressed, this proposition underpins the necessity of establishing a comprehensive framework of basic rights capable of ensuring at least uniformity of protection throughout the whole country. In order to supersede the current model, a set of proposals is put forward, the more important being those listed below:

- a more compact union organisation according to branches of economic activities;
- legal safeguards to protect and enable workers to organise freely at the point of production;
- articulation of the levels of collective bargaining from workplace up to national general level;
- elimination of compulsory arbitration by the labour court;
- full union autonomy and liberty;
- supportive legislation to foster union organisation and direct bargaining;
- maintenance of a basic set of individual statutory labour rights that would protect the sectors not covered by collective bargaining.

Besides the CUT, a similar view has recently been espoused by other actors involved in the debate, particularly in those that took place in the mentioned Forum, as happened with Força Sindical, PNBE (a modernising current of employers), Sinfavea (the employers national union of the motocar industry), and Anamatra (the national association of the judges of the labour court).[28]

6.2.2 *The Proposals Concerned Exclusively with Direct Bargaining*

This group of proposals has in common an exclusive concern with introducing free collective bargaining, markedly at the decentralised level of enterprise, in order to cope with the need for restructuring and modernising the productive apparatus. The competitive pressures stemming from the opening up of the economy initiated by President Collor and continued by Presidents Franco and Cardoso require a more flexible and adaptable management of the labour force, free from state-imposed constraints. The logic is to value a direct relationship of management with employees in the particular setting of the company, dispensing with the State and the union whenever possible. As a corollary, such an approach aims to deregulate the labour law and has no concern with the less developed sectors where bargaining is less feasible.[29] Given the objective of terminating the current excessive intervention of the State through the detailed labour law and the labour court settlement of conflicts, some of the concrete measures advocated by this group partially coincided with those of the so-called 'global reform proposal' group. This partial coincidence, though inspired by distinctive assumptions, helps to justify some initial consensus registered in the 'Forum'. Among the leading advocates of this proposal are FIESP, FENABAN, CNA, CNI, CNC and ABRH.[30]

6.2.3   The Proposals for Partial Modification of the Model

The third group of proposals is put forward by the more traditional actors who are only interested in partial reform of the existing hybrid corporatism. On the one hand, the survival of a number of entities of the union movement depends upon the corporatist inducements (monopoly of representation, union tax and normative power of the labour court), particularly the top official federations and confederations: this is the case of the CGTs, CNTI, CNTM, CNTC, CONTEC, CONTAG and CNT. The discontinuance of these inducements would jeopardise workers' organisation in the middle of an adverse political and economic conjuncture (Andrade, 1994, 1995). For them, the debate on the reform of the system is an opportunity for some partial improvements such as the introduction of protection against unfair dismissal and the reform of the labour court. On the other hand, there is a diffuse position within some entrepreneurial sectors (expressed by the Commerce Federation of São Paulo or by the National Confederation of Agriculture, for example – see *Folha de São Paulo*, 09.08.93) demonstrating no strong interest in changing a model that has maintained union organisation outside the enterprises and has not challenged the traditional paternalist and authoritarian pattern of administration of the labour force (Siqueira, 1994b; *Boletim Informacut* 250; and Ministério do Trabalho, 1993).

6.3   Labour Relations under the Government of Fernando Henrique Cardoso

The overwhelming victory of Fernando Henrique Cardoso over Lula and the other candidates in the first ballot of the presidential election held on 5 October 1994 speeded up the modernising agenda which had been slowing down during the Itamar Franco government. Having enacted a stabilisation programme in July when acting as Finance Minister, Cardoso came to power in a wave of strong popular support. His initial measures aimed at keeping inflation down, accelerating the privatisation programme, reducing the fiscal deficit, reforming the pension system, curbing the number of civil servants and redefining the responsibilities among the three levels of the Brazilian federation. Because the enforcement of most of these measures was prevented by Constitutional provisions, the government stressed the need for constitutional change as a prerequisite of the continuation of its programme of reforms. By the end of the first half of 1995 Cardoso had succeeded in passing some amendments to the Constitution allowing the termination of the state monopoly in telecommunications and oil. In the former case, Congress approved the amendment after the government had defeated the strong Oil Industry Workers' Union, a CUT affiliate. In May the oil workers of 'Petrobrás' had launched a general strike protesting against the government's decision not to pay the wage correction agreed in September of the previous year in a negotiation in which the then President Itamar Franco took part. The stoppage lasted 30 days and the country's 11 refineries' output fell by nearly 11 per cent, giving rise to a loss estimated in US\$ 200 million. But the government faced the movement in the light of its strategy to confront one of the strongest adversaries of its project to lift the state monopoly of oil. On May 24th, 1,600 army troops took over four of the paralysed refineries, following the decision by the labour court declaring the strike illegal and imposing a fine of US\$ 100 thousand a day on the unions whose workers failed to return to their jobs.[31] Following the occupation, the government laid off a hundred strikers, among them some union leaders.[32] The crack-down on one of the strongholds of the labour movement thus paved the way to the reforms pursued by the government.

The opening phase of the Cardoso presidency was thus marked by the endeavour to advance the programme of reforms on the assumption that the stabilisation plan would not keep inflation down unless the reforms were concluded. In regard to the process of reform of the system of labour relations initiated by the Itamar Franco government, two factors are noteworthy. First, the context has forced the government to concentrate on the already referred to set of measures, given its priority to push ahead with the stabilisation. The long and complex changes required in labour relations, although important for the restructuring of the economy, are not perceived as one of the first priorities. Secondly, the initial relationship with the CUT was marked by the confrontational stance adopted in the episode of the oil workers, probably with the aim of weakening resistance against certain measures such as the breakup of the state monopolies in oil and telecommunications and the reform of the pension system. In consequence, the steps already taken towards reform of the system of labour relations under the auspices of the former Minister Barelli have been awaiting a more suitable conjuncture.

During the electoral campaign and in its first declarations in office, Fernando Henrique Cardoso manifested a vague concordance with the proposal of introducing the 'collective labour contract'. But as already noticed, the label has been used in several different perspectives. An early hint was given when he mentioned the issue as a means of replacing the then existing wage indexation (*Folha de São Paulo*, 06.10.94). In fact, in July 1995 the government enacted the Provisional Measure ('Medida Provisória') no. 1053, eliminating the indexation of wages and trying to boost direct negotiation through mediation and the imposition of certain obstacles to the intervention of the labour court (*Jornal do Commercio*, 04.07.95). These measures however fell short of introducing the comprehensive set of changes necessary to supersede the current hybrid corporatist system and were undertaken with no consultation with the relevant actors.

Although the issue of the future system of labour relations has not yet been fully introduced into the government agenda, the parties have already accumulated a considerable set of concrete proposals as well as some consensual points. On the part of the core sector of the labour movement, the CUT, the willingness to negotiate the reforms proposed by the government and Congress has been reasserted. At the meeting of its national directive body held on May 5th, the CUT officially decided to create a commission charged with initiating negotiation with the government and Congress on the programme of reforms. At the same meeting, the 'central' presented its own proposal for the reform of the pension system and decided to urge the government to start such a programme with the issues of the tax system and labour relations (*Folha de São Paulo*, 06.05.95, and *Jornal do Commercio*, 06.05.95). In respect of the tax reform, ratifying its 'propositive' attitudes, the CUT took an active part in the elaboration of a set of proposals in common with the main business associations (Federation of Industrialists of São Paulo – FIESP, National Confederation of Industrialists – CNI, the 'National Thought of the Entrepreneurial Grassroots' – PNBE). Whilst some other workers' confederations adhered to the document presented to the government in May 1995, the initiative was credited to PNBE, FIESP and CUT due to their involvement in its elaboration. The document also urged the government to place the issue of labour relations on its immediate agenda (*Folha de São Paulo*, 07.05.95). In short, recent developments suggest that the reform of the current model of labour relations has not been cast aside by the main protagonists of the system.

3 The CUT's Model: Structures, Practices and Proposals

1 THE GROWTH OF THE CUT

1.1 The CUT's Confrontational Strategy

The changes in the Brazilian socio-economic structure during the military rule were highly significant in shaping the new grounds on which the emerging unionism was to develop. The modernisation of the productive structure of the country and the concentration of manufacturing industry in some specific regions and sectors (motor-vehicles, petrochemicals, durable consumer goods, etc.) had little impact on in-equalities of income distribution even when the economy was growing fast. Between 1960 and 1980, migration from the countryside amounted to around 28 million people, São Paulo alone accounting for 4.5 million people of those (Alves, 1994). The establishment of a modern industrial core in some metropolitan regions of the great cities opened up massive opportunities of employment for that large contingent of migrants, including their sons and daughters. Such a population concentration generated increasing demands from a new generation of workers eager to get their share of the benefits of the economic miracle. In this context, the initial mobilisations of the late 1970s were precipitated by the socio-economic strains experienced by the huge contingent of workers belonging to a fresh generation employed in the new industries (Oliveira, 1994: 498). Those workers no longer shared the deferential attitude of the country-bred parents nor the union culture which characterised populist politics prior to military rule. They were prepared to experiment with novel forms of expression of their grievances, both economically and politically. The new unionism that arose in the late 1970s was both an expression of and a response to a new generation of workers in a completely different economic context from that of the 'populist unionism' prior to military rule.

The role of the new unionism in the definition of the strategies of the labour movement in the last decade is salient from the records of the attempts at general strikes. The first occurred on 21 July 1983, called by the National Commission Pro-CUT, the national body which had been set up in the first Conclat held in Praia Grande in 1981 with participants drawn from all the currents of the labour movement. In this massive strike, the first since the early 1960s, between 2 and 3 million workers stopped working in protest against the high cost of living, government economic policies, wage squeezes, government interventions in unions and payment of the external debt (Sandoval, 1994).

The second sprang from the collapse of the 'Cruzado' Plan and took place immediately after the announcement of the 'Cruzado' Plan II, which had frozen prices and changed the wage escalator. Thus, on 12 December 1986, the labour movement launched the second general strike after the initiative of the CUT and the subsequent adherence of all then existing national organisations, CUT, CGT and USI. Whilst the movement did not reach all the work force, it was, however, sufficiently widespread to justify its characterisation as the largest mobilisation hitherto achieved by the labour movement. The CUT records claimed about 25 million participants, whilst military intelligence (National Service of Information – 'SNI') and the print media estimated they were around 10 million.[1]

The third general strike was once again called to protest against a shock policy package of the government which adversely affected real wages. The 'Bresser' Plan was announced in June 1987 and the strike called for August, after successive postponements and the exposure of the fissures between the various currents of the movement. Opposed by the 'unionism of results' (then a current within the CGT), the strike was considered a failure even by its organisers.

The CUT again had an important role in the fourth general strike of the period. This time the movement was successful, involving around 35 million workers according to its organisers (CUT and CGT). As stated by Sandoval (1994: 193), who draws on data collected by both *O Estado de São Paulo*, issue of 15 March 1989, and *Revista Veja*, issue of 22 March 1989, such a participation reached 37 per cent of the urban work force or 22 million workers. Protesting against another 'heterodox' shock package, the so-called Summer Plan, this general strike took place on 14 and 15 March 1989. It urged a fresh economic policy and the recovery of the wages lost as a result of the Summer Plan (varying between 41 per cent and 49 per cent). Most sectors of industry, transport, services and civil servants ceased working in almost all the capitals of the states. The movement was, according to the general evaluation, the most inclusive general strike ever registered in the history of the Brazilian labour movement.[2]

Another attempt at a general strike was made by the CUT on 12 and 13 June 1990, during the first semester of President Collor's mandate. It brought together the struggles of the many categories then mobilised in partial strikes for wage readjustments and against the harmful effects on wages caused by the economic policy. On the eve of the movement, the CUT changed its character into a 'national strike of the categories which were already in wage campaigning'. This recognised that the conditions were not suitable for a real general strike. Around 2 million workers of about 30 categories were involved in the movement, which, however, was judged unsuccessful.[3]

Yet again, on 22 and 23 May 1991, the CUT called a general strike to protest against Collor's economic policies epitomised in the so-called Collor II Plan (freeze of prices and wages, fiscal and monetary adjustments). Again, the movement proved a failure as a general strike, but was quite significant as a protest. There were stoppages in all the capitals of states and many other cities. According to the CUT's report,[4] about 18 economic branches were involved in the actions and several street demonstrations were performed throughout the country.

These movements, strongly influenced by the CUT, afford weighty evidence of the confrontational strategy adopted by the new unionism. If they represent a reactive defence against one-sided policies which had an adverse impact on real wages, they were also important means for increasing recognition in the public arena. They were, therefore, part of a broader tendency of widening industrial action. Tables 3.1 to 3.3 give an overview of the patterns of the strike rates since the rebirth of the labour movement in 1978, by focusing on the three basic strike indicators: number of strikes, number of strikers and non-worked days.

Some features of industrial action in this phase are worth noting. Take the distribution of the strikes in the public and private sectors. The pioneerism of the urban industrial workers, particularly the metalworkers, is clearly depicted by the figures that show the prevalence of the strikes in the private sector in the years from 1978 to 1980. In this initial phase of labour unrest, the number of strikes, the number of strikers and non-worked days are consistently higher for the private sector. From 1981 to 1983, when both the recession and the employers' reaction had caused a temporary retreat of the movement, the initial mobilisations of civil servants accounted for the increase of the public sector's share in the total of both non-worked days and

Table 3.1   Strikes per aggregate sectors urban areas, 1978–92

Years	Public sector		Private sector		Both		Total	
	Number	*%*	*Number*	*%*	*Number*	*%*	*Number*	*%*
1978	8	6.8	108	91.5	2	1.7	118	100.0
1979	38	15.4	184	74.8	24	9.8	246	100.0
1980	33	22.9	94	65.3	17	11.8	144	100.0
1981	40	26.7	87	58.0	23	15.3	150	100.0
1982	40	27.8	97	67.4	7	4.9	144	100.0
1983	114	29.0	274	69.7	5	1.3	393	100.0
1984	142	23.0	467	75.6	9	1.5	618	100.0
1985	289	31.2	622	67.1	16	1.7	927	100.0
1986	403	24.2	1,197	71.9	65	3.9	1,665	100.0
1987	838	38.3	1,344	61.4	6	0.3	2,188	100.0
1988	1,116	52.2	947	44.3	74	3.5	2,137	100.0
1989	1,298	32.9	2,540	64.4	105	2.7	3,943	100.0
1990	826	35.0	1,460	61.9	71	3.0	2,357	100.0
1991	649	46.4	733	52.4	17	1.2	1,399	100.0
1992	315	55.5	239	42.1	14	2.5	568	100.0
Total	5,834	35.5	10,154	61.8	441	2.7	16,429	100.0

Source: NEPP/UNICAMP, Research 'Acompanhamento de greves no Brasil; Desep/CUT for 1992, in Noronha (1994).

Table 3.2   Strikers per aggregate sectors, urban areas, 1978–92

Years	Public sector Number	%	Private sector Number	%	Both Number	%	Total Number	%
1978	26,806	18.9	115,75	81.1	0	0.0	141,981	100.0
1979	175,990	9.9	1,253,826	70.8	340,974	19.3	1,770,790	100.0
1980	220,533	27.2	533,624	65.8	56,935	7.0	811,092	100.0
1981	351,943	56.5	171,922	27.6	99,030	15.9	622,895	100.0
1982	262,105	54.8	116,532	24.3	100,000	20.9	478,637	100.0
1983	504,502	57.7	369,574	42.3	550	0.1	874,626	100.0
1984	871,538	65.9	426,213	32.2	25,636	1.9	1,323,87	100.0
1985	2,901,889	47.6	2,401,147	39.4	790,250	13.0	6,093,286	100.0
1986	3,478,498	56.4	1,991,505	32.3	692,745	11.2	6,162,748	100.0
1987	5,453,873	63.5	2,397,345	27.9	737,160	8.6	8,588,378	100.0
1988	6,236,689	75.9	1,740,334	21.2	241,523	2.9	8,218,546	100.0
1989	10,912,568	59.4	3,981,395	21.7	3,484,660	19.0	18,378,623	100.0
1990	14,258,304	70.3	4,588,486	22.6	1,449,566	7.1	20,296,356	100.0
1991	9,139,239	54.7	5,014,956	30.0	2,547,440	15.3	16,701,635	100.0
1992	2,044,747	69.9	849,410	29.1	29,315	1.0	2,923,472	100.0

Source: NEPP/UNICAMP, Research 'Acompanhamento de greves no Brasil; Desep/CUT for 1992, in Noronha (1994).

Table 3.3   Non-worked days per aggregate sectors, urban areas, 1978–92

Years	Public sector Number	%	Private sector Number	%	Both Number	%	Total Number	%
1978	443,489	24.4	1,366,649	75.0	11,100	0.6	1,821,239	100.0
1979	4,072,537	19.6	11,611,194	55.9	5,100,884	24.5	20,784,615	100.0
1980	4,945,247	35.5	7,683,344	55.2	1,282,516	9.2	13,911,106	100.0
1981	3,761,313	53.9	2,428,749	34.8	790,314	11.3	6,980,376	100.0
1982	3,406,838	65.9	1,285,318	24.9	474,678	9.2	5,166,833	100.0
1983	10,900,699	82.5	2,298,783	17.4	14,406	0.1	13,214,087	100.0
1984	11,621,737	82.7	2,363,557	16.8	63,008	0.4	14,048,303	100.0
1985	56,336,016	73.6	15,570,512	20.3	4,652,822	6.1	76,559,350	100.0
1986	40,133,423	75.6	11,351,228	21.4	1,598,951	3.0	53,083,602	100.0
1987	106,312,661	80.4	19,506,813	14.7	6,482,413	4.9	132,301,887	100.0
1988	75,549,895	85.3	12,482,883	14.1	531,589	0.6	88,564,367	100.0
1989	189,210,807	76.8	47,560,165	19.3	9,651,476	3.9	246,422,449	100.0
1990	126,056,642	67.3	43,814,198	23.4	17,407,883	9.3	187,278,723	100.0
1991	181,127,159	80.0	40,881,609	18.1	4,271,439	1.9	226,280,207	100.0
1992	19,593,646	86.8	2,901,305	12.8	84,365	0.4	25,579,316	100.0
Total	833,472,109	75.2	223,106,308	20.1	52,418,043	4.7	1,108,996,460	100.0

Source: NEPP/UNICAMP, Research 'Acompanhamento de greves no Brasil; Desep/CUT for 1992, in Noronha (1994).

number of strikers. But attesting that the industrial workers
continued to mobilise, the number of strikes was still higher
in the private sector during those three years of recession.
More precisely, the real initiation of the civil servants in
the strike activities should be located in 1983, when the
election of a number of state governors belonging to the
main opposition parties (PMDB, PDT) brought about a new
atmosphere for the expression of their demands. This is
confirmed by the figures shown in Table 3.1 for 1983, when
the number of strikes for the public sector almost trebled
in relation to the average of the previous years.

A clear turning point was the 1985 inauguration of the
democratic government after two decades of military rule.
Demands that had long been repressed came to the fore,
leading a huge number of occupational categories to start
their first industrial action in years. Thus, in 1985 the total
number of strikes leaped from 618 to 927, and both the
number of workers involved in strikes and the total of lost
days were multiplied by five. All the three indicators went
up steadily from 1985 onwards, reaching all-time peaks in
1989. This year exhibits the paroxysm of a period when
high inflation, wage deterioration and unfulfilled democratic
expectations coupled with a new sense of union legitimacy,
produced an unprecedented level of worker collective action.
It is interesting to note that these mobilisations were carried
out by workers belonging to both public and private sectors
of the economy. If one considers the number of strikes,
one will observe that there were more strikes in the private
sector, yet, since strikes in the public sectors are longer
and tend to encompass broader groups of workers, the other
two indicators are higher for the civil servants. The data
suggest that the entrance of public sector employees in
the labour struggle does not mean that they replaced the
private sector workers. Rather, the former's mobilisation
added up to the latter's.

Another discontinuity in the path of strikes could be
located in the ascent of President Collor in 1990, who
promptly advanced the neo-liberal anti-labour agenda.
Although the labour movement attempted to resist by calling
both general strikes and more localised initiatives, the
indicators for the period display a decrease in labour's ability

to mobilise. The noticeable exception is the high number of strikers in 1990, around 20 million, confirming the hypothesis that the behaviour of the labour movement at this time can best be understood as if it were pursuing a strategy of broad strikes involving whole categories and groups of categories (Noronha, 1994). In that year the impressive number of public employees on strike demonstrates the strength of civil servants' opposition to the dismantling of public administration attempted by the Administration. The figures for 1992, significantly lower than the two previous year, are interpreted by Noronha in part as underestimates due to the change of source and methodology,[5] and in part as a result of the uncertainties stemming from the process of the impeachment of president Collor (from May to September). Even though the levels of strikes in the early 1990s were still not low, it has been commonly agreed that a new phase was inaugurated after the steady expansionist cycle of the 1980s. As we pointed out in Chapter 2, this new cycle marked a combination of the resort to strike, still a constant, particularly in the 'CUTist unionism', with the utilisation of other channels for settling labour conflicts.

In overall terms, it should be remembered that the mobilisation initiated in 1978 marked the biggest wave of strikes ever engaged in by the Brazilian working class. Nonetheless, some strike patterns of the past have been maintained. According to Sandoval's analysis of the strikes in Brazil in the period 1945–90, the most constant strike pattern in the country has been the decentralised one, category-wide or enterprise-wide. He stresses, however, the extraordinary importance of the resort to broader mobilisations at certain special conjunctures. Thus, in the 1950s and early 60s, what he terms the 'massive strike' became the most prominent characteristic of Brazilian workers' stoppages. Aiming at pressuring the government and the entrepreunerial elites for political and economic changes, the 'massive strikes' accounted for 90 per cent of the total number of workers participating in such activity in the period from 1961 to 1963 (Sandoval, 1994: 108). Comparing such patterns with those of the 1980s, one could note a rough parallel. The massive or general strikes of the 1980s, still urging political and economic reforms, are very significant phenomena in trying to understand the strategies of the labour movement. But the most common pattern was the decentralised collective action. And among the decentralised strikes, the company-wide stoppages clearly prevailed in the period 1978–87, accounting for 75 per cent of the strikes as against 15 per cent for those per occupational categories or groups of categories, and 10 per cent per groups of enterprises (Noronha, 1994: 328). In terms of geographical distribution, the general pattern of concentration in the south-east was also maintained, despite a clear tendency to include other regions. Hence, the 82.7 per cent south-east share of the total number of strikes from 1945 to 1968 had merely been reduced to 65.4 per cent in the period 1978–87, São Paulo alone accounting for 56.9 per cent and 45.2 per cent, respectively, in the two periods. As for the duration, Brazilian strikes continued to be rather long in the period 1978–92, varying from an average of 3.4 to 10.4 days (Noronha, 1994: 328–9; Sandoval, 1994: 36).

This record of spectacular upsurge in strike activities in the 1980s provides an idea of the extent of the confrontational strategy pursued by the labour movement, particularly by the sectors gathered in the CUT. In a context of widespread labour retraction in most of the industrialised world, even in Latin America, the Brazilian workers were at odds with the general trend. Such a frequent resort to strikes proved to fulfil at least three objectives of labour during the redemocratisation. First, it helped to enhance workers' ability to resist wage deterioration. Second, it made feasible the insertion of labour into the public arena as an independent actor. Third, it put pressure on both the State and employers to alter the system of labour relations. In Chapter 7 we address these three important consequences of the confrontational strategy pursued by the new unionism in particular, trying to emphasise that it has thus contributed to developing workers' citizenship. To these effects, one could add the impact of the confrontational strategies on the union member's own attitudes and values, a point that we further develop in that chapter. Now we restrict ourselves to mentioning the importance of this sort of impact: in the case of the new unionism in Brazil, as with other social movements in Latin America, 'goals, tactics and strategic choices not only have impacts on the political environment but also shape the way issues are regarded within the movement, and so achieve lesser or greater degrees of loyalty and cohesion' (Foweraker, 1995: 50–1).

By comparison with the growth of the other sectors of the labour movement during the 1980s, the CUT's record is most impressive. Its accomplishments are even more remarkable when we consider the historical background of organised labour in Brazil. Its tradition and the legal framework then still entirely enforced did not furnish a helpful explanation for the CUT's performance. The corporative organisation used to be a considerable obstacle against autonomy since union leadership and workers themselves were inclined to trust in paternalistic attitudes either from the State or employers.

The confrontational strategy adopted by the CUT in this phase was chosen both to overcome the traditional subaltern position of labour in the public arena and to transform their living and working conditions. Such objectives were deemed incompatible with the CONCLAT's and CGT's emphasis on class alliance and moderation of workers' demands as the way to achieve democracy. For the CUT, workers' objectives could only be pursued by constructing an autonomous trade unionism and by developing the class autonomy of workers. In so doing, in view of the authoritarian tradition of the Brazilian elites, the new unionism had no choice but to adopt a militant attitude. To put it in other terms, the confrontational strategy was a means to assert the social citizenship of the workers. As Moisés observed (1982: 61), the working class had just begun to construct its own citizenship.

This strategy of conflict produced far-reaching results which laid the basis for future changes both in the Brazilian labour relations and in the wider democratic institutions. As Almeida argued (1988), the confrontational choice introduced collective bargaining into a system whose framework had been designed to prevent it; the stronger control mechanisms, such as the strike law, lost efficacy; the social question came to the public agenda, becoming at least rhetorically acknowledged by almost all the actors; and union life was revitalised with membership involvement and the renewal of leadership.

1.2 Acting within the Existing Framework

The upsurge of labour mobilisation had been firmly grounded upon the grassroots. We saw that even where the official union remained inert before workers' aspirations, several enterprise commissions were created by an emerging determined militancy. The question arising out of that development, therefore, was what to do with the increasing organisational achievements of the rank-and-file. The context in which the independent sectors of the labour movement appeared in the late 1970s and early 1980s theoretically offered two possible strategies. The factory commissions and groups in opposition to the union official leadership could become the nuclei either for a new and parallel union structure or for winning over existing corporatist unions in order to change their character.

The independent leaders opted for the second strategy as the only feasible one under the whole set of restraints then still imposed on workers' mobilisation. The chosen alternative implied the destruction of the state-sanctioned union structure from within, as Luís Ignácio Lula da Silva asserted as far back as in 1978:

> If there is a legally constituted union to represent the workers, what must we do? We must bring into the unions the best that there is within the factories. . . . there can be as many commissions as there are groups of workers, but they should work within the union, either to get rid of the union leadership or to make the union leaders work, whatever. But, I repeat, within the union, if what they want is to change unionism. Because in union assemblies, it's the union members who make decisions. If there are 1,000 workers from different groups and these people decide to change the rules of the game, then these people can come and change the rules of the game. What has to be done is to create conditions for these people to begin to participate.[6]

A similar view was expressed by Jair Meneguelli, the president of the CUT from 1983 to 1994:

> We did not want to create more unions. Our goals were just the other way round. It had to be a long journey. We were already talking about the proposal of the 'collective labour contract'. And it is impossible to introduce it with excessively scattered unions (today we have around 19,000 unions). Then what we had to do was to penetrate the official structure in order to change it.[7]

This choice was made in the beginning of the new unionism when there were some tendencies toward developing opposition groups into the embryo of a new framework to be built up (sectors of the 'Union Opposition'). However, when the CUT was founded in 1983 this path had already been undertaken by the new unionism. At that time, many official unions were under the control of unionists who had created the national organisation.

The CUT's strategy of acting within the existing union apparatus seems motivated, among other things, by two orders of factors. For one thing, the conceptions connected with the official unionism were substantially diffused among the workers by the early 1980s. As Erickson (1977) pointed out in discussing labour practices in the period up to 1964, the unions were regarded by the workers, in good measure, as an apparatus supposed to provide a number of welfare services. Usually workers felt themselves still too weak to organise on their own without employing some means available by the State.

For another, the effects of the brutal military repression of union life left a deep imprint on the workers' consciousness. The former activists were dismissed, often arrested and tortured. During military rule up to the 1980s, any sign whatever of militancy was branded as subversive; participation in union activity became very dangerous and could be sanctioned at least by dismissal. All these contextual restraints on the participation in union or political life had deeply marked the collective perception of the workers. In order to reorganise militant action, the leaders were confronted with the legitimisation of their initiative. A suspicious collective attitude had to be overcome in order to boost workers' mobilisation. Under those constraints it would be utopian not to employ the existing union as a resource to legitimise militant initiative.

Given the structural context, the CUT took a major policy decision to struggle for rupture with the corporatist or statist union structure and for developing an autonomous and militant unionism. Such a choice, however, was determined by the restrictions noted above. In consequence, the process was perceived to work through the existing union structure with the purpose of altering it. Even within the inherited organisations, there was a kind of 'vacuum' to be filled. That strategy of 'rupture from within' probably also explains the fast growth of the CUT to the detriment of both the old unionists (pelegos), who in reality did not want to change the structure, and of the traditional combative sectors, which were less critical about the actual union structure and were limited to seeking to liberalise it.

A strategy of this kind was seen by some authors as compromising the socio-political innovations of the new unionism, which would be strongly permeated by the conceptions related to corporatism. Criticising the CUT's choice, Boito Jr. (1991a) recalls this strategy of gaining control of the official union. He argues that union opposition groups, hitherto organised only in some enterprises within the category, usually the biggest ones, had a real chance of bypassing the official union apparatus. The only suitable alternative to fulfil the CUT's general objectives would have been the option of developing the embryonic structure so as to create a parallel union system. He argues that even the new unionists shared the populist ideology which sees the workers as weak and dependent on state protection to neutralise powerful employers. Consequently they failed to grasp the potential available for building up independent and parallel union structures. The option of working within existing unions to organise the whole membership of a given category is the result of a limited criticism of the received corporatist conceptions.

However, the already mentioned context in which the strategy was matured suggests that the alternative course would border on mere wishful thinking. Rupture from within was the path adopted, based on both objective and subjective constraints. At that time there was a widespread idea that the seizing of the official unions would be the most suitable way to extend the leadership of union opposition groups over the whole category, and to provide a material structure to support the struggle against the State and employers. This was regarded as the best solution to fill the vacuum left by previous authoritarian suppression of workers' organisation and mobilisation. A similar strategy was pursued by the South African new unionism, in another important instance of renewal of the labour movement in the 1970s and 80s. As Seidman points out in her comparative study of both new unionisms (1994: 189–90), the legal framework of the Apartheid state imposed a number of restrictions to workers' organisation (e.g. racial segregation). Up to the early 1980s, the non-racial trade unions which represented the black workers had refused to apply for registration and remained outside the state structures. But when the State relaxed certain constraints over the registered unions, such as the imposition of segregation of membership, the benefits of remaining outside the industrial system were outweighed by participation. Most black unionists came to conclude that, by registering their hitherto unofficial unions, they could prevent the high costs involved in forcing reluctant employers to recognise the unions whenever collective bargaining was to be attempted. Once their unions were registered, they could benefit from access to labour courts and recognition by employers for bargaining purposes. On such considerations, the argument that participation in state structures would narrow the unions' action to economic demands and would lead to bureaucratisation was gradually replaced by the consideration that registration was a convenient tactical decision rather than a matter of principle.

1.3   The CUT's Organisational Growth

The 1980s were marked by an overall decrease of the role of the unions in developed countries. In contrast with the sharp decline in the strength of unions in these countries, however, the Brazilian unions enjoyed rapid growth throughout a decade of general awakening of the labour movement.

Nevertheless, their relative position still presents a structural weakness, with a relatively low unionisation ratio.[8] Before the 1988 Constitution, union membership had remained at under 20 per cent of the working population.[9] A survey published by the IBGE in 1988 showed that from a working population of 51.73 million, about 9.09 million were affiliated either to a union or to an association. In this case, the ratio would be 17.6 per cent. If only the officially existing unions were taken into account, the 7.12 million members would represent a ratio of 13.8 per cent, although the former figure is more accurate due to the fact that most associations worked as 'de facto' union under the formal restrictions of the legal regime enforced up to 1988. The IBGE survey of 1990 showed that the unionisation ratio has been maintained in modest levels even after the huge mobilisations of the 1980s. In 1990 the ratio had reached 24.6 per cent of the economically active population.

The new Constitution lifted both the ban on unionisation of civil servants and the statutory requirement of prior authorisation by Ministry of Labour before unions could be set up. As a consequence, the number of unions virtually exploded. Between 1988 and 1990, the number of urban unions increased by 31.3 per cent, that is, one-third of the total was created in those years. In the same years, 1,311 worker entities were created. As the monopoly of representation was maintained, there still existed 255 of those new unions under legal challenge in the courts concerning alleged breaks of the principle of 'union uniqueness'. Therefore, between 1988 and 1990, 1,056 entities were definitively registered. Bearing in mind that the unions existing in 1987 were 5,648, there was a total of 6,703 worker entities in 1990. These figures imply a growth of 18.7 per cent.[10] Data for the more recent period are rather controversial for the current legal framework provides a strong incentive for the creation of a huge number of unions with scarce representative power, whose functioning is ensured by the union tax and the monopoly of representation. Data collected by the IBGE in 1991 and published in the official statistical year book in 1994 points to the existence of 10,750 unions (6,260 urban organisations and 4,445 rural ones) and 16,748,155 voluntary members. If one allows for the 1,705 employers' organisations (comprising 305,793 affiliated) one concludes that for the IBGE the number of workers' unions in 1991 amounted to 7,505, comprising both urban and rural entities; such employees' unions joined together 15,766,298 voluntary members. For 1994 the estimates vary from 9,000, according to some officials of the Ministry of Labour, to 19,000 unions, according to the CUT (Oliveira, 1994: 504, and interview no. 35, with 'Vicentinho', the CUT national president from 1994).

Although the democratic transition was conducted under the hegemony of the elites and the moderate sectors of the democratic forces, which reproduced both the subordinate role of labour and its structural weakness, one should not neglect the notable growth of unionism. A certain 'vacuum' inherited from the authoritarian period had to be filled in. Additionally, there was a rhetorical consensus at least about the necessity of relaxing the control of the State over union life. Thus, the decade witnessed both several general strikes (or attempts at general strikes) and an increase in industrial disputes, as we have already noted.

True, the growth of the labour movement is still insufficient for overcoming the structural fragility of organised labour in Brazil; but its general performance since its revival is impressive, even more when one considers the CUT. In June 1990, its 1,117 affiliated entities covered a total of 12,422,885 workers. Out of those, 3,536,947 were voluntary members of their unions, which implies a unionisation ratio of 28 per cent, substantially higher than the general ratio in the country. In August 1991, 1,679 unions were affiliated, representing 4.5 million unionised workers. Those unions recorded approximately 15 million workers in their base, which gave a unionisation ratio of 30 per cent (CUT, 1991). In June 1993, the number of affiliated unions had already risen to 1,917 (Comin, 1994: 379). More recently, in January 1995, the CUT's representation comprised 2,238 unions, with 17,592,189 workers at grassroots. Out of this base, 5,252,587 workers were voluntarily affiliated to their respective unions. The union density ratio in the CUT ranks, therefore, was 29.82 per cent in the early 1995, still higher than the figure for the entire country (*Informacut* no. 250, 1995). Figure 3.1 depicts the CUT's increasingly representative scope.

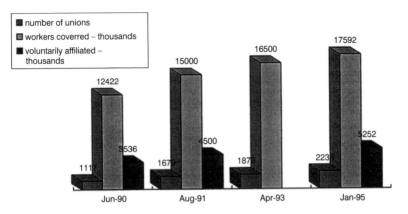

Figure 3.1 The growth of the CUT

Sources: CUT (1991); Comin (1994); and CUT (1995).

Obviously the mere number of entities affiliated or even the union density ratios are not enough to account for the real size of the CUT's share of the growing organisation of labour in Brazil. Since union tax and monopoly of representation were maintained, there still exists a notable dispersion of unions in the municipal or inter-municipal areas, as well as in the very large number of categories defined according to the main activity of the enterprise. Thus, very often the same economic branch, even in the same territory, is divided into many categories.

One must keep in mind, therefore, that the real organisational strength may not be gauged by the artificial figures of such a dispersed structure. As the actual presence of any organisation may only be assessed by its real capacity of mobilisation, we have to take stock of such fundamental factors as the nature of the sectors organised, the number of workers covered and affiliated, as well as the strategic position of the category in the production. In short, the qualitative profile of the representation cannot be forgotten.

Finally, before entering into the analysis of the alternative proposals elaborated by the CUT through its twelve years of existence, let us present a summary of the six national congresses it has held so far. As we observe in Table 3.4, in each congress the reasserting of the struggle for the workers' rights was combined with the maturation

Table 3.4 CUT's congresses

	Date	Number of delegates	Number of unions	Main decisions
Foundation	1983	5,054	911	Foundation; statutes; election of provisional executive committee, struggle for improving working rights.
1o.	1984	5,522	937	Priority to the horizontal structure (national and regional general branches); election of the national executive body; national campaign for the reduction of the work week to 40 h, land reform, union autonomy and freedom, and three-monthly wage adjustments.
2o.	1986	5,564	1,014	Definition of the vertical structure (department per economic branch); the collective labour contract as a new conception of negotiation; rejection of the social pact called by the government; general strike proposal against the government's economic policies.
3o.	1988	6,247	1,143	Struggle against the payment of the foreign debt; continuity of the struggle for workers' rights and for land reform; organisational consolidation with the definition of a whole alternative structure from the base to the top, to supersede the corporatist apparatus; criteria to choose delegates to the congresses according to the number of members affiliated instead of that of the category whose monopoly of representation is ensured by law; reasserting the collective labour contract; assertion of the role of the 'central' as organiser and contractual representative of labour; superseding of the conceptions about the 'Central' as merely a movement or articulation of the workers' struggle.

4o.	1991	11,554	1,679	Reasserting of its directive and contractual role; characterisation as a 'classist', autonomous, democratic, unitary, massive and 'basist' 'central' of workers; definition of the current challenges: to advance its implantation as an organic entity with its own structure, and articulate the struggle for immediate claims with the pursuit of a democratic society from the workers' standpoint; struggle against the neo-liberal project of Collor's government; articulation with other sectors of civil society in order to elaborate an alternative project of development with a more equitable income distribution; emphasis on the democratisation of the mass media.
5o.	1994	11,918	22,300	Mobilisation against the economic programme of the government; participation in the 'sectional chambers', Mercosul and other tripartite 'forums'; financial restructuring based on the union contributions of 5%, 8% and 9% of their revenues, respectively in 1995, 96 and 97; ratification of the proposal of the 'collective labour contract' or 'democratic system of labour relations'; neutrality of the entity in the 1994 presidential election combined with the recommendation of individual militants' involvement in the campaign for Lula; ratification of the struggle for land reform and other popular-oriented public policies (education, communication, health, housing, children, and informal sector work, anti-racism and gender).

Sources: 'Caderno de Teses ao 4o. Congresso da CUT', edited by CUT, 1991, mimeo; 'Resoluções do 4o. Congresso da CUT', edited by CUT, Set/1991, mimeo; 'Resoluções do 5o. Congresso', edited by CUT, Jun/1995; *Revista Istoé*, issue no. 1286, 25.05.94; and *Folha de São Paulo*, issue of 23.05.94.

of an alternative conception of both the union organisation and the collective bargaining. Under all sorts of political and economic constraints, the new unionism had also
to concentrate on the formulation of an alternative for the
old pattern of industrial relations still maintained to a
considerable extent by the 1988 Constitution. Equally noticeable is the deliberation about the formal links between
the 'central' and the affiliated unions in the third congress
held in 1988. Leading to a more organic structuring of
the CUT, which implied the definition of more precise sets
of duties and rights, including monthly dues, the resolutions of the third congress marked a turning point. From
then on, according to the former finance director of the
CUT in the state of Pernambuco, Cláudio Ferreira, 'the
"central" ceased to be a mere movement and became an
institutionalised representative of workers imbued with a
classist and unionist nature' (Interview no. 7). Another direction of evolution, equally noticeable, is the progressive
assertion of the 'central' as the representative of workers
in all spheres of negotiation, including tripartite bodies
such as the 'sectoral chambers' and managerial councils
like the FGTS. In sum, what clearly emerges from the
deliberations of its successive congresses is the maintenance
of a strong commitment to mobilisation of the grassroots
in pursuit of better working conditions and standards of
living for the whole popular sector, even though this commitment has recently been combined with an awareness of
the need to negotiate with governments and employers. In
order to give a more consistent idea of the CUT's growth
and awareness of the evolving challenges to the assertion
of workers' citizenship, Table 3.4 provides a summary of
the six congresses it has held up to 1995, by detailing
participation and resolutions.

2   DEVELOPING AN ALTERNATIVE MODEL OF INDUSTRIAL RELATIONS

The CUT was born out of the workers' struggle for higher
wages and better working conditions as well as for the
extension of citizenship towards the whole popular sector.

Since the beginning, the economic and political constraints were perceived to be strengthened by the existing model of industrial relations. To change patterns of behaviour was a difficult task in the Brazilian context. High inflation rates, unemployment, the unequal wealth and income distribution and authoritarian attitudes of both the State and employers towards labour explained the low level of union insertion into the public arena. In addition, the state-sanctioned union structure stood as a prominent obstacle to the self-organisation of labour which simultaneously helped to reinforce those adverse conditions.

Hence the CUT unionists viewed the overcoming of the corporatist model as a means to enhance both the workers' general standard of living and the labour insertion into the public arena. To tackle the reform of corporatism involved the removal of the obstacles it posed to autonomous union organisation and the democratic expression of the conflict with employers. The question then arose as to which should be changed first: the union organisation or the system of collective negotiations and conflict settlement? In other words, did the corporatist and fragmented official unions have to be replaced as a prerequisite to the struggle for an autonomous collective bargaining framework?

Awareness of the highly organic integration of the elements of the system induced the conclusion that neither organisation nor negotiation could be addressed separately. If one intends to develop an autonomous system of negotiation capable of expressing the claims of the parties according to the effective correlation of forces, it is not possible to employ an organisational framework which was fashioned for different purposes. In fact, the corporatist assumption that conflict is pathological does not require a representative and mobilised union. Rather than a union fit to express workers' claims, it requires a body capable of keeping the conflict within certain limits and, therefore, prepared to channel the workers' demands through the institutional apparatus of the State. Hence, the new pattern of collective bargaining would not be achieved with the old official union. In other words, any effective collective bargaining would be unfeasible without a suitable union organisation designed to promote it.

To conclude, the fragmented organisation and negotiation divides the work force, impedes perception of their common claims, and weakens the solidarity among the categories. The combating of such an atomised negotiation entails the re-examining of the union organisational framework which at present represents different sides of the same coin. If unions are to acquire bargaining power both union organisation and the collective bargaining structure cannot be addressed separately. For the CUT's strategy, therefore, collective negotiations are the lever with which to change the entire system of labour relations in the country. Through the formulation of another structure of negotiation to replace the existing one, the complete overhauling of the organisational framework is simultaneously assumed and developed.

3   SUPERSEDING THE CORPORATIST 'INDUCEMENTS'

3.1   Dispensing with Union Tax and Monopoly of Representation

Although criticism of state intervention in labour relations is widespread, its depth varies markedly among the relevant actors. Some currents of the labour movement tend to reject only the interventionist features regarded as negative (cf. the third group of proposals put forward in the 'Forum for the Collective Labour Contract' held in late 1993 – Chapter 2, Section 6.2). So they merely denounce the more repressive components of the union structure. On the other hand, the so-called 'positive aspects of the model', such as the monopoly of representation, state-provided resources through union tax and the normative power of the labour court are perceived as achievements of workers worth being assured by law. Indeed, this standpoint springs from a misconception about the intrinsic contradiction between, on one side, aspiration to union freedom and autonomy and, on another, union unity (monopoly of representation) and other manifestations of the structure imposed by the State upon workers' organisation.

This contradiction became rather apparent when, on the

eve of the presidential election of 1994, a debate arose in the country about the legitimacy of the material support the CUT unions had allegedly granted the candidacy of Lula and other PT representatives. In November 1993 a strong wave against corruption galvanised public opinion in revulsion against the bribes members of Parliament belonging to the 'budget committee' were said to receive from big companies in the process of approval of the federal budget. Well-known as the 'scandal of the budget committee', the event led Parliament to install a special committe to investigate the affair. While civil society became particularly sensitive against corruption, none of the members of Parliament affiliated to the Worker's Party (PT) were involved with those misdeeds. By that time, the PT presidential candidate was well ahead in the opinion polls. A conservative reaction was then orchestrated, Parliament having authorised the setting up of a special committee to investigate the contribution of the CUT unions to PT-candidacies. In contrast to countries like Britain, where unions' contributions to their candidates are not illegal, part of the press and the conservative political forces argued that the alleged electoral donations by the unions to their candidates were unconstitutional. Some Brazilian constitutional lawyers claimed that the union tax, being warranted by the State, was equal in nature to any other tribute and was liable to monitoring by the State through the Legislative and the Judiciary. They also argued that unions were not free to assume partisan positions because they were legal representatives of the entire occupational category, and not just of the members (*Folha de São Paulo*, 27.11.93). These arguments used at that time to attack the labour movement cast further light on the fragility of union autonomy as long as the corporatist union tax and monopoly of representation remains in place. Awareness of the impossibility of solving this contradiction without renouncing any 'protector state' intervention in union structure is at the core of the development of the unions organised around the CUT.

Considering the close ties between union organisation, structure of collective bargaining and resolution of conflict, the alternative approach views the whole set as a coherent and articulate one. The endeavour to alter it, therefore, must simultaneously address all the features of a system which is analysed by the CUT as completely artificial, composed of unions lacking representativeness and supported by the union tax awarded by the State. Combining paternalism with authoritarianism, the model impedes the emergence of new militants and leaders and fails to involve membership in union life.

The CUT has rejected the 'juridification' of union organisation. Regarding the issue of the uniqueness of representation which derives from the monopoly granted by the State, the CUT's approach is quite clear. It welcomes the unity of workers as an important source of strength, but also realises that the unity imposed by law is artificial. Moreover, it is provided by the State at the high cost of the real representativeness of the union. Unity increases the workers' power only when it results from their conscious deliberation. If unity means the sharing in the same goals and endeavour, there is no sense in obtaining it by means other than the free willingness of workers. The uniqueness imposed by law omits to take into account the relevant requisite of representativeness. Between formal bureaucratic procedures and the strength of real representativeness, the unity imposed by law chooses the former.

For identical reasons, another important aspect of the corporatist union organisational structure is rejected by the CUT. The union tax is regarded as a major pillar of a bureaucratic and unrepresentative unionism. Its maintenance by the 1988 Constitution has perpetuated an apparatus whose life is not dependent on the real consensus and participation of the work force. The artificial unions, federations and confederations are allowed to exist, despite their inability to organise, mobilise and maintain the real support of the employees. In this case of the union tax, however, the new unionism still displays some contradictions. Many unions still critically depend upon the resources of the union tax and even unions affiliated to the CUT feel unable to forgo such contributions despite the CUT's stance. Although in the short run it is admittedly difficult to replace such a vast amount of resources, many unions are making no attempt to create alternative mechanisms. However, some others, following a decision taken in their general assembly, have returned the revenues collected as union tax to the workers and based their expenditures on voluntary contributions from them. The metalworkers of São Bernardo, the plastic industry workers of São Paulo, the chemical industry workers of São Paulo, the metalworkers of Campinas, the oil workers of Camaçari and the telecommunication workers of Pernambuco are among those which have initiated such a practice (Gianotti and Sebastião Neto, 1990: 66; *Informacut* no. 215, interview no. 27). Given that such initiatives are as yet few and limited, the issue is regarded as a major challenge to be addressed by the CUT. The complete elimination of the union tax is therefore urged to take place in a gradual fashion to allow time for the unions to adapt.

Bearing in mind this sort of reasoning and the concrete experience of the Brazilian labour movement, the CUT has therefore pressed for the full application of the principles of union freedom and autonomy. The foregoing discussion suggests that the current union organisation, 'protected and chartered' by the State, is not functional for developing a system based on autonomous relations. Hence, the new unionism's proposals have always stressed the need to overcome the corporatist official union. The monopoly of representation and the union tax, regarded as the main organisational constraints of the old system, are to be terminated. To replace the corporatist union, the CUT has developed another framework whose lineaments we shall analyse in Sections 4 and 5.

3.2 Dispensing with the Normative Power of the Labour Court

In the light of an analogous assessment, the CUT formulation stresses that the weak state-sanctioned union in Brazil could not be expected to take part effectively in collective bargaining. Its fragmentation implies that each category performs its negotiation in an isolated way. Moreover, since the law stipulates a compulsory deadline for the parties to initiate negotiation – the so-called 'base-line date' ('database') – what happens is that parties, in practice, tend to negotiate only once a year. Thus, the bargaining process has a very restricted scope, for there are neither grounds nor time to address all the complex matters connected with the working conditions. The lack of articulation of the different categories and levels of collective negotiation implies that the workers' power remains considerably reduced.

In the event of conflict, the State promptly intervenes through the labour court's normative power and thereby reduces the incentive for employers to take seriously a negotiation process which ultimately may be settled by the labour court. An autonomous system of collective bargaining, under such a constraint, cannot survive. The authoritarian features combine with the paternalist ones. In fact, the weak categories are often 'helped' by the labour court when the 'normative award' grants them some benefits that otherwise they would not obtain. This consideration has allowed a positive evaluation of the labour court both by some union sectors and by part of the literature (Rodrigues, 1980 and 1990b). It has been argued that the normative power of the labour court offers a sort of minimum guarantee for weak and not-well-organised categories. Taking away such a protection would enable only the strong workers' sectors to benefit from expanding collective bargaining. Moreover, the set of rights attained by bureaucratic unions merely by resorting to the labour courts, even when they fail the organisational strength requirement, enables them to appeal to workers on the grounds of the benefits obtained on behalf of their constituencies (Souza,1990). Such arguments, however, leave unanswered the crucial objection that a union 'helped' by the court award has no incentive to involve membership and thus reproduces the lack of organisational strength that ultimately makes them dependent on the labour court.

Elsewhere, compulsory arbitration has also given birth to controversy. In England, it has been argued that some occupational groups – such as nurses – have benefited from having their pay determined by independent review bodies of arbitration in a context as unfavourable to collective bargaining as that of recent years (Bailey, 1994). Looking back at pre-Nazi Germany, one could note how Hugo Sinzheimer, a founder father of the German Labour Law, advocated compulsory arbitration in 1929 and 1932 in the hope that such a means of conflict-settlement would endow the German unions with political resources they desperately needed at a time of massive unemployment. Sinzheimer's view was nevertheless resisted by Kahn-Freund, to whom compulsory arbitration worked to undermine trade union autonomy and, consequently, to weaken an important demo-cratic counterpower to Fascism. In regard to Australia and Nigeria, two of the most visible cases of widespread adoption of compulsory arbitration, alongside New Zealand, Singapore, Malaysia, India and Brazil, it has been shown that its in-troduction in both countries was part of a broader process where the State intervened in industrial relations with the purpose of controlling and disciplining labour through both paternalistic and coercive means. Not surprisingly, the in-stitutionalisation of compulsory arbitration in those coun-tries followed large waves of labour unrest, respectively in 1890–4 and 1963–4, and thus were closely connected to the goals of tightening the control of labour and the labour market (Omaji, 1993). Be that as it may, the comparative record at best does not indicate that compulsory arbitra-tion is particularly supportive for the labour movement.

Back to the Brazilian context, the CUT formulation argues that the positive assessment of compulsory arbitration neglects the full impact of this kind of conflict settlement. Experience has shown that the normative power tends to function as a mechanism for eliminating collective conflict and, hence, has a greater impact upon the mobilised and strategically strong sectors of the labour force. Although enjoying enough power to impose their claims even with-out the court arbitration, the mobilisation of those sectors tends to be geared to the perspective of securing an award from the labour court and is very often mitigated by the latter's intervention. Under such constraints, the general level of wages and working conditions of those sectors does not fulfil its potential growth. As a result, the example of the accomplishments of those strategic sectors is clearly neutralised and the potential positive impact on the labour market derived from the action of the strong categories is reduced.[11] The general share of labour income as a pro-portion of the total of income of the country is artificially kept down. Such a structure is prone to level unions' strength 'from below' because it confines the strongest unions within the parameters affordable by the enterprises or branches whose unions are weaker.

4   ORGANISATION WITHIN THE WORKPLACE (OWW)

Since the revitalisation of the labour movement in the late 1970s, organisation within the workplace (OWW)[12] has been perceived as crucial to enable workers to attain their claims. It emerged as a response to the increasing mobilisation of workers by-passing the official union, then dominated by non-militant leadership. From the late 1970s onwards, demands for recovering and increasing real wages shifted the negotiation with employers towards the enterprise. This movement produced a special concern with organisation and negotiation within the shop floor. Many factory commissions arose from groups chosen 'ad hoc' in the workers' meetings to negotiate with the enterprises' representatives, and to cope with the immobilism of official unions. Despite employers' suspicion about organisation of workers within the workplace, the factory commissions were often institutionalised through the settlement of collective disputes. They were therefore an accomplishment of workers through mobilisation.[13]

An important question pertinent to the factory commissions is the character of their relationship with the corresponding union. From the standpoint of the official union headed by the old type of unionist, the growth of such commissions was deemed a challenge. Only under pressure were they incorporated after trying to respond to the need for organisation within the shop floor through the shop steward. The São Paulo metalworkers' union is an example of this kind of reaction. In 1980 their traditional leadership included the demand for a factory commission in their platform. Nevertheless, they were conceived in a somewhat different way, as mere union commissions within the enterprise and without any autonomy.

The moderate labour movement grouped in CONCLAT–CGT proposed the commission as the union extension within the enterprise, lacking autonomy and sometimes even without direct election by the workers. The CUT's proposal, in turn, proved to oscillate according to the position of its proponents within the union and the two currents of the new unionism: the independent or authentic unionists and the opposition groups. In cases where the union was still under control of the sectors regarded as pelegos, the autonomy tended to be stressed. When the official union had been seized by the new unionists, the relationship was apt to be more nuanced, as noted by Keller (1986). In such cases, although maintaining the autonomy of the workers' commissions and its election by all the workers in the respective base (not only those affiliated to the union), some articulation with the union was always preserved.

The commission within the workplace is understood, in sum, as the first step of workers' organisation in articulation with other levels of organisation. In the CUT's field there has been a gradual maturing of the concept of commissions. The complete autonomy imagined by some groups hitherto opposing the unions ('Union Opposition') as an embryo of a parallel union structure was replaced by the idea that they are autonomous and that sovereignty rests with the whole set of workers, but at the same time they should be articulated with union as part of the whole organisational structure. Hence, Article 13 of the CUT's statute reads that both the union and the base organisation within the workplace constitute the associated members of the entity (CUT, 1991a, 1991b).

In brief, the CUT's approach to factory commissions seems close to the kind of OWW which developed in some Western countries, particularly in the aftermath of the Italian workers' cycle of struggles known as 'Hot Autumn'. The Italian 'consiglio di fabrica', or 'consiglio dei delegati', emerged as independent structures of employees' organisation in the work place, representing all the workers, unionised or not. Then they were incorporated by the main national organisations (CGIL, CISL and UIL) within their own organisational framework (Giugni, 1991: 41–50). In the CUT's experience, similarly, the 'comissões de fabrica' emerged independently of the unions, and sometimes against them. They also tended to group all the workers irrespective of their union affiliation. With the evolution of the struggles, they were recognised as 'base organisms' of the unions.

What initially was an imposition of the context was later understood and elaborated as the strategic key to bolster the changes in the industrial relations system. The proposed type of collective bargaining had as a prerequisite the representation of the workers within the workplace. The strength required to negotiate, the flow of information about the methods of work, the introduction of new technology and the authentic claims of the workers are heavily dependent on the inputs derived from such a representation. In its absence, collective bargaining loses its efficacy (Braga and Miranda, 1991).

Additionally, OWW and its protective rights are said to play an important role in the construction of an autonomous system of labour relations as a whole. Indeed, the engendering of a legitimate organisation of workers at the shop-floor provides the basis upon which both the bargaining process and the 'promotional' legislation can build. As Lord Wedderburn notes in his analysis of the Italian 'rappresentanza sindacale aziendale' enacted by Article 19 of the Legge 300/70 ('Lo Statuto dei Lavoratori'), the absence of a protected 'substructure of trade unionism' within the enterprise is a powerful hindrance to the development of a system of autonomous collective bargaining and the related legislative programme (1991: 249).

In the Brazilian labour relations of the 1990s, the observation made by Tavares de Almeida (1980) about the difficulty of the official unions in operating effectively in the large enterprises due to lack of organisation within the workplace is certainly still valid. Demands appropriate to modern large companies, concerning careers, rhythm of production, personnel selection and reward systems are complex matters that can only be addressed by specific knowledge provided by close acquaintance with the work environment. OWW is therefore the crucial requisite for developing a re-shaped collective bargaining.

The factory commissions' experience has matured to fulfil their role in autonomous collective bargaining in the more developed sectors of the labour relations system. The fifty commissions existing in 1991 amongst the metalworkers of São Bernardo do Campo evolved from an initial accent on organisation and mobilisation within the workplace towards a role in the negotiation process (Benites Filho, 1991: 35). The factory commissions secure detailed information about the matters upon which the bargaining evolves and thus improve both the quality of representation and the bargaining process itself. Besides being the basis for an autonomous collective bargaining, representation within the enterprise has a fundamental role to play in the enforcement of the collective contract, as Castro reminds us (1991: 23).

By expanding the contact between the leadership and the rank-and-file, as well as by mobilising workers, the OWW has contributed to the achievement of crucial demands which go beyond the existing structure and engendered conditions for a new type of union organisation (Negro, 1991: 81). Not surprisingly, representation within the workplace has been defined as 'a strategic goal of the CUT', according to the resolution adopted in its national meeting held in 1993 ('6a. Plenária Nacional').[14] To summarise what has been argued, let us present the key objectives pursued by the CUT alternative proposals through the OWW:

• mobilisation and involvement of the rank and file;
• democratisation of the enterprise;
• improvement in the quality of workers' representation;
• betterment of the quality of the bargaining process by providing inputs about the working conditions and the grievances to be settled;
• enforcement of the collective agreements;
• enabling unions to compete with employers' conceptions put forward at the point of production;
• construction of an alternative union structure, articulated from the workplace up to the top level;
• articulation of different levels of bargaining by empowering workers' representation;
• acting as a basis for the further development of a set of 'supportive legislation' to union activity and collective bargaining.

Despite the CUT's awareness of the strategic importance of the expansion of workers' representation within the enterprise, the issue has been an Achilles' heel for the further superseding of corporatism. As late as in 1992, the CUT officials recognised that only a small minority of the CUT unions had actually installed an organisation within the workplace (Almeida, 1992). Recognising the problems, the CUT organised the 'First National Meeting on Organisation Within the Workplace' in November 1993 following a decision adopted in its '6a. Plenária'. Resulting from the discussions at that meeting, the 'central' issued a 'white paper' outlining the principles and strategies to be pursued in order to boost the setting up of OWWs among its affiliates (CUT, 1994: 60–4). The autonomy of the OWW in relation to the union was reasserted in that the former represents not only union members but also non-unionised employees working at a given workplace. The resolution did not seek to impose a pre-moulded form upon unions but explicitly allowed for the diversity of forms such as factory commissions, shop stewards and 'CIPAs'.[15] Such diverse and autonomous bodies were not meant to create a competitor to the union at the shop floor but rather to act in articulation with it. Such an articulation with the other levels of union organisation proposed by the CUT stands in total contrast to certain recent proposals by employers (FIESP, CNI, etc.) which circumscribe workers' representation to the isolated level of the enterprise. Finally, it was recognised that there is a need to struggle for promotional legislation to enforce workers' right to organise at the shop floor.

5   THE CUT'S PROPOSAL ON ORGANISATION

5.1   An Alternative Framework

The corporatist organisational framework engendered a vast bureaucratic union apparatus remote from the rank-and-file. To overcome its unrepresentativeness, the CUT has elaborated an alternative framework for the union organisation, starting from the representation within the workplace whose genesis we described in Section 4. Although the factory or enterprise commissions are autonomous and group all the workers in the shop floor (not only those affiliated to the union), they are supposed to act in accord with the union. The union, in turn, is expected to undergo important alterations, the foremost being the democratisation of its internal life and the redefinition of its base.

Even after the 1988 Constitution, the base of the union remained determined by the corporatist concept of the 'occupational category' defined by the main activity of the enterprise, for most unions were founded under the state-imposed definitions of the CLT and the 'Comission of Union Chartering' ('Comissão de Enquadramento Sindical'). Following those criteria usually an economic branch was divided into many groups according to the activity of the enterprise. Instead of only one union for commerce, for example, there were unions representing several categories accounting for slight differences such as the retail or whole-sale trade. The case of the workers in the ports is illustrative: there is a union for the workers who load goods, another for those who inspect the shipment, another for those who look after it, and so forth. To overcome this fragmentation, the CUT proposes to widen the current jurisdiction of the unions by organising categories which correspond to each economic branch. This change is expected to stimulate consciousness of the common situation of all those in the same economic branch.

5.2 The Vertical Structure

The aforementioned unions, defined through branches of the economy (metallurgical industry, banking, education, health, chemical industry and so forth), were supposed to be grouped in departments at national, regional and state level. The department was then conceived as the second-level vertical structure of the CUT, designed to replace the federation of corporatism. A major difference consisted in the organisation of the department of a whole economic branch, rather than the mere category of the former federation. It represented an effort to overcome the atom-isation of the official framework, since it was an inter-category organisation.

The definition of this vertical structure was formalised

in 1986, in the second CUT's congress. Confirming the assertion that the processes of both organisation and negotiation come together, the initial departments arose from categories which were able to carry on a unified wage campaign. The first one, the National Department of Bank Workers, was formed in 1986 as an outcome of the national campaign initiated in 1985. The Metalworkers' National Department came after, as a result of the experience of the unified mobilisation of the metalworkers of São Paulo. Subsequently there appeared the National Department of the Workers in the Oil Industry, which also had a national wage campaign.

A further development occurred after the '5a. Plenária' in 1992. While defining the eighteen economic branches of the CUT alternative vertical structure, that meeting decided that the departments should evolve into national entities of the 'central', becoming either a national union, a federation or a confederation. In contrast to the old corporatist federation, the CUT's encompassed the entire economic branch and represented workers in proportion to their actual affiliation in their respective unions. The process of constitution of the CUT federations and confederations, therefore, followed a twofold strategy. Either they were the result of the 'conquest' of the old federation and its subsequent transformation, or they were founded in parallel to compete with existing official entities. In both hypotheses, the department played the role of co-ordination and articulation of the process of either 'conquest' or constitution of the CUT federation and its further democratisation. Such a strategy was summarised by the national secretary of the CUT for organisation:

> As for the federations we should indicate a transition that takes its complexity into account. Our tactic contemplates the dispute for the control of the official entities and subsequent democratisation, along with the consolidation of the entities created in parallel to the official structure. . . . It also considers the creation of national entities out of the national departments. In this latter case, the transition consists of evolving from the department per economic branch (national or regional)

towards the federation per economic branch. . . . In this transition, all the unions affiliated to the CUT should integrate one of the economic branches already defined. The department should continue as an internal level of the CUT organisation up till the further constitution of the new federations and confederations. The superseding of the department cannot be achieved by decree, prescinding of a broad debate. (Oliveira, 1992)

The mentioned economic branches and other broad categories defined by the fifth 'Plenária', and ratified by the fifth congress held in 1994, are the following:

- Agriculture, plantation and agro-industry (rural);
- Metallurgy, metal-mechanic, steel industry, and electric-electronic (metalworkers);
- Bank, financial sector, insurance, stock market (bank employees);
- Chemical industry, plastic, paper, petrol-chemical, oil (chemical industry workers);
- Textile industry, dress, leather, shoes (dress industry workers);
- Commerce and services (commerce employees);
- Education, teaching and culture (education employees);
- Health care and welfare (health employees);
- Administration and public service;
- Building industry, furniture and wood (building industry workers);
- Mining extraction and transformation (miners);
- Food, drink and smoking (food industry workers);
- Communication, newspapers, radio and TV broadcast, publicity and printing (communication workers);
- Liberal professionals, technicians and administrative employees;
- Utilities – water, sewage, gas and power (urban workers);
- Transport – air, road, rail and ship (transport workers);
- Self-employed urban workers;
- Retired.

By the fifth congress of the CUT, held on 19–22 May 1994, some steps in the consolidation of the vertical structure had already been taken. The National Confederation of Metalworkers, the National Confederation of the Bank Employees, the National Confederation of Chemical and Oil Workers and the National Federation of the Building Industry had by then been founded out of the respective national departments and were prepared to compete with the old confederations and federations of the official apparatus (CUT, 1994: 28). Some other sectors, however, had not reached an agreement among themselves on whether to set up a unified national federation, as was the case of the workers in public utilities, civil servants, education employees and health workers. Facing such a reality, the fifth congress agreed to continue with the departments and co-ordinations in those sectors until the further unification in national federations or confederations became possible.

5.3   The Horizontal Structure

The so-called horizontal structure of the CUT, on the other hand, reinforces the 'classist'[16] and democratic basis upon which the 'central' is supposed to be constructed. Until 1986, the horizontal structure was the only existing one. It was the main evidence that the new unionism had resolved to overcome the state-sanctioned union structure that was based only on the vertical structures, namely, from the union representing a given occupational category up to the confederation representative of the same category. The horizontal structure, in turn, is formed at the state, regional and national level embracing all workers at the respective level independently of the category to which they belong. Each level has its own leadership elected in the appropriate congress and all levels are expected to act in articulation with each other.

This type of structure, also acting in connection with the vertical one, helps to end the segmentation of the workers within their categories or economic branch. Thus, in principle the entire working class might be organised within a structure which highlights the common interests of all its sectors. The alternative organisational proposal, in short, seeks to cover the organisation of the workers from the rank and file up to the inter-category national levels (Castro,

1991: 23). This whole alternative organisational framework, it is worth stressing, has been elaborated on the assumption that freedom and autonomy are goals to be achieved through increasing mobilisation and practice of collective bargaining.

5.4 The Move Towards the 'Organic Union of the CUT'

How far the alternative framework put forward by the CUT has replaced the corporative institutions and practices is a controversial matter. Some analysts have argued that the CUT has not been able to overcome the obstacles to the consolidation of its alternative project, among other factors, because it has gradually relied on the official union structure, perhaps even has lacked the will to destroy the old arrangements (Rodrigues and Cardoso, 1993: 149). A certain resignation to the egoistic 'ethos' of the divided corporatist categories has been recognised by the CUT itself. According to the Resolutions adopted in the fifth congress of 1994, such an accommodation to the official union structure stems from the difficulties of organising within the workplace, of consolidating the alternative structure and addressing the global reform of the system of labour relations. These shortcomings are understood as flowing from the same constraints that initially induced the new unionism to adopt the strategy of winning the official union to alter it from inside: the institutional weight of the existing official unions in workers' perceptions combined with the legal prerogatives and resources (CUT, 1994: 26–7).

The fifth congress of the CUT realised that the question of transforming the internal structures of the unions had been left to their individual initiatives rather than been impelled by general policies advanced by the 'central'. It was recognised that excessive efforts had been devoted to the internal structuring of the CUT both in its horizontal and vertical levels. The time had come to address the union level, making feasible the transition from the 'central' as a 'co-ordinator' of the unions towards the 'central' constituted by 'organic unions' (cf. 'Textos à 6a. Plenária', CUT, 1993). Instead of unions merely affiliated to the CUT, the 'CUT union' was urged. The 'organic union', therefore,

was conceived as arising from the workers' exercise of freedom and autonomy in order to build up the union at the
level of economic branch in order to overcome the restrictions of the category-wide union. This process of aggrega-
tion of representation was designed to go hand in hand
with the definition of basic common criteria such as electoral
rules, fairness procedures governing factional struggles within
unions ('regras éticas') and democratic rules of functioning.
Such criteria are intended to meet the requirements of the
CUT alternative model and, thus, to advance the transition
from the official type of union towards a democratic, renewed
union capable of enhancing membership involvement and
of promoting fair play in internal disputes. The campaign
for the development of the 'organic union' of the CUT
was formally launched in the '7a. Plenária Nacional' held
in September 1995, starting with the above outlined criteria
as guidelines for the transformation of the existing unions
affiliated to the 'central' (CUT, 1995).

As in other levels of the consolidation of the CUT alter-
native model, some unions have already led the way. On
March 5th 1993, the Metalworkers' Union of ABC was born
out of the merging of the unions of Santo André and São
Bernardo. The new union brought together around 104
thousand voluntary members out of a base of 161 thousand
workers, which yielded an affiliation ratio of 64 per cent.
The other metalworkers' union of the region, that of São
Caetano, refused to join, although a survey conducted by
IBOPE showed that 86 per cent of the workers would like
to be members of the new union (*Informacut*, 211, 1993).
Other unions that have already started to merge with others
in order to set up big unions encompassing the whole economic branch include the chemical and plastic workers of
São Paulo, the chemical and petrochemical industry workers
of Bahia and the oil industry workers at national level (CUT,
1994: 28; Oliveira, 1994: 505; and interviews nos 5 and 19).

6   THE COLLECTIVE LABOUR CONTRACT

Strictly speaking, the 'collective labour contract' is the
instrument which results from collective bargaining freed

from the current constraints. In the early 1980s, however, the new unionism selected such a designation as a sort of slogan for a new approach to the country's entire system of labour relations. Seeking to contrast 'collective labour contract' ('contrato coletivo de trabalho') with the current expressions 'acordo' and 'convenção coletiva' enshrined within the corporatist law, the label hints at the idea that free collective bargaining is the lever to override the received legal arrangements and construct another framework for labour relations. Hence, it was originally conceived as part of a complex alternative proposal to previous arrangements. In the second congress of the CUT held in 1986, it formally became the banner through which the new unionism intended to display its distinctive conception of labour relations.

From the early 1990s onwards, especially with the appointment of Wálter Barelli to the Ministry of Labour in 1992, different actors presented their proposals to change the system employing the same expression 'collective labour contract'. Although the initial association with the changing of the system was preserved, the expression gained as many connotations as there were proposals brought into the debate (Siqueira Neto, 1994a). In Section 6 of Chapter 2 such distinctive approaches were addressed and related to their respective proponents. This section, in turn, concentrates on the CUT's formulation. Given the above mentioned fact that 'collective labour contract' has been assigned a variety of meanings, the CUT has come to prefer the expression 'democratic system of labour relations' to characterise its proposal of 'collective labour contract'. Such more comprehensive designation has been emphasised in the recent resolution where the 'central' spells out and updates its proposals of change (CUT, 1995). Since the set of proposals that make up the CUT alternative model has already been commented on in the present chapter, this section will focus particularly on the new unionism's proposals regarding collective bargaining. Reference to 'collective labour contract', henceforward, will denote the new unionism's proposal for altering the bargaining system.

The CUT's proposal for collective bargaining attempts to overcome the limitations of the current model. Instead of holding negotiations once a year as established in the current system of 'base-line date'('data-base'), the proposal incorporates the principle of permanent bargaining. The piecemeal negotiation that emerges from the fragmented system of the occupational categories is to be replaced by integrated negotiation within each economic branch or even inter-categorial. Regarding territoriality, the proposal advocates the co-existence of contracts at the national, state, regional, 'municipal' and even plant levels, co-ordinated among themselves. Settlement of collective conflict is expected to be left to the direct agreement between the parties, with the option of recourse to voluntary arbitration in case of deadlock. If the latter occurs, the clauses of the hitherto existing collective contract should continue to be enforced until the parties reach another settlement. For the CUT's strategy of replacing the current labour relations system, the process of collective negotiation is the crucial point as far its re-designing will force both union organisation and the attitudes of the parties to change accordingly. This implies the recognition of the tight connection between organisation and bargaining, which, according to the established literature on industrial relations, shows that increasing workers' strength fosters bargaining and vice-versa (Crouch, 1993: 287).

The collective labour contract meets the crucial objections to the existing system. Against the exclusively corporatist negotiation by the category-wide union, the proposal advocates a national negotiation articulated by departments or federations which embrace several categories, simultaneously with unification of the so-called 'base-line date'.[17] Against the system of only one negotiation per year, the permanent negotiation is seen as a way of taking into account the dynamics of the conflict. Against the limitation of the contents of the negotiation, which has been restricted almost to recovering the previous real wage levels, the CUT proposals widen its scope to cover work relations as a whole, including participation in the choice of work methods, introduction of new technology, objectives and rhythm of production, and so forth (Braga, 1991; Oliveira, 1992). Such a conception is based on the assumption that the full democratisation of the work process is a goal worth pursuing.

This proposal lays a particular emphasis on the need to transcend the fragmentation of the corporatist contractual system. The strengthening of the centralised and articulated organisation through the 'central' is crucial to combat that fragmented pattern of collective bargaining, thereby highlighting the articulation of the several levels of categories. Having as its lever the negotiation at the workplace, the system conceives of the levels of union, department or federation per economic branch and 'central' to be closely articulated. From the minimal standards to be addressed at the national level, the idea is to develop a gradual process of specialisation towards the regional, state, sector and enterprise levels (Castro, 1991).

Yet the concept of an articulated process of negotiation is not a closed or exhaustive theorisation. Its justification lies in the need to demolish the existing model and to extend the workers' achievements to the less organised sectors of the labour force (Ramos Filho, 1991). The quest for articulation is resisted by the employers' formulation through their preference for decentralised negotiation at the level of the enterprise supposedly to enhance companies' productivity (Magano, 1992; Pastore, 1993; Zylberstajn, 1993). For the CUT and some analysts of labour issues (e.g., Medeiros, 1994), on the other hand, given the persistence of large areas of the labour market outside the unionised and even the formal sectors, the new arrangements must seek higher levels of bargaining beyond the enterprises and branches. Only through more centralised 'loci' of bargaining can the actors address the issues of basic rights, wage policies and other relevant economic policies in a way which takes into account the interests of those excluded sectors. An articulated pattern of collective bargaining, together with the role of the top organisations to spread demands initially raised by the strongest unions, are then perceived as crucial to address what many people would see as the segmentation of a dual labour market.

Although having to cope with daunting obstacles to an alternative collective bargaining process, some initiatives have been undertaken. The first concrete proposal adopting the concepts of the collective labour contract appears to have been put forward by the CUT Department of Metalworkers of São Paulo in February 1988 (Siqueira Neto, 1991: 32). Then, the list of demands included the main outline of a different type of negotiation. Presented to the Federation of Industries of São Paulo State (FIESP), the proposal aimed at introducing the voluntary exclusion of resort to the labour court in the case of conflict, the discontinuance of the one-year negotiation, the validity of the clauses of the former contract until the adoption of a new one, the duty of enterprises to inform the unions about the firm's business activities (profits, level of employment, investment plans), articulation of levels of negotiation,[18] and so forth. Although the proposal met with employers' initial resistance, some results began appearing in 1990, when a compromise between the Autolatina (Ford Brasil S.A. and Volkswagen do Brasil S.A.) and the Metalworkers of São Bernardo's Union was signed ('Protocolo da Autolatina'). According to it, the parties agreed to start the negotiation of points aiming at introducing the collective labour contract within a two-year deadline.[19]

Other initiatives of a similar kind worth noting are the agreements reached in the São Paulo's City Council (August 1990) and the Hospital of the Civil Servants of the State of São Paulo (May 1989). Both 'Protocolos' established a system of permanent negotiation. The principle of the articulation of the several levels of negotiation is introduced by the mention of the possibility of contracts by sectors or other entities of the administration. The commitment of the public administration and civil servants to improving the services offered to the community is especially emphasised.[20] A further instance of pioneering experimentation with the collective labour contract is the national contract that has annually been signed by the National Federation of Banks (Fenaban) and the CUT-affiliated National Confederation of Bank Employees together with the regional unions.

7 SUPPORTIVE OR AUXILIARY LEGISLATION AS PREREQUISITES FOR THE COLLECTIVE LABOUR CONTRACT

Even countries whose legal system is founded on the Common Law, in contrast to the Roman Law tradition of detailed legislative intervention, have recognised the necessity for the law to intervene in support of certain aspects of the labour relations system. Britain's case could be regarded as the best example. Notwithstanding its long-lived tradition of 'collective laissez-faire',[21] Britain's law has accepted the need for enacting some legal provisions to encourage collective bargaining and even union action. Its well-known voluntarism, often highlighted as the main feature of the 'collective laissez faire', has been qualified by some authors such as Lord Wedderburn (1995:1–63) and Kahn-Freund himself (1968: 7), who acknowledge that an auxiliary legislation has always been in place. For the former, a pure abstentionism has never been more than a 'myth' in England. An example of auxiliary provision is the British Wage Councils. Despite variations about its aims, the Wage Councils often targeted the fostering of collective bargaining (as under the Trade Boards Act 1918 or the Wages Councils Act 1945) up till their extinction by the Tory government late in the 1980s. Another interesting precedent in British Labour Law is the Fair Wages Resolution of 1946, according to which the legal enforcement of 'fair' wages and conditions of labour is considered with reference to the agreed patterns in the collective bargaining (Davies and Freedland, 1993). The incentive to collective bargaining, reinforced through the 'Order 1376' of 1951, for example, continued to exist in certain limited areas up till the 1980s, having helped to develop bargaining through arbitration by the 'Industrial Disputes Tribunal' on the basis reached by successful existing agreements. Such precedents of a highly voluntary system of industrial relations bear witness to the widespread conviction that collective bargaining must be combined with certain legal provisions essential to its feasibility.

The reinforcement of the auxiliary legislation has recently been advocated by some British authors after the legislative programme pursued by the Conservative government since

1979 (Wedderburn, 1991, 1995; Davies and Freedland, 1993; Ewing, 1988; Dickens and Hall, 1995). For them, a return to a system of 'pure abstentionism', indeed never entirely practised, is not appropriate for the future of the British Labour Law. The introduction of a basic set of statutory positive rights in support of union autonomy and freedom, and the bargaining process itself, is urged to restore a reasonable equilibrium among employers and employees. It has been noted that these proposals are quite similar to the CUT's demand for supportive legislation as a precondition for the introduction of the collective labour contract in Brazil, although both experiences spring from very different starting points and traditions (Barros, 1995b). The support legislation, rather than protecting the employees as individuals, seeks to equilibrate the power relation between workers and employers both within the enterprise and in the wider society. As Dickens and Hall suggest (1995: 178), an auxiliary legislation may facilitate union organisation and recruitment and then indirectly impel the enterprise to engage in collective bargaining. In short, the promotion legislation aims at boosting union activity and collective bargaining, thus enhancing the workers' latent power (Ghera, 1990: 24; Barros, 1995a).

Perhaps the most developed initiative of such a legislative programme is the Italian 'Statuto dei Lavoratori' ('Legge' no. 300/1970). For Gino Giugni (1991), its inspirer, the body of provisions on sustaining the union activity is linked to the principle of substantial equality in contradistinction to the principle of merely formal equality. Such measures are not confined to the employers' capacity to interfere in the sphere of union freedom. Rather than imposing negative obligations on the enterprise, the auxiliary legislation provides the workers in the workplace with instruments for performing their organised union activity.[22]

The enactment of supportive provisions both in Britain and in Italy attests that a collective bargaining system cannot work properly unless there exists a complex and many-stranded array of labour-related and employee-related legislation. It seems therefore that the CUT is right in urging a promotional or supportive legislation as a strong instrument to transform the current state's and employers' attitudes.

In order to abandon a heteronomous system of labour relations and move toward voluntary negotiation, such an auxiliary body of laws is indispensable. In its absence, the organisation and activity of workers at the shop floor are not attainable. And collective bargaining at this basic level and the associated organisation are regarded as further prerequisites for setting up the collective labour contract (Braga and Miranda, 1991: 63).

According to the CUT's formulation, then, there is no incompatibility between promotional legislation and the self-settlement of the conflict by the parties; rather, such legislation is strictly required since autonomous collective bargaining must be sustained by the guarantee of the contractual role and capacity of the union. Some of the urged legal changes were laid down in the set of bills elaborated by the CUT legal aides in 1994 and submitted to internal discussions. According to the principles outlined above, the proposals contemplate changes both in Constitutional and ordinary legislation. Basically, three bills were drawn up. The first deals with the support for the union organisation ('Projeto de lei sobre garantia da organização sindical brasileira'), targeting workers' rights to define the scope of the union, the opportunity for its creation, the representation within the workplace, the right of 'procedural substitution' of workers by unions in legal cases, the contractual role of the union, and job stability for workers' representatives at all levels and so forth. The second draft bill lays down a number of provisions to guarantee free collective bargaining such as the obligation on the parties to negotiate, the workers' right to get information from employers, the continuity aspect in the bargaining process, the right to strike, the negotiation at national level by the general confederations of the national collective contract, the articulation of the levels of bargaining, the adoption of bargaining in the public service and the introduction of mediation and arbitration to settle collective conflicts, among others. The third bill addresses the constitutional changes necessary to implement the directives outlined above (CUT, 1994a).

Following the same perspective, the guarantee of the right to strike is conceived as another essential prerequisite to a free system of collective bargaining. Beyond doubt, the legal treatment of collective conflict is a crucial feature of a system of labour relations. If one seeks to build a system resting upon pluralist assumptions that accept conflict, the right to strike has to be asserted. It would be a nonsense to conceive a system grounded on free organisation and autonomous collective bargaining, but without the full recognition of the right to strike. If conflict is deemed legitimate, the means to express it cannot be limited. Otherwise, one of the sides of the collective negotiation would be condemned to acting with tied hands.

8   OBSTACLES TO THE ALTERNATIVE PROPOSALS

From the analysis of the alternative proposals, it is not difficult to realise the scale of the task of transforming Brazilian labour relations. Obstacles range from the external context and correlation of forces in the wider society to the penetration of the old conceptions even into the new unionism. As we have seen, the functioning of the system itself is a powerful obstacle to its renewal, since it reproduces a model of unionism which does not develop autonomously.

The alternative proposal relies on its new approach to collective bargaining as the lever to shape both collective conflict and union organisation. But the collective labour contract, as the crucial element to transform the system, depends on prerequisites which have not yet been established. Although the strategy of implanting it through practice has produced results, it cannot dispense with certain legislative changes, even at the constitutional level. The supportive or promotional legislation is a substantial element to lend feasibility to the union organisation, and thus to promote autonomous collective bargaining. The intervention of the labour court in the conflict, in turn, is an institutional feature that hinders the growth of alternative practices.

These changes in the law have not been enacted. As we noted in Section 6 of Chapter 2, the structural reforms advanced by President Fernando Henrique Cardoso have concentrated on the question of the State, the pension system and privatisation. By the end of the first year of the government few changes had been implemented in the field of labour relations. Nevertheless there is a growing feeling among all the relevant actors that the current hybrid corporatism is not functional to the new phase in national development. The case for change had been reaffirmed in the conclusions of the 'Forum of the Collective Labour Contract' in 1993. At this stage, few observers bet on a long survival to the current framework. The nature and intensity of the changes, however, are matters that remain to be seen.

Apart from the priorities of the agenda of the incumbent government, the perception of public opinion and the chief institutional agents are further hindering factors that will play a part in the rhythm and character of the ongoing changes. They still tend to reproduce entrenched values of the corporatist framework as exemplified by their ambiguities concerning the role of the labour court in settling collective disputes (and thus in stamping out conflict and deterring free bargaining). A survey carried out by IDESP ('Instituto de Estudos Econômicos, Sociais e Políticos de São Paulo') showed most members of Congress in favour of stimulating free collective bargaining and the implementation of the collective labour contract (63 per cent). Nevertheless, in an apparent contradiction or misperception of the meaning of the collective labour contract, a larger majority support the maintenance of the compulsory settlement of the conflict by the labour court (76 per cent). These figures represent the opinion of a Congress that remained in office until 1994 from a sample that rigorously corresponded to the parties' and regions' representations (Souza: 1992). If we assume that the Congress elected in 1994 did not represent much change in the political culture of its members, we may realise the difficulties facing the task of altering legislation on the issue. Furthermore, although the institution of the 'classist judge' or 'classist representation' in the labour courts (cf. Section 1.4, Chapter 2) has been widely regarded as one of the elements of the corporatist framework strictly connected to the current role of the labour court, as many as 57 per cent of the members of Parliament lent their support to its maintenance during the constitutional revision held (and aborted) in 1994, according to a survey carried out by the 'Departamento Intersindical de Assessoria Parlamentar – DIAP' (Barreto, 1994).

In addition to the difficulties external to the industrial relations system, as indicated above, the internal factors are strong obstacles to its changing. The corporatist framework is responsible for the lack of a culture of negotiation. The parties are prone to rely rather on the heteronomous patterns of conflict-settlement than on autonomous direct bargaining. In addition, even when collective bargaining develops, its scope and periodicity are quite limited. There is a general tendency to concentrate on recovering real wage levels, which is supposed to take place once a year on the occasion of the 'base-line date'.

Still at the internal level of the system, the fragmentation of the categories and negotiations shows an added negative feature. The alternative stance advocates that the union in the base should be organised by economic branch as a strategy to overcome fragmentation. Nevertheless, the economic branches have not fully reshaped the union structure. This fault was clearly recognised in the '7a. Plenária' of the CUT (1995), having led to the campaign for the generalisation of the so-called 'organic union of the CUT' (see Section 5.4). Consequently, the fragmented union organisational framework is still the rule, reinforcing the limits to collective bargaining and frustrating the emergence of a culture of negotiation.

The general weakness of the official union also hampers the consolidation of free collective bargaining. We have seen how the union contribution, the monopoly of representation, and the normative power of the labour court have produced an artificial union lacking real representativeness, and absent from the workplace. This defect is itself a serious factor in inhibiting the alternative proposal's potentialities, since it yields a strong attachment of important union sectors to the paternalism of the state-provided organisational resources and court settlement of conflict. Against the replacement of state protection, some analysts argue that the small unions would be easily dominated by the employers. However, this argument misses the point that attachment to the current model will imply the perpetuation of the structural dependence of the unions on the State and of union weakness (Siqueira Neto, 1991).

Strictly connected with the pattern of state-led industrial relations is the development of a bureaucratic community with a heavy interest in the maintenance of the system. Some union leaders perpetuated in the union apparatus, the career judges, the 'classist judges', the civil servants of both the Ministry of Labour and the Labour Court, the lawyers and other advisers of the parties, altogether compose a large bureaucratic community. As the literature has stressed (Simão, 1981; Rodrigues, 1990b; Crivelli, 1991), the impact of the opposition of these influential social groups to changing the model can hardly be neglected.

Finally, one more obstacle to innovation deserves attention. It concerns some 'new unions'' own attitudes. Although those sectors grouped in the CUT are expected to develop and practise the new conceptions, they are often pervaded by the official ideology. This circumstance has diminished the impetus toward grassroots organisations and the abandonment of statist tutelage. On this topic, one should note the analysis of the labour movement by the Workers' Party in its congress held in December 1991 (PT, 1991). In fact, while addressing the party line on the labour issue, the resolutions of that congress highlight the difficulties of overcoming corporatism and its contamination of the CUT itself. This document goes further, identifying the exacerbation of internal disputes as a hindrance to the pursuit of the new model. The heterogeneity within the CUT sometimes has degenerated into self-destructive disputes over the control of the apparatus, to the neglect of the implementation of alternative policies.

The problems with internal disputes, their implications for the democratic functioning, and misconceptions of the CUT's stance, have also been recognised in its documents. The resolutions of its fourth congress held in September 1991, taking stock of the recent period, are very assertive about those issues. There is an explicit criticism of those sectors which do not entirely accept the negotiational role of the CUT and tend to see it as a mere movement that, in practice, restricts its action to direct economic mobilisation. Still, the new line stresses that this conception has been superseded by one which combines negotiation with mobilisation and addresses broader policies affecting the whole popular sector. Furthermore, the present line also aims at building an alternative model of development for the country, which implies unified action with other sectors of civil society (CUT, 1991). Similarly, in the resolutions of the fifth congress held in 1994 (CUT, 1994b), the insufficient transformation of the internal life of the unions is identified as a major challenge to the labour movement in its struggle to convert to a more pluralist mould which is regarded both desirable and inevitable (CUT, 1994b).

4 Trade Unionism in Pernambuco

1 RESURGENCE

1.1 Antecedents

In Chapters 2 and 3 we looked at the rebirth of the Brazilian labour movement. The CUT's strategy of seizing the official unions in order to change them from the inside proved successful. So the first workers' mobilisations since the military-imposed silence came both from inside and outside the union structure. Where the old union leadership remained asleep, a new generation of young unionists managed to provoke workers' collective action. Very often those militants that came together during wage campaigns subsequently formed opposition groups challenging the old leadership through electoral disputes.

In the state of Pernambuco the process followed a similar path. The state itself had been marked by political turbulence in the democratic period that preceded the military rule. The famous 'peasant leagues' ('ligas camponesas'), one of the first initiatives to mobilise rural workers in the country, had been set up in the state under the leadership of the lawyer Francisco Julião in the 1950s and subsequently developed into a nation-wide movement for defence of land reform. A National Council of the Peasant Leagues was created to articulate the 'base nuclei' ('núcleos de base') where the peasants resisted landowners' arbitrariness with the advice of lawyers and intellectuals committed to their struggle. As a former lawyer of the 'leagues', Joaquim Ferreira Filho, puts it, the 'mere enforcement of the Civil Law to protect the peasants' rights would amount to a revolution' (interview no. 20). The 'peasant leagues' were responsible for some famous episodes, such as the occupation of the sugar mill known as 'Engenho Galiléia', whereby the peasants seized its control in Vitória de Santo Antão, Pernambuco, and the rural workers' struggles of Sapé, in the neighbour state of Paraíba, where the famous leader João Pedro Teixeira was killed by gunmen hired by the landowners. Some of the leagues eventually developed into legally established rural unions as exemplified by the case of the league of Sirinharém, PE. The increased political radicalisation of the period pre-1964 led the leagues to adopt a platform of armed struggle and to create the 'Movimento Tiradentes' with the aim of conducting the 'Brazilian Revolution' in a Cuban fashion.[1]

The 1964 coup hit the state immersed in a radicalised political environment. The state was economically and socially marked by sugar cane plantations which generated a powerful oligarchy accustomed to exercise its power with violence and tight control of the state apparatus. In 1962 Governor Miguel Arraes had been elected through a coalition known as the 'Recife Front', which grouped democratic and nationalist political forces, among them the influential Brazilian Communist Party, and embraced popular-oriented policies. In 1960 Arraes had already won the election for the mayorship of the capital of the state, Recife, with the backing of the labour movement expressed in a manifesto signed by forty trade unions. In the 1962 election for the state governorship he was afforded the support of another manifesto representing around two hundred thousand workers (Soares, 1982). The endorsement of the labour movement shaped the character of the government of Miguel Arraes. In contrast with the repressive attitude of the previous governors, the state started trying to mediate labour conflicts. During this period, thanks to the mediation of the state government, the sugar cane landowners and the rural unions signed the historic 'countryside agreement' recognising certain rights for the rural workers for the first time.

The labour movement in Pernambuco at the time, although within the limits of the populist relationship between the people, the politicians and the state (Weffort, 1986), was one of the most active in the country. Unions representing the workers in the port of Recife, in the 'Pernambuco Tramways', in the textile industry, in the rural sugar cane plants, in the state-owned railway company (RFFESA), in the printing industry, in metallurgy and others had a considerable mobilisation power. Despite all sorts of obstacles, ranging from the lack of material resources to deep-rooted traditional attitudes displayed by workers, entrepreneurs and state institutions, they succeeded in putting labour into the political arena. Their influence reached legislative bodies in the three spheres, the municipality of Recife, the state and the federation, with the election of workers representatives to the three correspondent legislative bodies. Among the workers holding elected offices in the state parliament were deputies Gilberto Azevedo, Cícero Targino and Cláudio Braga, respectively a bank employee, a worker in the Port of Recife and a railway worker, all of them members of the 'Partido Comunista Brasileiro' (*Jornal do Commercio*, 10.11.94). In the 1960s, this political party had members occupying important positions in the state government and in the government of the city of Recife.

Such a high visibility of the labour movement was not matched by a commensurate degree of real power. The key features of unionism at national level were reproduced in the state. Demonstrations and penetration in the state apparatus emerged hand in hand with the lack of grassroots organisations. According to Soares (1982: 124), despite huge mobilisations for economic demands, the unions acted within the limits of state tutelage. Thus both the relationship with the Arraes government, at the state level, and with the federal government under Goulart, were subjected to the limits of the institutional arrangements prevalent at that conjuncture. The table presented in Appendix 4 gives us an overall idea about the main labour conflicts of the period before the military coup.

1.2 The First Mobilisations in Pernambuco

The new political environment of the late 1970s had significant effects in the labour movement. The re-emergence at national level was matched by a number of initiatives in the states. In Pernambuco the seeds sown by the former rural unions and peasants leagues started producing fruits in 1979. In that year, led by the Rural Workers' Federation ('Fetape'), the rural workers mobilised for the annual collective bargaining, demanding wage increases and the enforcement of certain elementary workers' rights. Among those rights were the statutory obligation for the landowners to allow the workers to enjoy a small piece of land for subsistence agriculture and the recognition of union delegates. The registration of the employment contract as well as a better measurement for the task-related wage (the equivalent to the piece-work pay of industry) were other basic items of the successful rural workers' platform. The resistance of the sugar producers was strong. Union leaders and their aides had to struggle even to get access to the workers within the sugar plantations, being exposed to all sorts of threats, including murder. Because the peasants were decisively mobilised for the first time in years – around two hundred thousand workers went on strike – their movement yielded a positive deal for the unions after an eight-day stoppage. The event drew nation-wide attention, being regarded as a mark of the labour movement renascence precisely in a sector marked by brutal exploitation and long-standing authoritarian relationship between workers and employers (interview no. 8).

Other occupational categories started behaving in the same way. A nucleus of what constituted an opposition slate, struggling to win election in the union, emerged often out of groups formed in order to discuss the situation of workers and their grievances. The role of the workers' branch of the Catholic Action ('Ação Católica Operária') is well known, as exemplified by the way a number of future union leaders initiated their careers. Severino Antônio de Lima, a member of the directorate of the Metalworkers' Union of Pernambuco since 1980, is a good example of this process. He was induced by a relative to attend some meetings held by Catholic Church groups in order to debate workers' problems and from then on became an activist (interview no. 33). In 1978 a group of printing workers, shop assistants, metalworkers and weavers, with the sponsorship of the Catholic Church, was already meeting regularly to discuss ways of influencing their unions, controlled at the time by the pelegos (Morais, 1992: 78).

Other workers became militant as a result of the influence of the small Communist parties and fractions that had survived the struggle against the military, most of which having taken part in the army struggle against the military regime. The Brazilian Communist Party (PCB), the Communist Party of Brazil (PC do B), the dissidents of the Brazilian Communist Party led by the famous leaders Luís Carlos Prestes and Gregório Bezerra (called the 'Prestes Line'), the Brazilian Revolutionary Communist Party (PCBR), the Revolutionary Movement October 8th (MR-8) and other parties with 'Leninist' or 'Trotskyist' persuasions concentrated on what they used to call the 'mass front'. Their strategies for the 'mass front', of course, included developing and securing control of a strong and massive union movement. Many groups of militants entered the creeping labour movement through this channel, as exemplified by Izaías Bastos da Silva, a metalworker (interview no. 17), and Daísa Amador, who was for a long time an aide of the Rural Workers' Federation – Fetape (interview no. 8)

Another common source of militancy was the student movement which had great visibility in the years immediately preceding the military coup in 1964 due to its role in the resistance against the regime. Urging the restoration of democracy, the student movement staged huge demonstrations in the mid-1960s led by student organisations such as the then proscribed National Student Union (UNE). Perhaps the most massive initiative of the students was the famous 'Rally of the One Hundred Thousand' called to protest against the murder of the student Edson Luís by the police. The liberalisation of the regime in the mid-1970s again saw the students in a position of great visibility. Long stoppages and meetings were common, the case for democracy being the axis of the movement everywhere. Such a political initiation subsequently led many student activists to migrate to the labour movement and play an important role in its resurgence. Interview no. 29, with Ricardo Estêvão de Oliveira, a labour lawyer who has worked since 1980 for the unions and the CUT in Pernambuco, provides a good example of such a trajectory. He had held the presidency of the student directorate of the Law Faculty of Recife.

In 1979, the presence of those fresh labour militants was already contributing to shaking workers out of their passivity. In May both the private schools' teachers and those of the state schools organised to demand wage increases and job stability. In spite of the reluctance of the old-style leadership then controlling both unions, the rank and file pushed the union (in the case of the private schools' teachers) and the association (in the case of the state schools' teachers) towards mobilisation. After several general assemblies, all of them with high attendances, the two occupational categories decided to go on strike. The stoppage lasted seven days, having reached the largest schools mainly in the capital Recife. The private schools' teachers won an important victory. For the first time they had paralysed the sector and won certain rights and benefits through mobilisation rather than merely obtained unimportant concessions from the employers. Among the benefits secured, partial job stability, a 58 per cent wage hike, and the right to attend union assemblies during working time without loss of remuneration may be listed as the most important ones. After this movement, the occupational category launched a strike almost every year in the dates fixed by law as the adequate moment for collective bargaining, the so-called base-line dates ('datas-base').

The state schools' teachers, instead, had to cope with the radical intransigence of the state governor Marco Maciel, a docile follower of the military who had been appointed to the post without election. After persistent mobilisation, the teachers had to return to work without any of their demands having been met. For them, however, a positive step had been achieved in terms of organisation (Morais, 1992: 82).

Another significant sign of the coming unrest in the labour movement in the state of Pernambuco was the great mobilisation of journalists. Gathering professionals from both the audio-television and print media, the journalists' unions had a salient role in the struggle against the authoritarian regime. A number of national leaders of the journalists' unions had already achieved national prestige, some of them succeeding in becoming Members of Parliament, as in the cases of Audálio Dantas and Fernando Morais. In Pernambuco, however, the union had been turned into a 'recreational association' with officials initially appointed by the government securing a tight grip on the union and avoiding any kind of political involvement.

In the first half of 1979, discontent with the union's officials came to light in the process of renewal of the annual collective agreement scheduled to take place in August. Led by informal opposition militants, the occupational category met in several assemblies both inside editorial rooms and in the headquarters of other civil society organisations' headquarters such as the Brazilian Lawyers' Association (OAB). The waking up of so many professionals whose jobs granted them high visibility was strong enough to break the union officials' resistance. Against the latter's will, the movement reached its peak on 8 July 1979, in the largest assembly of the whole history of the union with 259 journalists out of 419 union members taking part in the voting (union archives and interview no. 10). If one considers that retired members and other journalists were affiliated to the union even without acting as journalists, one may conclude that almost all the active professionals attended and voted in that assembly. The proposal favouring the strike was defeated by a small margin and the occupational category struck a reasonable pay rise anyway. This was regarded as a great achievement for a professional group that had remained passive for so long a time.

Following the wage campaign of 1979, the 'opposition group' contested the union election in July 1980. The old group in power used the union apparatus and had the support of the governor, a support that made a great deal of difference because the 'official slate' could employ all the necessary means to reach the electorate, ranging from cars and buildings (both belonging to the state government) to financial resources. Despite such an unequal distribution of resources, the opposition won the first ballot but without an absolute majority. Because at that time union elections were regulated by the Ministry of Labour, the rules imposed a second ballot that was won by the old pelegos after all sorts of pressure. The seeds had been sown and in 1986, after a complicated process of bargaining between the two groups, the former opposition managed to gain control of the majority of the directorate of the union. Subsequently a number of mobilisations allowed the occupational category to obtain important benefits in the annual bargaining.

In 1987 the union led a successful 34-day strike in 'Jornal

do Commercio', a media group whose assets included radio stations, television and the newspaper. This industrial action, demanding payment of three months' overdue salaries, included occupation of the enterprise headquarters and interruption of normal broadcasting. The television and radio aired only strikers' bulletins, explaining their reasons to public opinion. After the occupation, responding to the owner's request, the police came to rescue the enterprise's assets. Only after skilful mediation by the head of the Regional Office of the Ministry of Labour in Pernambuco (DRT-PE), did the workers escape being arrested and beaten (interviews nos. 10, 14 and 15). During the movement, responding to the employers' allegation that radio operators and journalists were jeopardising the wages of the printing workers in the enterprise, the strikers won the support of other unions, politicians and public opinion to raise funds. As a result of this solidarity they could pay the printing workers' wages during all the 34 days of the stoppage.

The negotiation was highly complex because it was not limited to the wage question. The very control of the enterprise was at stake. Since its financial situation was one of almost definitive bankruptcy, the proposal put forward by certain militants of taking over the enterprise and turning it into a co-operative was defeated due to the difficulty of raising funds for the necessary investments. But both occupational categories, journalists and radio operators, got involved in discussions about selling off the enterprise. The current owners had gained control of the company through a negotiation favoured by the State which awarded the owners a privileged financial scheme to enable its recovery. As the President-elect Tancredo Neves defined the deal to one of the owners, Deputy José Mendonça (according to interviews nos. 14 and 15), not without irony, it was a 'heterodox one'. The strike came to an end when, with the consent of the workers, a powerful entrepreneur from the supermarket sector decided to buy the company, agreeing to pay the overdue wages, in a negotiation that had a small businessman serving as an intermediary.

In the second half of 1979, the rise of new-unionism materialised in the two power companies operating in the state of Pernambuco. The first one, 'Companhia Hidroelétrica do São Francisco – Chesf' was a mixed-capital enterprise, controlled by the federal government, acting mainly as a generator and supplier for big consumers and for the state-controlled companies. The second one was the 'Companhia de Eletricidade de Pernambuco – Celpe', whose capital was dominated by the state of Pernambuco. The employees of both enterprises were represented by the Urban Workers' Union which by the time was directed by pelegos appointed by the military. As the grassroots, following the tracks of labour resurgence all over the country, started pressuring the companies for maintaining the real value of wages, the formal leadership refused to stimulate the movement. In August, the employees of 'Chesf' constituted an 'ad hoc' committee for negotiation and declared the first strike of the electricity sector in the country and the first one in a federal state-owned company after 1964. The platform included recovering of the purchasing power of wages and job stability. As the military regarded the electricity sector as a matter of national security (strikes in this sector were forbidden by Decree 1632/78), repression was the chosen strategy. Threats of dismissal and even physical violence were common. The union headquarters in Paulo Afonso, where the main power generator plant was installed, was invaded by the Army leaving several workers injured and arrested. The Army arbitrariness went on by taking control of the whole of the company's headquarters in a confrontation rendered harder owing to the support of the workers by the population of the city of Paulo Afonso whose lives were mainly concentrated around the company's activities. After having extracted important concessions out of 'Chesf', the workers decided not to yield on the demand for job stability for the members of the negotiation commission as long as they were aware of the federal government's intention of dismissing all the leaders of the movement. Some of those leaders were already answering an enquiry led by the federal police into alleged breaking of the National Security Law for striking in a sector regarded as important for national security. After intensive negotiation at the level of the Ministry of Energy Affairs, the government agreed to maintain the jobs of the beleaguered leaders. This strike was widely seen as a landmark in the new unionism even in national terms (interviews nos. 6 and 32).

If the strike in the state company – 'Celpe' – was less clamorous than the 'Chesf's one, certainly it was not less important for the awakening of the occupational category's consciousness and growing militancy. After a five-day stoppage, the state government conceded most of the workers' claims, including wage recovery, although it refused to cancel the sacking of five leaders of the movement (they were finally reinstated in 1987, after a long campaign led by the Urban Workers' Union) (interviews, nos. 6 and 32. Following these two historical strikes, the urban workers managed to win the union election held in August 1980 by a overwhelming majority of votes. This was the first big union conquered by new unionism militants in Pernambuco.

Another occupational category that launched important campaigns in the wake of the new unionism in Pernambuco was the metalworkers. Since their union was controlled by old-style trade unionists as well, they first set up an 'opposition group' that had roots in the Catholic worker groups. As early as in 1979 they managed to gain the participation of two thousand workers in an assembly for launching a wage campaign even against the will of the union officials. This assembly elected a wage commission formed by members of the 'opposition'. After a strike threat, the employers agreed to grant a 70 per cent pay rise and job stability for the commission's members (Centro Josué de Castro, 1988: 41; and interviews nos. 17 and 33). On 29–30 June and 1 July 1981, for a majority of 506 votes out of a total of 3,719 votes (2,077 against 1,642), the opposition that had adopted the nickname 'Zé Ferrugem' assumed the union directorate (Centro Josué de Castro, 1988; and interview no. 33).

Securing access to the union structure, the new unionism militants went on to organise active groups in several enterprises within the geographical area of the union. As for strategy, they chose to profit from certain aspects of the labour law such as the election for the Accident Prevention Commission (CIPA).[2] Since the law confers job stability on the workers' representatives in the CIPA, they benefited from such a privileged situation to carry out the union organisation work. In addition, they managed to set up commissions chosen at the grassroots for bargaining with the employers alongside union officials. Thus the Metalworkers strategy consisted of employing such emerging leadership to organise rank and file. The members of both the CIPAs and the negotiation commission, having some legal protection against retaliation, eventually constituted the nuclei of activists performing the union duties related to mobilisation within factories. Some of them subsequently yielded the 'factory commissions' as exemplified by the 'Cosinor's Commission', the first in the North and North-east regions of the country. This commission was set up in 1981 with effective members and eleven substitutes but initially most of its members were not militants and did not challenge management. After 1984 a more activist attitude was achieved by gathering members from CIPA and from 'wage commissions' and the employer was forced to recognise its independence. The strategic importance of that model of organisation inside the plant produced relevant achievements for the work force such as the reduction of the working week from 48 hours to 46 hours, a quarterly wage recovery, and several reinstatements of sacked workers (Centro Josué de Castro, 1988). Despite the success of the factory commission of 'Cosinor' or perhaps because of it, the company decided to stifle this pioneer experience by firing its members after the end of their job stability and sometimes disregarding such stability. By 1986 the experience was over (interview no. 33).

The first industrial action carried out by the Metalworkers was the strike of 'Reciferal' (a bus carriages producer) in November 1981. During the 1980–3 recession, Reciferal's management planned to sack around forty workers while restricting the already squeezed wages. The reaction of the company was marked by crude repression, no dialogue and reliance on police abuses. Workers faced strong intimidation, with the police and enterprises watchmen physically forcing them to enter work. At a certain point during the five-day strike, the enterprise parked the bus for commuting workers in front of the police headquarters and forced them to ride. Several workers were beaten, among them one of the union officials. Under this overwhelming pressure, the union had to call off the strike without even securing the quashing of the dismissals and with no wage increase. Again, the evaluation of the activists was that the 'conscious balance' was positive in that the last workers' illusions had crumbled.

Following the strike at 'Reciferal', the Metalworkers were involved in the three-day strike at 'Monor' in the first quarter of 1982. Manufacturing micro-motors, the company had announced a scheme for dismissals. The workers stopped working for three days, succeeding in forcing management to drop plans for dismissals and promise wage increases. Although the latter commitment was not honoured by the company afterwards (forcing another stoppage), the movement was plainly successful. Intimidation had been overcome by a massive participation in the movement.

In July 1982, the Metalworkers' Union launched a strike at 'Renda Priori'. With the mediation of Gentil Mendonça Filho, the head of the Regional Office of the Ministry of Labour in the state of Pernambuco ('DRT/PE'), the company agreed to stop lay-offs, committed itself to correcting wage distortions and paying wages in arrears. Once again the role of intimidation was performed by the police during the two days of stoppage.

Another landmark in the history of metalworkers' mobilisations that helped to assert the new unionism in Pernambuco was the strike at 'Volnor', a producer of steel cutlery and trays. For fifteen days in March 1983, the workers downed tools urging the company to halt lay-offs and improve their pay. Demonstrations in the centre of Recife, camping in front of the State Governor's Palace and occupation (and camping with relatives) of the plant were some of the mobilisation means deployed by strikers thus succeeding in forcing management to pay wages owed and to desist from the planned lay-offs.

In 1985, another violent movement was led by the Metalworkers' Union at 'Açonorte', a steel producer owned by the strong Gerdau group. Several militants were beaten up by the police and arrested. After three days of stoppage, management conceded part of the pay rise demanded by the union, re-engaged some of the previously dismissed workers and awarded the negotiation commission a six-month job stability. This was the first wage commission to achieve job stability in the private sector in the state of Pernambuco.

Still in 1985, an important strike worth mentioning is the bank workers' one. The movement was conducted by the combination of unions from both the CUT and CON-CLAT. But the most militant attitude was undoubtedly held by the unions and militants gathered in the Bank Employees' National Department of the CUT.[3] This movement was deemed the largest national strike by one occupational category in the whole history of the Brazilian labour movement up to that time, encompassing around 700,000 labourers on September 11, 12 and 13. Although the Labour Minister Almir Pazzianoto supported the Labour Court ruling which declared the stoppages unlawful, the workers eventually won a 12 per cent real pay rise and the payment of the non-worked days. This was deemed one of the greatest successes of the labour movement at that time. In Pernambuco, the union was still controlled by the former leadership affiliated to CONCLAT and refused to perform most of the preparative tasks. At the last moment, the union took part in the strike which, nevertheless, was led mainly by the 'opposition group'. Several branches in the state were closed, particularly those owned by 'Banorte', 'BNB', 'Banespa' and 'Banco do Brasil' (CUT/PE, 1985).

In 1986, a strike hit one of the oldest sectors of Pernambuco's working classes: the textile industry. Led by the new directorate that had defeated the old pelegos in 1985, around nine thousand weavers (92 per cent of the occupational category) stopped working for four days, reaching all the enterprises of the sector. Besides economic achievements, they succeeded in forcing management to grant the payment of one full-time union official for each enterprise (cf. interview no. 1).

The brief mention of some of the most important mobilisations that signalled the labour movement's rebirth in Pernambuco allows us to make a number of analytical points. Morais (1992) has stressed that the main leadership of such movements was not the union officials. In fact, as we have seen in the case of metalworkers, urban industry workers, private school teachers and journalists, their movements became reality because of the decisive intervention of militants outside the union ranks. This was a clear sign of the emergence of the new unionism in the state, whose initiatives were strong enough to sweep away the resistance of the old pelegos in mobilising the rank and file.

The data aforementioned offers a list of the most significant mobilisations of the workers during the revival of the movement in the state of Pernambuco. From such an account one might observe that the following stoppages were performed in the private sector: rural workers in 1979, private school teachers in 1979 and subsequent years, metalworkers ('Reciferal' in 1981, 'Monor' in 1982, 'Renda Priori' in 1982, 'Volnor' in 1983, 'Açonorte' in 1985), journalists and radio operators ('Empresa Jornal do Commercio') in 1987, and weavers in 1986. The mentioned strikes hitting the state sector were those in 'Chesf' (1979), 'Celpe' (1979) and state schools' teachers (1979). The 1985 banking strike, in turn, reached bank branches in both the private and the public sector. The literature has discussed the character of the sectors where the new unionism first flourished. Bearing in mind the initial mobilisations of São Paulo ABC's metalworkers at the heart of the most technologically developed sector of the country's industry, authors such as Almeida (1980) and Sader (1988) maintain that the phenomena were typical of those modern sectors. Taking issue with this view and drawing on data he collected for the new unionism in Pernambuco in the period between the late 1970s and the late 1980s, Morais (1992) argues persuasively that the labour revival was not confined to the modern sector as long as it reached both traditional sectors (such as the rural) and the state. But the examples presented by Morais could mislead the observer, for they might be interpreted as supporting the view that the new unionism in Pernambuco was primarily an affair of the public sector. Our data, however, suggest that both the private and the public sector, as well as both the traditional and the modern sectors, were hit alike by the initial mobilisations proper to the new unionism in the state of Pernambuco.

A further conclusion arising from such labour mobilisations concerns the role of the state. In the public sector strikes the militants were directly confronted by state authorities, very often by violent means. In the case of the private sector strikes, the state was not absent or neutral. The police always exerted pressure and in certain occasions physical violence. The role of the Regional Office of the Ministry of Labour in Pernambuco ('DRT-PE') was paradoxical. While the legal constraints that put the unions' internal and external life under control of the Ministry were still enforced, its head in Pernambuco, Gentil Mendonça Filho, had a different conception of state intervention (interview no. 14). Within the legal limits, he managed to serve chiefly as a mediator of labour conflicts throughout the 1980s, as exemplified by the metalworkers' strike in the first half of the 1980s and by the 'Jornal do Commercio' strike in 1987. It is widely accepted by unionists and employers (interviews nos. 15 and 30) that he anticipated most of the policies that would be adopted subsequently in the late 1980s by the Labour Ministry during Almir Pazzianoto's term in office.

1.3 The First Articulations

We have already noticed that the emerging set of rank and file union members forming opposition groups had sought to act together since the beginning. From both the so-called 'organised left' and the Catholic workers groups, militants often met to discuss problems and actions related to different occupational categories. This character of the initial actions favoured the broader articulations reproduced in the state in parallel with the national ones.

In 1981 the labour movement began to prepare the first national meeting held since 1964 – the 'Conferência Nacional das Classes Trabalhadores' (CONCLAT). In Pernambuco, the emerging militants called a state-wide meeting, the 'Encontro Estadual das Classes Trabalhadoras' (ENCLAT). This meeting was held on 18–19 July 1981 in the city of Olinda. Among the main unions organising the event were the Rural Workers' Federation – 'Fetape', the metalworkers opposition group, the Urban Workers' Union, the private schools' teachers opposition, the Watchmen's Association, the State Schools Teachers' Association, the Insurance Workers' Union, the bank employees opposition and other groups in opposition to the incumbent officials in their unions (interviews nos 8, 29 and 30). Their pursued goal was the articulation of unions and opposition groups as well as the discussion of the participation of the state in the national meeting to be held in 'Praia Grande – São Paulo'. The 165 delegates taking part in the first 'Pernambuco's ENCLAT' represented 55 occupational categories, through their trade unions, associations and opposition groups already organised. This meeting chose the representatives of the state in the CONCLAT as well as approved the platform of the labour movement in Pernambuco which included the main banners: (a) amnesty for the militants punished on the grounds of the 'National Security Law' for their participation in strikes; (b) land reform; (c) a wage policy of quarterly automatic readjustment; (d) job stability; (e) union autonomy and freedom; (f) reduction of the working week to 40 hours (CUT, 1984: 29; and interviews nos 8, and 28).

The representation of the labour movement of the state to the national meeting comprised 186 delegates from the fifty-six occupational categories that had participated in the First ENCLAT (CUT, 1984: 33). However, the number of unions which actually sent delegates to that first national meeting of the labour movement was quite limited as yet. Most unions did not take part in those initial articulations, as demonstrated by a survey carried out in 1986/87 among the urban unions of the state of Pernambuco (CEAS and Fundação Joaquim Nabuco, 1989: 69). According to the collected data, only 16.7 per cent of the unions surveyed sent delegates to the first 'CONCLAT' in 1981. By 1987, from a sample with the most important urban unions of the state, the same survey indicated that merely 42.9 per cent of the unions lent support to one of the national top organisations of the time. Table 4.1 shows how this support was distributed.

As already mentioned, the First National 'CONCLAT' decided to form a national commission responsible for the creation of the single national top organisation of the labour movement – The National Commission 'Pro-CUT'. The participation of the state's representatives was significant, as one may infer from the election of four members from Pernambuco state among the fifty-six total members of the 'Commission Pro-CUT' (Medeiros, 1992: 63; and Pró-Cut, 1983).[4]

Table 4.1   Unions' relationship with the national top organisations, 1986/87 (percentage)

Kind of relation	CUT	CGT	CUT/CGT	CUT/CGT/UIL	None	No answer	Total
Support	16.7	19.0	4.8	2.4	54.7	2.4	100
Affiliation	7.2	4.7	N.A.	N.A	83.3	4.8	100
Participation at directive boards	9.5	8.3	N.A	N.A	77.4	4.8	100

Source: Ceas/Fundaj Survey, 1986/87.

The initial years of the resurgence of the labour movement in the state were also marked by an informal articulation called 'Intersindical'. Holding weekly meetings, this union articulation played an important role in a number of workers' initiatives in the period. Discussions used to be intense because differences of conceptions were already strong. Watchmen, state schools' teachers, insurance workers, metalworkers opposition group, private schools' teachers, rural workers, bank opposition group, and urban workers were the most regular attendants (interviews nos 8 and 28). Among the main concerted actions of Intersindical and CONCLAT at the time was the celebration of May 1st in 1981. Breaking with the meetings called by the state authorities, the new unionism militants gathered in the small stadium of the soccer club 'Santo Amaro', holding the first massive independent meeting of Pernambuco's workers after many years (interviews nos 8, 28 and 32). In the same year another significant unified action took place on the occasion of a national day of struggle against workers' hard conditions called by CONCLAT. The demonstration held in Recife, the capital of the state, was widely acknowledged as one of the most sizeable of the country, having gathered around 4,000 workers in the main rally (Medeiros, 1992: 59).

Still under the military restrictions, the labour movement used to turn the annual celebrations for the workers' day – on May 1st – into an opportunity for protesting through huge mobilisations. The process of preparation for the demonstrations and rallies was itself an occasion for mobilising workers and tightening the inter-categorial links. 'Ad hoc' committees were set up in order to raise funds among grassroots and other institutions. Initially the emerging 'combative' sectors of the movement adopted the strategy of attending the official celebrations for protesting against the authorities that staged them. Then, as the control of some unions was gained by militant groups, they organised their own events. The May 1st celebrations initially unified the whole movement in the state. Then, after the 1983 split between the sectors that founded the CUT in August and those that created the CONCLAT in November, such ceremonies became decentralised, each group staging their own ones.

Just before the split of 1983, the labour movement had succeeded in carrying out the General Strike of 21 July 1983 against the Decree-law 2.045 that reduced real wages. In Pernambuco the stoppage was considered a watershed, having reached several occupational categories and with a unified rally in the city centre of Recife which gathered several thousands of workers, virtually paralysing all the activities, especially shops. The preparation of the movement involved a great number of meetings generally held at the headquarters of the Metalworkers' Union. Owing to police infiltration, repression proved to be not so difficult a task. Early in the morning the main factories whose workers had already decided to stop were surrounded by troops. Having decided to carry out the movement, the workers faced aggression. Thirty-two of them were arrested and jailed in the hated DOPS (political police). Only late in the night were they freed, after pressure from demonstrators and the intervention of democratic politicians (interviews nos 17 and 33).

That strike was the last great initiative called by the unified labour movement before the split of 1983. In Pernambuco the differences between the two factions were quite sharp. On one side, the militants integrating the so-called 'combative bloc' (mainly formed by new unionism activists) had their representatives in the National Commission Pro-CUT and controlled several unions and opposition groups. They set up a provisional commission to found the CUT in Pernambuco in the second semester of 1983. This provisional commission had members from the Metalworkers' Union (José Alves de Siqueira, a member of the union's directorate, was its general co-ordinator), the State Schools Teachers' Union and the Insurance Workers (Raimundo Ananias) (*Folha Sindical*, Oct. 1984 and interviews nos 8 and 30).

On the other side, the 'Unidade Sindical' section insisted on emphasising the need for the unity of the whole labour movement. This section had their more active tendencies in the unionists affiliated to the communist parties, to the MR-8 and the rural unions. In Pernambuco they set up the local branch of 'Conclat' (the National Co-ordination of the Working Classes), the top organisation founded in November 1983 in Praia Grande as a result of the division of the Brazilian labour movement. The first years of Conclat in Pernambuco had the urban workers, the weavers, the private school teachers, the bank workers and the rural workers' federation as its most active members. They also had representatives in the former 'National Commission Pro-CUT' and continued to exert influence at both the national and the state levels of workers' articulations (interviews nos 1 and 8).

Immediately after the 1983 split, the labour movement in Pernambuco continued to include a number of unions that either remained neutral or did not take part in any sort of articulation. Among the unions that kept themselves in a neutral position because of political differences within their directive bodies were the Data Processing Workers' Union, the Engineers' Union (whose control was gained by the new unionism militants in November 1983) and the Telecommunications Workers' Union (this one just up to the first half of 1984, when it decided to affiliate to the CUT) (interviews nos 7 and 32).

1.4 Consolidation

The consolidation of the labour movement in Pernambuco roughly coincides with the second half of the 1980s. By 1984, during the national campaign for direct election for the Presidency of the Republic, the two labour currents were already consolidated. Initially certain important unions failed to opt for one or the other of the confronting sides, as noted above. This was a result of differences in political persuasion within the directorates of those unions. The

Communist officials favoured the continuation of the former alliance between the 'combative' trade unionists and the old conservative groups, while the new unionism fraction decided to build up the CUT by dispensing with those 'backward' sectors. However, the large majority of the trade unions remained under the influence of the so-called 'Unidade Sindical' (Union Unity) section grouped in Conclat and, later on, in the CGT (General 'Central' of Workers). Urban Workers, Textile Industry Workers, and Bank Workers continued to be the leading unions of the sector in the state.[5] Their policies were twofold: on one side they concentrated on the official union's leadership; and on the other, they adopted an amenable criticism of the union structure which combined the campaign for elimination of state intervention on unions but accepted some of the fundamentals of the corporatist framework such as the union tax and the monopoly of representation. On the broader political matters, the CGT's activists defended a 'democratic alliance' of all the sectors fighting to end military rule, generally through the then major opposition party MDB ('Movimento Democrático Brasileiro').

The 'Unidade Sindical' section of the labour movement in Pernambuco decided to found the state branch of the CGT on 2 March 1986 during the first 'Enclat' ('Encontro das classes trabalhadores') of the state of Pernambuco. The decision to create the CGT's branch in the state anticipated by one month the foundation of that organisation at national level. Ratifying the existing platform, that congress of foundation elected the state directive board, whose president was Pedro Silva, a textile worker affiliated to the MR-8. Among the other members of the directorate were José Carlos Andrade, another textile worker, Luís Carlos da Silva, then president of the Industry Workers' Federation, Severino Lourenço, the president of the Food Industry Workers' Federation, Hercílio Ferreira, from the Building Industry Workers' Federation, and Manoel Ribeiro, then secretary of the Textile Industry Workers' Federation. Among the principal unions taking part in the CGT's foundation congress were those of drivers, bank workers, building industry workers of Recife and textile industrial workers (CGT's archives and interview no. 24).

Table 4.2 The foundation congress of the CUT in Pernambuco: delegates per categories

Unions	Number of delegates	Unions	Number of delegates
Metalworkers	26	Psychologists	10
Insurance workers	10	Social assistant workers	05
Engineers	17	University lecturers	06
Chemical industry workers	15	Data processing workers	05
Escada textile workers	02	Petrolândia building industry	14
Igarassu rural workers	02	State schools teachers	08
Petrolândia rural workers	02	Union opposition groups	
Serra Talhada rural workers	05	Urban workers	17
Belmonte rural workers	05	Bank workers	10
Pre-union associations		Retail shop assistants	18
Domestic workers	05	Private schools' teachers	16
Watchmen	14	'Agua Preta' rural workers	08

Unions participating as observers: Medical professionals, Rubber industry workers, Building industry workers and Telecommunication workers

Invited observers: Neighbourhood Associations of 'Petrolândia' and 'Brasília Teimosa', Neighbour Federation of 'Casa Amarela' and 'Cabo' Rural Workers' Union Opposition

Source: Recife, *Folha Sindical*, October 1984, Special Edition.

The CUT's state branch in Pernambuco, in turn, was created with the decisive participation of the metallurgical workers, the Watchmen's Union, the insurance workers and the sympathetic sectors of other unions, the majority of which were still affiliated to the CGT (engineers, private schools' teachers, urban workers, retail shop workers and some rural unions).[6] The foundation congress was held in Cecosne, a cultural centre in the city of Recife, on 27–29 July 1984; 183 delegates took part in the event, representing 13 urban organisations (associations and unions), 4 rural unions and 4 rural unions' oppositions, as Table 4.2 shows.

Among the chief items of the platform approved in that foundation congress were: support for 'union opposition groups', creation of factory commissions, helping the struggle of the unemployed, union democracy through general assemblies, strengthening of links between the labour and 'popular' movements, supporting all mobilisations of workers in the state of Pernambuco and setting up an institution for political education of workers.

The second congress of the CUT in Pernambuco was held in Recife, in late November 1985. The 235 attendant delegates represented the following organisations: (i) rural workers' unions of Igarassu, Amaraji, Cabo, Chã Grande, Serra Talhada, São José do Belmonte, Petrolândia, Itacuruba, Floresta; (ii) the urban unions of the insurance workers, the engineers, the urban workers, the port workers, the telecommunication workers, the rubber industry workers, the metallurgical workers, the psychologists, the private schools teachers, the textiles of Paulista and Igarassu, the state schools teachers, the watchmen, the social workers; (iii) the pre-union associations: mail workers, civil servants of Olinda, urban train workers; (iv) and the opposition groups: bank employees, building industry, and the commerce employees. Although many of those unions were not formally affiliated to the CUT, the list shows its growth since the first Congress (CUT/PE, 1986).[7]

The process of consolidation of the labour movement in Pernambuco was far more visible in the ranks of the CUT owing to the more militant practices and strategies of the new unionism sector. Such a combative stance is apparent from data collected by the already mentioned survey carried out by CEAS and Fundação Joaquim Nabuco in 1987 with a sample of 84 urban unions in Pernambuco. Figure 4.1 shows the responses to the question asking whether those unions had ever received any kind of support from the national top organisations.

The CUT's policy of changing the union structure from inside proved sucessful. Its activists combined the tactics of disputing official unions' elections and, where there was no union, creating a new one. This last manoeuvre is well exemplified by the Data Processing Workers' Union founded on 2 October 1985 after three years of existence as a pre-union association (*Boletim Cut*/PE, October 1985). The majority of unions created under the auspices of the CUT in Pernambuco, however, were those in the public sector after the 1988 Constitution authorised the civil servants to

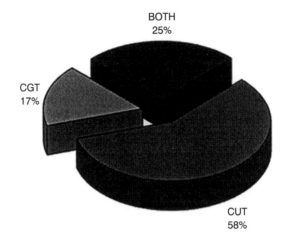

BOTH
25%

CGT
17%

CUT
58%

■ CUT
▣ CGT
■ BOTH

Figure 4.1 Percent of unions in Pernambuco receiving any kind of support from the top organisations

Source: Ceas/Joaquim Nabuco Survey, 1986/87.

unionise. Such was a deliberate policy of the CUT after 1988 ('we spent the whole year of 1989 creating unions in the public sector', said the former finance director of the CUT in Pernambuco, Cláudio Ferreira – interview no. 7). These initiatives were backed by a national project that transferred funds from the national board of the CUT to its state branches. As a result, a number of unions were born already affiliated to the CUT, the most important being the Federal Civil Servants in Pernambuco's Union (19.03.89), the Federal Civil Servants in Medical Care and Welfare in Pernambuco's Union (17.03.89), the State Civil Servants of Pernambuco's Union (1989), the Civil Servants of Recife's Union (13.07.89), the Civil Servants of Olinda's Union (21.06.89) (archives of the CUT/PE and interviews nos 3, 7, and 31).

The new unionism policy of taking over existing unions through electoral means was decisive in enabling it to seize control of the most prominent unions of the labour movement in Pernambuco. In 1984 the 'opposition' won the Telecommunication Workers' Union and a few months later decided to affiliate to the CUT after a short period of formal neutrality. In 1984 a disputed election in the Engineers' Union was also won by the slate sympathetic to the CUT. In 1985 it was the turn of the important Rubber Industry Workers' Union; in 1987, the Joiners' Union, the Federal Railway Company Workers' Union and the Radio Operators' Union; in 1988, the powerful Bank Employees' Union (representing around thirty thousand workers) and the Chemical Industry Workers' Union; in 1989, the Airways Workers' Union and the Sugar Industry Workers' Union.

2   THE CURRENT PANORAMA: CUT, CGTs AND FORÇA SINDICAL IN PERNAMBUCO

2.1   A New Cycle

The first half of the 1990s marks a new phase of the labour movement both at national and state level. The cycle of assertion, legitimisation, mobilisation and fast growth seems to have reached a halt. In March 1990, President Fernando Collor inaugurated a government committed to privatising state enterprises, opening up the economy and curtailing the power and influence of the labour movement; as a result of deep recession, high unemployment levels ensued thus making working-class resistance even more difficult. He tried to co-opt part of the labour movement, as the appointment of Antônio Rogério Magri to the Ministry of Labour epitomises. Magri, together with Luís Antônio Medeiros, was an exponent of the so-called 'business unionism' or 'unionism of results'. Instead of helping to shift the balance of power towards labour as one might have expected from a union leader, Minister Magri agreed with the policies put forward by President Collor.

By the end of the 1980s, the allegiances and alignments of the different persuasions were, roughly speaking, consolidated. The CUT consolidated as the larger top organisation, representing workers both in the public and private sector, urban and rural areas, being present in all the states of the country. Its policy continued to be the most militant in the entire labour movement. On the other side of the political spectrum, both CGTs suffered a process of stagnation, having lost positions to Força Sindical. Gradually the latter imposed itself as an alternative to the alleged radicalism of the CUT. It claimed to practise a non-ideological unionism concerned with the pragmatic material improvement of the working class mostly secured through means of negotiation rather than strike action.

2.2 The CUT

The CUT's trajectory had a turning-point at the third Congress held in Belo Horizonte from 7th to 11th September 1988. Among the main resolutions adopted, the congress resolved to oblige the unions to affiliate formally and contribute regularly if they were to qualify for the right to participate in the CUT's decisions. This apparently formal resolution implied that, from then on, the CUT ceased to be a loose movement capable of gathering unions without many formal links. Through such a clause, which enabled it to act through regular contributions by the affiliated unions, it approximated more closely to the type of an 'organic general union'.

In Pernambuco, as the former finance director of the CUT in the state points out, 'up to 1988 the CUT managed to survive through the revenues produced by projects and conjunctural campaigns' (interview no. 7). For every planned action, the directorate in the state had to raise funds from external sponsors, from the national board and from occasional contributions by the unions. After the third national congress, the sympathiser unions had to affiliate and to contribute regularly with 2.5 per cent of their receipts if they were to take part in the life of the 'central'. As a result, the number of affiliated unions grew fast. By late 1989, taking stock of its financial situation, the Pernambuco's branch of the CUT realised that for the first time around 60 per cent of the expenses were met by regular contributions from the unions.

The process of strengthening the CUT in Pernambuco is also apparent from Table 4.3 which shows its representation at the national congresses of the 'central'.

A relative reduction in the representation of the unions of the state of Pernambuco in the CUT's national congresses,

Table 4.3   Pernambuco's representation in the CUT's congresses

Congress	No. of entities	No. of delegates	No. of represented workers
I – 1983	24	114	370,425
II – 1986	44	223	445,977
III – 1988	34	209	N.A.
IV – 1991	N.A.	73	N.A.
V – 1994	31	84	300,000*

* Estimated by the author on the basis of raw data from the mentioned archives.

Source: Resolutions of CUT's Congresses and CUT/PE's archives.

particularly after 1988, may be explained by the more rigid criteria of participation adopted after the third national congress held in that year.

The consolidation of the CUT's branch in Pernambuco led it to attain a position of hegemony in the labour movement in the state. By 1994, almost the totality of the public sector unions were under its control. The same happened in the private sector, as exemplified by some of the main occupational categories: banking, sugar industry, data processing, printing, journalists, engineers, rubber industry, cultural activities, radio operators, metalworkers, joiners, chemical industry, and others. At that time, the state branch of the CUT counted 75 affiliated unions.

2.3   The CGTs

Section 5.2 of Chapter 2 thoroughly describes the evolution of the CGT as the sector of the labour movement which developed in contrast to the new unionism organised in the CUT. Seeking to maintain the unity of the movement, the CGT initially gathered both the old pelegos and some left-wing leaders attached to the traditional communist parties (PCB and PC do B). The split in the second congress in 1989 which led to the creation of two CGTs (the 'Confederation' led by Antônio Rogério Magri, and the 'Central', by Joaquim dos Santos Andrade and the MR-8 activists) obviously was reproduced at the state level. The 'Confederation' kept the majority of the unions affiliated to the CGT in the state of Pernambuco. Even some activists from the MR-8 (then aligned with Joaquim dos Santos Andrade in the 'Central') started dissenting. In the second congress of the CGT in Pernambuco, held in September 1989, the differences became clear at last. The president-elect, José Carlos Andrade, headed the directorate with no MR-8 activists. Other unions included in the directorate were Ceramic Workers', Caruaru Building Industry Workers', Paper Industry Workers', Glass Industry Workers' and Drivers'. By the 1990s, the 'Confederação Geral dos Trabalhadores' comprised around thirty unions and federations affiliated in the state of Pernambuco. Their policies, although continuing to be less adversarial, tended to identify with the CUT's, as may be inferred from a number of initiatives carried out together (the successful general strike of March 1989, and the actions against the government of President Collor, being good examples) (interviews nos 1 and 24).

The minority fraction, the 'Central', remained controlled by MR-8 activists, whose main unions were Building Industry of the Metropolitan Region of Recife Workers' and Shoe Industry Workers'. Due to the clear-cut preponderance of the CUT and the already considerable presence of the 'Confederação Geral dos Trabalhadores', the 'Central Geral dos Trabalhadores' has been isolated from the main currents of the labour movement in Pernambuco.

2.4 Força Sindical

Having first emerged in the late 1980s as merely one of the currents within the CGT, Força Sindical adopted a rhetoric of pragmatism as opposed to what it regards as the ideological stance assumed by the CUT. Later on, its leaders elaborated a more comprehensive programme, identified with the betterment of the 'Brazilian savage capitalism', published with the ambitious title *A Project for Brazil* (Força Sindical, 1993). Data presented in Section 5.3 of Chapter 2 and in this section likewise suggest that the document represents more an intellectual effort by some scholars than a compilation of debates conducted within the ranks of the 'central'. As a consequence, there is a huge gap between the ideas advocated at the theoretical level and the understanding (and even adherence) of the ordinary Força Sindical's union officials.

In the state of Pernambuco, by 1994 Força Sindical was still in the process of consolidation. In April 1992 the state branch was formally set up by a number of unionists that had either formerly integrated into the CGT or remained independent from the main confederations. In both cases, those unionists had always belonged to the so-called traditional sector of the labour movement. The main unions involved with the setting up of Força Sindical in Pernambuco were the Federation of Bank Employees, the Federation of Workers in the Wheat Industry, the Watchmen's Union and the Commerce Employees' Union in Recife. Even allowing for the erosion of the power of the Federation of Bank Employees caused by the loss of control over the Bank Employees' Union of Pernambuco in 1988 (to the CUT), those unions comprise a powerful administrative machine which has been principally directed towards the provision of social and medical benefits to the membership (interviews nos 13 and 26). The Commerce Employee's Union came to serve as a strategic stronghold for the consolidation of the Força Sindical in Pernambuco. Its president, Severino Ramos, rapidly assumed the co-ordination of the entity in the state. In the second quarter of 1993, the group of unionists led by José Cassiano de Souza that had defeated the CUT's incumbent leadership in the Watchmen's Union attained an expressive electoral victory over the CUT's slate. It was a remarkable achievement because that union had been founded by CUT's militants and had been regarded as a CUT's stronghold up till 1990. This election was lavishly financed by the national board of Força Sindical and consequently its relationship with the Watchmen's Union was reinforced. By 1994 the unions affiliated to the Força Sindical in the state of Pernambuco were the following:

- Commerce Workers' Union in Recife
- Watchmen's Union in the State of Pernambuco
- Union of Workers in Conservation and Cleaning of Buildings in Pernambuco
- Union of Workers in Hotels and Similar Establishments in Pernambuco

- Wheat Industry Workers' Union in Pernambuco
- Union of Workers in Papers Distribution in Pernambuco
- Nurses and Similar Workers' Union in Pernambuco
- Job Safety Professionals' Union
- Rural Workers' Union in Carpina

Besides the better established CUT and CGT-Confederation, the representation and strength of Força Sindical in Pernambuco are still marginal. Apart from commerce, security services (watchmen's union) and wheat industry, the occupational categories represented are not expressive in economic or political terms. The 'central' does not have a formal structure in the state, not even headquarters or other material means. It has worked mainly as an articulation of some unions whose leadership came from the more bureaucratic sectors of the labour movement. Even this mere articulation is regarded as a rather 'loose one' (interview no. 26).

3 THE OCCUPATIONAL CATEGORIES INCLUDED IN THE RESEARCH SAMPLE

3.1 The Unions whose Members were Surveyed

Chapter 5 will discuss the statistical test employed in this research. The test, a multiple regression one, was designed with the purpose of assessing how different models of unionism currently practised in Brazil have influenced the political culture of their members. Specifically, our test aims at finding out whether the alternative model developed by the CUT unions has had any impact on a particular kind of political culture: the culture of active citizenship.

The development of a certain political culture may be the result of a large number of factors. Our research aims exclusively to look into only one of the possible independent variables: the union model. Thus we had to describe different models of unionism actually existing in the country and in the state of Pernambuco. In order to understand the research setting, this chapter presents facts and analysis on the trade unionism of the state of Pernambuco since its revival in the late 1970s. The preceding sections focused on that history. This Section 3 presents the seven unions whose members were selected for the sample of our survey.

3.2   The Telecommunications Workers' Union

Founded on 29 May 1934, the Telecommunications Workers' Union, from now on named simply by its acronym SINTTEL, represents all the workers in telecommunications in the state of Pernambuco. Most workers included in its base of representation are employees of the three federal government-owned companies of the telecommunications sector: 'Telpe', 'Embratel' and Telebrás'. Besides them there are thirteen private companies that act as permanent tenderers for contracts offered by the state sector. The distribution of occupational categories among those companies is as given in Table 4.4.

The 1964 military regime imposed and supported a docile pelego that ran the union for several years without undertaking any sort of mobilisation. Collective bargaining was just a formal matter, performed every year with no significant benefit to workers. We have already referred to the process of winning over of official unions by new unionism militants. SINTTEL is one of the best instances of this strategy of gaining control over unions from inside. In 1980 two groups of workers from grassroots decided to run for the union election. Lacking any sort of experience both groups were defeated by the old pelegos. Later on, in 1983, already merged, the opposition managed to win that year's election, after a complicated process in which the new-unionism group had to wait for an extra round due to fraud carried out by the union officials. Six months later, the opposition succeeded in winning the second ballot and inaugurated a new administration. Differences in accountability, legitimacy and involvement of workers were soon quite apparent. Collective bargaining became a matter of participation. Huge assemblies preceded by small meetings at workplaces afforded the sense of strength and real bargaining power missed by workers for so long (Medeiros, 1992; and interviews nos 27 and 31).

Table 4.4   Distribution of the telecommunications workers per enterprise, July 1994

Companies	Number of employees	%
Telpe	2,310	63.4
Embratel	400	11.0
Telebrás	64	0.017
Private firms	870	23.9
Total	3,644	100.00

Source: SINTTEL archives.

From 1984 the same group has led the union, triumphing in every election held since then. Only one of the original political factions, those militants affiliated to the former 'Convergência Socialista' (a Trotskyist group that abandoned the PT in the early 1990s to create the PSTU – 'Partido Socialista dos Trabalhadores Unificados'), have split and disputed elections on two occasions.

Although the occupational category is a relatively small one (merely 3,650 workers), SINTTEL today boasts a lot of achievements. The financial situation of the union is fairly balanced. Putting into practice the CUT's claim to dispense with the union tax, SINTTEL introduced the principle of calling workers to vote on whether the resources are to be returned to them. Since then, they have voted to hand over the equivalent amount as a voluntary contribution to the union.

The unionisation ratio is quite significant, well above the less than 20 per cent Brazilian average. From 3,644 workers at grassroots, 2,787 were voluntarily affiliated to the union in July 1994, which yields a union density of 76.5 per cent. Even if one considers that only a small part of the occupational category is in the private sector, one cannot underestimate such an index.

Being one of the unions closest to the CUT in the state of Pernambuco, SINTTEL has contributed to formulating the CUT's proposal to change the current industrial relations system. In practice its leadership has tried to develop a union model which relies on mobilisation of grassroots, direct bargaining, democracy and accountability. In the day-to-day endeavours, the union has always introduced themes that go beyond mere economic claims. The following data help to clarify such a conclusion. Out of 37 collective bargaining negotiations in the last five years, only four were submitted to the labour court. It demonstrates the union's option for direct bargaining, in line with the CUT's platform to abolish the court power to interfere with autonomous negotiations.

Among the main benefits currently enjoyed by telecommunications workers are: meal tickets, provision of nurseries, medical and dentist assistance, basic food baskets, democratisation of the accident prevention commission (CIPA), paid leave for carrying out union duties, the right of employees to attend courses and congresses promoted by the union without deduction from wages, the right to retraining for technological innovation, job security in the cases of modernisation of working processes, joint definition (employer and union) of productivity criteria, consultation on investment and tariff policies. Some of these benefits have a democratising meaning, enlarging workers' participation and control.

Its archives show that the union has held around 24 general assemblies per year, attended by around 240 members on average. Besides the elected union officials (9 members in the executive committee and 41 in the directive council), SINTTEL has counted on a network of 40 informal militants at the grassroots.

Two of the last campaigns sponsored by the union are emblematic of the new-unionism's determination to go beyond the limits of economic claims. In 1992 and 1993 it led a successful struggle against corruption in 'TELPE' (Telecommunications of Pernambuco), combining grassroots mobilisations with media, and even the utilisation of the Judiciary. The campaign ended with the ousting of the then president of the company. Another initiative was the defence of the state monopoly on telecommunications. Although a rather controversial matter, one has to point out that the campaign warned that only the most profitable segments of the state companies would be sold, leaving no resources to be invested in services in poor communities. Such a campaign serves to show a union developing a role rather different from that reserved by the corporatist union structure imposed by CLT, where unions are expected to advance economic claims to the virtual exclusion of others.

Another decision by the current leadership of SINTTEL seems to be in line with the alternative proposals advanced by the new unionism to change the current system. Having inherited a union with a relatively large 'assistential' structure, by 1994 the union had changed its administrative structure into an apparatus designed to carry out only tasks related to mobilisation, bargaining and political education. Medical care and other welfare provisions were left to the state (or to be demanded from the state). The only facility granted to members currently is legal aid, even if restricted to labour law matters. Concern for workers' education may be inferred from the huge printing equipment, the weekly paper and the large number of political education courses permanently available to the membership, given by professional staff hired for that purpose.

Such policies have had a considerable impact on members' attitudes towards the union and the broader political affairs. A survey of SINTTEL's members conducted by scholars from Universidade Federal de Pernambuco in 1993 yielded results that allow us to reach such a conclusion (Barbosa and Silva, 1993). Asked about the role of unions, 62 per cent answered that their main goal should be transforming society, as against 34 per cent who regarded them as concerned with economic betterment and less than 1 per cent who envisaged unions as associations for leisure activities. Asked if they considered the union important to their lives, 70.6 per cent replied that it was very important; 24.3 per cent, that it was rather important; and 4 per cent, that it has no importance for them. The sample pointed to an affiliation ratio of 80 per cent, which is consistent with data extracted from the union archives to which we referred above.

As far as political party affiliation is concerned, this occupational category appears to contradict the received general picture of Brazilian society. As is widely acknowledged, political parties in Brazil lack real penetration in the general society. Very few people have ever bothered to affiliate to them. Notwithstanding this general pattern, the telecommunications workers in Pernambuco show an uncommonly high ratio of affiliation to political parties. Although 90 per cent of them disclaimed any party affiliation, as many as 6.7 per cent answered that they have affiliated to the Workers' Party (PT), with all the other parties being mentioned by less than 0.5 per cent each. When the question was 'mere sympathy for a political party', the PT was mentioned by 34.8 per cent of respondents. Among the other parties, only PSDB and PMDB, with 2.2 per cent and 2.4 per cent, respectively, received more than 2 per cent of the preferences. On this question, still 56.9 per cent asserted no sympathy for any party.

A further issue has to do with the statistical test included in this work, being concerned with workers' attitudes towards citizenship. When questioned if they had any participation in social organisations, 81.9 per cent of the telecommunications workers replied affirmatively. Regarding participation in courses and seminars concerned with national problems, 45 per cent said they would like to take part, as against 41 per cent who said no; on that question 6.7 per cent declared that they had already participated in such courses. Another high percentage, if compared with the general patterns in society at large, was scored by respondents who admitted to participating in demonstrations and rallies. Even though 49.3 per cent answered no, as many as 20.8 per cent said yes, and 19.1 per cent replied they would like to participate in such events. The results of that survey clearly indicate that SINTTEL's goal of helping to develop workers' consciousness has been at least partially achieved.

3.3   The Metalworkers' Union

Like the Telecommunications Workers' Union, the Metalworkers' was created in the 1930s (21 November 1935), when Getúlio Vargas introduced the chief structures of unionism in Brazil. This is one of the most important unions in the state of Pernambuco, by far the major union in the private industrial sector. The occupational category it represents is spread over around forty enterprises. Table 4.5 gives the name and number of employees of the largest companies in the sector.

Table 4.5   Distribution of the metalworkers per enterprises, July 1994

Company	Employees	Company	Employees
Autolatina (Ford and Wolksw.)	1,200	Microlite do NE	550
Motogear Norte	480	Alcoa Aluminio do Br	600
Acumuladores Moura	495	Codistil do NE	80
Noraço	200	Maq. Piratininga	300
Phillips	350	Metal. Matarazzo	400
Açonorte	600	Leon Heimer	230
Continental	2001	200 Caio Norte	370
Rufino Ferreira	330	Industrias Villares	120
Grupo Guedes	189	Ind. Reunidas Renda	280
F.Conte S.A.	350	Other	–
Total			7,324

Source: Archives of the Metalworkers' Union.

From a total of around eighteen thousand workers at grassroots, 3,500 workers are members of the Metalworkers' Union. The ratio of 19. 35 per cent, though in line with the national average, has to be interpreted in the light of widespread anti-union policies pursued by the enterprises in the sector. As the president of the union points out, most companies in the metallurgical sector practise a deliberate anti-union policy which is apparent from the conflicts reported in Section 1, as well as from data that emerged both from interviews with the president of the union and from the human resources manager of Açonorte (interviews nos 2 and 34). The former reported particular cases of retaliation against employees who had adhered to the union recently, occurring in the following companies: Phillips, Icomacedo, Alcoa, Nave Sul and Autoguedes. The latter was very clear about Açonorte's (a company owned by the strong Gerdau group) deliberate strategy of granting certain welfare benefits to employees and, at the same time, maintaining a tough stance against the union. All of them provide examples of a general trend in private sector enterprises in Pernambuco.[8] In such a context, the Metalworkers' Union appears as one whose union density ratio is among the highest in the private sector in the state.

Despite the adversarial stance adopted by enterprises in

the sector, the Metalworkers' Union has managed to secure a number of rights and benefits through mobilisations
and stoppages. In August 1994, in the wake of the 'Real
Plan' of Stabilisation, and when consequently prices and
wages were practically frozen, the metalworkers won an
important wage hike. After a 5-day strike, which reached
twenty firms, the employers agreed to grant a 19.5 per
cent pay rise and a 3-month job security for the entire
category (union archives). Owing to an independent stance
and grassroots mobilisation, the metallugical workers managed to attain important benefits such as certain provisions against unfair dismissals, a wage hike and the return
of previously fired workers. Many of those rights were earned
through strikes and direct bargaining (70 stoppages in the
three years up to 1994). From the 215 collective agreements reached in the period 1990–94, none of them were
sent to the Labour Court.

Nevertheless, the union has sent a large number of individual cases to the Labour Court, seeking to secure the
employer's compliance with statutory rights of workers, as
well as with the collective agreements. By August 1994,
the law department of the union was dealing with 600 cases
before the Labour Court, many of them involving several
workers.

To make feasible this confrontational policy, the Metalworkers' Union has counted on a group of 27 officials and
another 130 militants without any formal post in the union
structure. They hold over 40 general assemblies per year,
with an average attendance of 450 members. All these features make it clear that the Metalworkers' Union, despite
strong opposition from enterprises, has managed to put in
practice the CUT's principles of union autonomy, mobilisation at grassroots level and the quest for benefits through
direct bargaining and industrial actions.

3.4   The Data Processing Workers' Union

This is a fairly interesting union to examine for the purpose of assessing differences of relationship between leaders and grassroots, with the possible effects on the latter's
attitudes. The union is a result of the technological inno-

vation experienced by the Brazilian economy in the 1980s. A fast growing new economic sector challenged some militants to try to organise an occupational category hitherto completely unstructured. In 1979 they managed to create an association that later assumed the nature of a 'pre-union association'. Part of the group that set up the association started participating in the first articulations of the labour movement in the state of Pernambuco. They took part in the first CONCLAT, and in the regional meetings of workers (ENCLATs). Because the original group gathered militants from different political persuasions (PT, PCB and PC do B), the entity initially failed to affiliate formally to either of the two great currents of the Brazilian labour movement. Only in 1987 did the union enter CUT officially. This does not mean, however, that it remained apart from the articulations that gradually consolidated the CUT in Pernambuco in the first half of the 1980s (Medeiros, 1992).

The Data Processing Workers' Union was founded in October 1985, when it was granted official recognition by the Ministry of Labour. Because it was created by militants already identified with the new unionism, the union was free from certain vices of the old structure. Thus, it refused to provide the membership with facilities such as medical and dental care and free lab tests. One should not forget, however, that the union, being recognised by the State, immediately enjoyed corporatist inducements' like monopoly of representation and the union tax.

The occupational category covers public enterprises in the three levels of Brazilian administration. At the federal level there are three great companies whose activities are in the data processing trade: 'Serpro', 'Datamec' and 'Dataprev'. At the level of the state of Pernambuco, the union represents workers from 'Fisepe', and at municipal level, workers from 'Emprel'. Besides these enterprises in the public sector, the category is spread over smaller private firms, almost all of them being small software houses. Although precise data are not available, the union reckons that there are around 120 of those firms in its base of representation. Table 4.6 gives us a rough idea of the branch in Pernambuco state.

Table 4.6   Distribution of the data-processing workers per main enterprises, July 1994

Public sector	No. of employees	Private sector	No. of employees
Federal	–	Mercantil	180
Serpro	610	MV Informática	97
Dataprev	189	Origin	74
Datamec	156	Elógica	63
Fns	30	Telesystems	49
State		Global	27
Fisepe	620	Procenge	25
Municipal		Gerdau	10
Emprel	440	Digidata	82

Source: Archives of SINDPD.

Since its foundation in 1985, the union has functioned with some organisational bodies which are rather unusual in the experience of corporatist unions. Immediately below the highest deliberative body, the general assembly, there is a 'deliberative council' charged with the formulation of general strategies to be carried out by the executive body. This feature has been said to represent a break with the 'official union' tradition of concentrating power in the directorate and its presidency (Medeiros, 1992: 79). Another innovation was the setting up of five enterprise commissions ('comissões de trabalhadores') in the main firms in the trade: Serpro, Dataprev, Datamec, Fisepe and Emprel. The members of those commissions, ranging from 4 to 8, are directly elected by workers at grassroots independently of affiliation to the union. Nevertheless, they work in close association with the union. The initiative, despite being limited to the firms in the public sector, has been regarded as another move of data processing workers towards overcoming the corporatist limits. As for the private enterprises, the union has managed to make workers elect a handful of union delegates albeit this is a very limited experience. In July 1994, for example, the whole occupational category had merely six union delegates (shop stewards).

Membership rose from 824 at the time of the creation of the union to 2,430 in July 1994. To assess union density, one has to split the occupational category into two broad groups. The first one, the publicly owned firms, presents an affiliation ratio of around 85 per cent (interview no.19). The private sector, being wholly broken up into very tiny firms, has allowed no data to be kept as long as membership is sporadic. To get in touch with the membership, the union has issued a fortnightly information sheet and a monthly newspaper of two thousand copies.

In line with the new unionism's proposals, the data processing workers have always emphasised direct bargaining backed by mobilisation. Apart from huge strikes in the publicly owned enterprises, since its first steps, the occupational category carried out a number of short and localised strikes even in private enterprises whose number and ownership obviously make it harder for workers to undertake industrial actions (Morais, 1992: 92). Collective bargaining with such a divided set of firms is not an easy task. The tactic adopted by the union is to call on 'demonstrative' short-term and localised strikes and then try to extend the agreed benefits to other firms. In this process of extension, the union has employed the Labour Court and its normative power to settle working conditions for those small firms where the union does not possess a sufficient organisation capable of improving its bargaining power. Notwithstanding such a residual utilisation of the Labour Court arbitration, the union has mainly relied on direct bargaining. From 39 collective bargaining processes initiated in the five years to July 1994, not less than 35 ended up with direct agreement with the business union or the companies. Only four negotiations were sent to the Labour Court arbitration. As for membership involvement the union boasts that it can rely on a group of around 500 militants (or quasi-militants). It has undertaken an average of twenty general meetings per year. The last three of those meetings had an average of 120 attendees.

Although the process of restructuring and stabilisation of the Brazilian economy in the early 1990s has hit the labour movement as a whole, the Data Processing Workers' Union has managed to adapt and keep its legitimacy even if rank and file participation has decreased since the late 1980s. As a result of the wage squeeze imposed by the several recent economic programmes, the union has sponsored numerous workers' cases before the Labour Court: such a court intervention is meant to force employers to comply with rights stemming from law or collective bargaining. In July 1994 there were 88 cases waiting for the court award, most of them grouping all the workers of a given firm.

All data presented above allow us to advance some conclusions about the data processing workers' experience. Although the main pillars of the Brazilian corporatist system of industrial relations are still enforced, this union has not concentrated all its strategies on them. It has tried to settle its model of organisation within workshops, as the creation of the workers' commissions testifies. Regarding the Labour Court arbitration power it has made a very limited and creative use of it, restricted to the extension or validation process; however, in certain cases, the firms themselves call in the court. Even if participation is not sufficiently widespread, the union has managed to create practices and channels of grassroots involvement. It seems reasonable to predict that the eventual transition of the Brazilian system from state interventionism towards a more contractual system is not likely to upset the Data Processing Workers' Union.

3.5   The Textile Industry Workers' Union

The Textile Industry Workers' Union is one of the oldest unions in the labour movement of Pernambuco. At the very end of the last century, there were some textile plants in several towns throughout the state. Workers started organising labour leagues and as early as 1890 the first industrial actions in Pernambuco were recorded in the textile industry (Morais, 1992). Not surprisingly, the textile workers played a prominent role in the very creation of the labour movement in all the industrialised regions of the country, as exemplified by the leading role of the factory commissions and the sector workers' union of São Paulo in the General Strike of 1917, the waves of strikes of 1934–35 and the equally famous 'strike of the 300,000' in March 1953 (Wolfe, 1993).

The union in the state of Pernambuco was founded on

29 May 1931 initially representing workers in the textile industry in the city of Recife. In 1936, the Ministry of Labour granted official recognition through Decree no. 24,694, in one of the moves which brought about the incorporation of the hitherto free labour movement by the corporatist Brazilian state. In 1939 a group of weavers attempted to set up another union within the same occupational category but the Ministery of Labour refused to grant it official recognition. Then, in 1940 both unions merged under the label 'Sindicato dos Trabalhadores nas Indústrias de Fiação e Tecelagem do Recife'. In 1945, during mobilisations for the end of Getúlio Vargas's dictatorship, the union suffered its first direct intervention by the state, appointees being designated by the Ministry of Labour to run its affairs. In 1952 the weavers undertook their first strike to back their demands for wage rises, a movement which lasted eight days. In 1958, taking part in a national movement, the union called a 49-day strike for improvement of workers' conditions, which triggered fierce employers and police reaction. The latter acted with the help of private security forces in order to repress workers' meetings and rallies. In 1964, the military imposed a docile leadership on the union after dislodging the former elected union officials. The union remained under control of the 'pro-government' officials up to 1985. During this pelego-controlled period, the union extended its base of representation to the cities of São Lourenço da Mata, Timbaúba, Cabo, and Camaragibe e Jaboatão, all of them being part of the so-called Metropolitan Region of Recife.

In 1984, the workers realised that the old-style leadership would not be able to lead the necessary mobilisations to improve the occupational category's living and working conditions. On February 27th ten thousand weavers took part in a massive rally in the centre of Recife protesting against the government's economic policy and its wicked effects on factory closure and unemployment. After that, the opposition group managed to win the election held in July. After controversies were brought to the court, the Ministry of Labour ordered another ballot to be held in January 1985. The opposition was made up of militants affiliated to the MR-8 and the MDB (Movimento Democrático

Brasileiro, the democratic front formed to fight against the military). The group won the second ballot by a 93 per cent majority and the new directorate presided over by José Pedro Gomes da Silva took office on 18 January 1985.

As for the labour movement's internal currents, the Weaver Union's new leadership made a clear choice for the so-called 'Union Unity' ('Unidade Sindical') that formed the CGT. Its most active militants belonged to the leftist MR-8 and they represented a break with the old-style pelegos. Nevertheless, they refused to join the newly born CUT, preferring to put emphasis on the unity of the whole official labour movement. Later on, in 1989, when the CGT split between MR-8 and the Rogério Magri's group, the Weavers' Union affiliated to the CGT led by the latter – the General Confederation of Workers ('Confederação Geral dos Trabalhadores'). Under the presidency of José Carlos Andrade, the union assumed a prominent role within the Confederation in the state of Pernambuco, managing to undertake a number of initiatives together with the CUT. From 1989 on, José Carlos Andrade was also the president of the General Confederation of Workers in Pernambuco.

Although the textile industry has progressively shrunk in Pernambuco, the Weavers' Union still represents a large number of workers. Table 4.7 shows the main companies in its constituency.

With a constituency of approximately 4,560 workers, membership amounts to 2,100, a union density of 46.05 per cent which is much higher than the national average of around 20 per cent. Workers in each company elect one shop steward per enterprise, whose duties consist of linking the union and the rank-and-file workers at the workshop. The union's press issues the monthly periodical *O Tecelão* ('The Weaver') once a month, reaching around 5,000 copies. In the five years to 1994, the union signed 23 collective agreements, 18 of them with individual companies and 5 covering the whole occupational category. In the same period it took part only in three 'dissídios coletivos' – the process through which the labour court settles the conflict in case of deadlock. As for the reaction of the union to workers' grievances, by 1994 it sponsored around 100 cases before the labour court and 15 administrative complaints to the

Table 4.7   Distribution of the textile workers per enterprise,
July 1994

Companies	Location	No. of employees
Braspérola	Camaragibe	900
Yolanda	Recife	700
Cotonifício J. Rufino	Cabo	600
Lipasa	Jaboatão	940
S. José do Nordeste	Jaboatão	800
Labortextil	Timbaúba	620

Source: Archives of the Textile Workers' Union.

Ministry of Labour regarding job safety. In the three years
to 1994, the union called two strikes in two of the enterprises which comprise its base of representation.

From the revenues estimated at 69,000 reais – approximately 72,000 American dollars – for the year 1994, 65
per cent comes from the voluntary contributions of the
membership, 26 per cent from the union tax and 26 per
cent from the contributions paid by the members during
collective bargaining as a means to strengthen the union.
The leadership of the Textile Workers' Union reckons around
one hundred known militants in its constituency. The
occupational category usually meets in general assembly at
least twice a year, with an average attendance of 200 workers.
All this data allows us to assume that this union has managed
to cope with the serious crises of the textile industry, even
if a decrease in its power and mobilisation is visible. It
remains as the main stronghold of the General Confederation
of Workers (CGT) in Pernambuco.

3.6   The Pharmaceutical Industry Workers' Union

The Pharmaceutical Industry Workers' Union was founded
a few months prior to the 1964 military coup, on September 1st 1963. Although in practice its activities are almost
restricted to the Metropolitan Region of Recife, the Ministry
of Labour granted it the monopoly of representation over
the occupational category of workers in the pharmaceutical
industry in the whole state of Pernambuco.

The eight hundred workers comprising this category are

spread over a small number of firms. The state of Pernambuco owns the most important enterprise in its base, LAFEPE – 'Laboratórios Farmacêuticos de Pernambuco', where half of the union's grassroots is concentrated. Merely six other laboratories employ more than twenty workers (Hebron, Cia. Industrial Farmaceutica, Laboratório Pernambucano, Diniz Brandao, Labortecne and Boehringer de Angeli). A score of tiny laboratories complete the composition of the pharmaceutical industry workers' category, all of them with a staff of a handful of workers or less.

The union records show that in July 1994 the affiliated members amounted to 480, which yields a union ratio of around 60 per cent. Such a ratio is well over the national average, albeit one needs to bear in mind that most of these unionised workers are employees of the state-owned LAFEPE. Although it is a small union, its financial structure is not entirely dependent on the union tax, the voluntary monthly dues paid by members constituting the most important source of revenues. As for the channels of resolution of collective conflicts, the union has relied on both the arbitration power of the Labour Court and direct settlement. Regarding general negotiation processes, in the five years to 1994, the union took part in five Labour Court arbitration cases and reached direct agreements in five other collective bargaining processes. In terms of the use of the labour court to settle individual workers' grievances, the records show just one legal action – although involving a large number of workers. In the five years to 1994, the pharmaceutical industry workers went on strike twice. The first strike, in March 1991, was to protest against the attitudes of the management of 'Lafepe' towards the rank-and-file. In the second one, in September 1994, the union called industrial action against the reneging of the collective agreement by 'Lafepe'. Among the most important benefits won in the last campaigns is the introduction of a new wage and task structure, in 1994.

To keep in touch with the grassroots, union officials have benefited from local meetings and a paper called *Informativo Sintrafarma*, with an irregular periodicity of 1,000 copies each issue. Among the most important events recently sponsored by the union, its leadership highlights the 'First Symposium of the Workers of Lafepe' which was held in December 1994. The symposium aimed at debating the firm's problems and elaborating a blueprint to improve its management. The final document was then handed out to the new directive board of the firm, appointed by the Governor-elect Miguel Arraes.

In the panorama of the labour movement in Pernambuco, the Pharmaceutical Industry Workers' Union has been aligned with the 'Confederação Geral dos Trabalhadores' – CGT. Its president in 1994, Israel Torres, was also the president of the 'Federação dos Trabalhadores nas Indústrias de Pernambuco', a second-level union organisation which is also affiliated to the CGT.

3.7 The Commerce Employees' Union in Recife

This union assembles the employees in the commercial retail sector in the city of Recife, a sector which is made up of a great number of scattered shops spread over the city. Only a few big shops, generally branches of large chains, employ a considerable number of employees in the same unit. Among those larger employers one might mention the variety shops 'Lojas Americanas', 'Lojas Brasileiras', 'Casas José Araújo', 'Primavera', and a handful of others. An important section of commerce, the supermarket national chains ('Bompreço', 'Pao-de-Açúcar'), is out of the representative reach of the Commerce Employees' Union in that their employees are covered by another union with exclusiveness of representation, as usually happens in the divided Brazilian union structure still influenced by legal requisites. The occupational category is reckoned by the union to cover as many as one hundred thousand workers in its territorial base. From those, around eight thousand employees are affiliated to the union, which gives a membership ratio of merely 8 per cent. Even among those voluntarily affiliated to the union only a minority pays regularly the 2 per cent of their wages monthly due charged by the union.

The very nature of the occupational category, therefore, provides at least an initial explanation for the lack of militancy traditionally displayed by this union. But since the 1964 military coup, its leadership has made no effort to overcome those 'natural' obstacles. The union has been ruled by officials concerned primarily with the handing out of welfare benefits to members, little attention being given to mobilisation and membership involvement, if any. The focus on the management of the apparatus built to meet that 'assistential' activity has concentrated strong powers in the hands of the union presidency. Up till the late 1980s, the union was managed by the well-known pelego Luís Generoso, a docile 'non-political' leader, who managed to hold office during the whole period of military rule, ensuring that 'his' union was never molested by the Ministry of Labour or by military officials themselves as happened to all the militant unions in the period. Meanwhile, Generoso obtained a place as a 'classist' workers' representative in the labour court, a post notorious for providing good salaries (little less than those of careeer judges) for merely two or three hours of work a day.

In the mid-1980s, a group of militants of the Catholic 'Ação Operária' unsuccessfully challenged the established leadership. Its failure might be attributed to both the lack of sufficient insertion into so scattered an occupational category and the incumbent group's strong control over the means provided by the union apparatus. After the election, most of the members of the opposition group were sacked by their respective employers and then kept out of the occupational category (interview no. 11). The current president, Severino Ramos, was elected in the early 1990s as a successor to Generoso. Concentration of power, and lack of stimuli to the emerging of new leadership from the grassroots such as shop stewards and enterprise committees, continued to be salient features of the union under the new presidency.[9]

The contention that the union is almost exclusively concerned with welfare provisions is supported by a recent publication issued in July 1994 (*Sindicato dos Comerciários*, 1994). Thousands of copies of the document were handed out to the union members with the aim of providing information about new collective agreements. Apart from giving the president all the credit for the recent union's achievements, the document lists a score of benefits provided by the union to the members. Among them, emphasis is put on the hiring of more doctors and dentists (raising the total of hired professionals to eighty), improvement of laboratories already installed, purchase of an ambulance, enhancement of facilities such as a leisure club, waiting rooms and other small facilities at the union headquarters. Not a word is said about advances in membership participation, accountability or any sort of representative channels to link the union bureaucracy to the rank-and-file. To be fair, the word 'militancy' is mentioned once: when describing the 'militant' efforts of the legal advice department in sponsoring members' individual suits before the labour court. Clause 19 of the 1994 collective agreement provides further evidence of the union's emphasis on welfare assistance. In addition to the union tax and the voluntary dues, most unions in Brazil charge an 'assistential contribution' from the occupational category. Despite the reference to 'assistance' in fact such a yearly contribution is paid during the collective bargaining procedures to meet the costs of mobilisation and strengthening of the category's bargaining power. In the case of the 'Commerce Employees' Union', according to clause 19, the contribution was imposed with the purpose of meeting costs of 'the maintenance of leisure and other facilities such as dentists, doctors and laboratories' (the very words of the 1994 Collective Agreement).

As already noticed in Section 2, this union played an important role in the articulations that led to the setting up of the branch of Força Sindical in the state of Pernambuco, its president having been acting as the regional co-ordinator of the confederation since 1992. This brief account of the features of the Commerce Employees' Union allows its classification in the fourth type of unions described by Hyman and Ferner in their influential discussion of the future of unions. They distinguish four categories of unions' identities and features: a union committed to 'political economism', one concerned with advancing the enterprise's productivity (the 'coalition partner' union), one involved with social movements, and finally a traditional type of unionism whose primary activities consist of providing services to their individual members (Hyman and Ferner, 1994). It would be hard not to identify the Commerce Employees' Union in Pernambuco with the latter.

3.8   The Bank Employees' Union of Pernambuco

Founded on 14 October 1931, this union has since become one of the most powerful of the labour movement in the state. Owing to its prominent position in the period prior to the military take-over of 1964, it was submitted to a succession of docile leaders concerned merely with the management of welfare provisions. Such a leadership secured control of the union's directive boards until 1988, having succeeded in setting up a strong 'assistential' structure which comprised an elementary school for the children of its members, a leisure countryside club and numerous doctors, dentists and lawyers. As described in Section 1.2, the administration of the pelegos tried to resist the pressure for a more militant attitude exerted by the grassroots in the mid-1980s, which led some of the mobilisations to be undertaken by emergent leaders other than the union officials.

As a result of such initiatives, the opposition group of militants which was born out of those initial struggles managed to win the election held in 1988 and gained control of the union. Since the early 1980s that group has been identified with the new unionism, having eventually affiliated the union to the CUT after consulting the membership through the general assembly. Initially the group managed to hold together the various currents within the new unionism. Later on, one of the groups, identified with the minority current within the CUT known as 'Cut Pela Base',[10] split with the ruling body majority and eventually launched its own slate to compete with the other group for the leadership. Following such a split, the election held in late 1994 was disputed by three slates in that the old group of more conservative leaders who had been ousted in 1988 decided to enter the election hoping to benefit from the division among the new unionism activists. The result of that election suggested a certain degree of discontent among the grassroots about the divisions of the group in power and possibly the 'overpoliticisation' of its policies. In the first ballot, the slate formed by the majority group of the direction gathered 4,161 votes as against 2,449 for the slate sponsored by the dissident former officials and 2,738 for the more conservative group who had been dislodged in 1988. In the second ballot, the slate linked to the majority fraction of the union leadership won the support of 4,965 members as against 3,912 votes cast to the conservative's slate. Such a result betrayed an irreversible split in the initial group which had renewed the union and also considerable backing for the group identified with the old 'assistential' and 'apolitical' policies.

Despite the conflicts among the factions which had seized control of the union in 1988, the new unionism leadership has developed its militant policies since then. A call for industrial action to support the workers' position in the national collective bargaining process has been very common, which testifies to the militant character of its initiatives. The union has taken part in the national articulation of the bank employees in the CUT-founded National Confederation of the Bank Employees (CNB) and in the Regional Federation of the Bank Employees in the Northeast (FETEC-CUT/NE) thus being one of the signatories to the 'collective labour contract' which has settled the collective conflict within the category every year in September. Such agreements advance the collective labour contract proposal through which the whole branch has negotiated without interference of the labour court. In fact, the only case of arbitration of a collective conflict by the labour court in the five years up to 1994 involving the Bank Employees of Pernambuco was due to the employer initiative, namely, the state-owned 'Bandepe' in 1991. The policy of not resorting to the labour court, however, is restricted to the settlement of the collective conflicts. As it has been highlighted in regard to the CUT's policies, the individual rights stemming both from statutory provisions and collective agreements have been reinforced by the union's initiatives before the courts and the Ministry of Labour. Thus, by 1994, the union was supporting around 700 cases in the labour court, out of which 85 involved workers on a collective basis. In 1993, the union had addressed 593 officials complaints to the Ministry of Labour, requesting the intervention of its inspectors in order to force employers to comply with the labour law.

With regard to organisation the union has sought to develop a set of structures designed to counteract the notorious weakness of the inherited corporatist structure. The union militancy include around 150 shop stewards elected by all the workers within the federal government-owned banks ('Banco do Brasil', 'Caixa Econômica Federal' and 'Banco do Nordeste do Brasil'), although the private employers' tough policies towards the union have precluded such workplace elections in the private sector (interview no. 36). In addition to the shop stewards in the public sector, there are other channels of participation, both formal and informal. The main decisions have been adopted in their congress (the highest level of the decision-making process) and in the general assembly and these have been called around 20 times each year, gathering an average of 100 attendants. Below the general assembly and above the directorate there is the 'colegiado', a wider body made up of the members of the directorate, the regional directors (officials of the unions elected with responsibilities for the regions of the state other than the Metropolitan Region of Recife), and the members of the audit commission ('conselho fiscal'), a body charged with monitoring of the financial matters of the entity. In sum, the congress, the general assembly, the 'colegiado', the directorate, and the 'conselho fiscal', together make up the directive system of the union which was conceived with the purpose of developing democracy, accountability, decentralisation of power and membership involvement.

In July 1994 the union archives reckoned 16,000 voluntary members from a total of 25,000 employees at the grass-roots, thus reaching the impressive unionisation ratio of 64 per cent, although one has to bear in mind that part of the category is employed in public-owned banks which obviously put no obstacle to affiliation to the union. Out of this contingent the union officials have counted on 300 known active militants who have helped to carry out the union's activities. The circulation of the union newspaper, which is printed weekly in its own press equipment, can reach 10,000 copies per issue.

A great deal of the union's revenue is still channelled to maintain its bureaucratic apparatus which comprises the headquarters (a cluster of three buildings in the centre of Recife), two other sets of flats in the centre of Recife, the leisure countryside club and 70 staff. The expenditures for this and for the union activities are supported by an annual revenue which in 1994 was estimated at R$ 1,742,000,00 (equivalent to US$ 1,672,000), with approximately 70 per cent coming from voluntary dues.

The data presented above suggest that the union has partially succeeded in putting into practice the militant stance advocated by the leadership elected in 1988 and successively re-elected with slight shifts of positions and individuals. The involvement of the membership has been pursued by the redesign of the functioning of the union as exemplified by the new directive stances, the election of shop stewards, the maintenance of the union's newspaper and the high frequency of assemblies called to discuss relevant issues (an average of 20 a year). These features combine with the emphasis on direct bargaining with employers through the 'collective labour contract' to start developing a mode of unionism whose practices and organisational arrangements tried to depart from the old official union. By 1995, however, the reduction of the financial sector of the Brazilian economy, leading to the merging of banks and the consequent cuts in personnel, loomed as the greatest challenge ever experienced by the union. Its capacity to cope with such a crisis is obviously an open question.

In this chapter we tried to give a picture, albeit largely descriptive, of the unions in our sample whose members were surveyed with the aim of measuring their attitudes. Both the account of the process of reorganisation of the labour movement in the state of Pernambuco and the description of the main characteristics of some of its main unions sought to provide the background for the shaping of attitudes which we have suggested may vary according to differences in the unions. The survey and its methodology are discussed in the following chapter.

5 The Survey: Measuring the Attitude of Active Citizenship

1 INTRODUCTION

The basic objective of this chapter is to examine the possible impacts of different labour relations models on the attitudes that form the culture of an active citizenry. An active citizen may be seen as someone who will 'consider oneself to have some sort of responsibility to be active in his or her community either in a formal or informal way, either in relation to local government or in relation to fellow citizens' (Almond and Verba, 1963: 164). It is hardly necessary to recall that if a model of labour relations helps to develop an attitude of active citizenship among workers, an important step to the development of citizenship in general may be said to have been performed. The participation of citizens either in the politics of society at large or in the spheres of production has been accepted by social thought as a means of overcoming social inequalities (Poole, 1986: 3; Pateman, 1970). All varieties of communitarianism hold in common the normative claim for citizens to involve themselves in public affairs and participate in community life (Avineri and De-Shalit, 1992). Although this study does not concentrate on testing the general hypothesis that participation of individuals in collective affairs contributes to extending citizenship and mitigating social inequality, it will nevertheless assume that this is a plausible working hypothesis. Consequently, we shall accept the idea that developing workers' citizenship in a country as socially unequal as Brazil has much to do with fostering participatory attitudes among subordinate social groups.

There is a further reason for us to concentrate more on the development of a culture of active citizenship rather than on citizenship indicators[1] themselves or even on a

156

civic culture broadly defined as a general recognition of democratic institutions and the attachment to the related political values by the majority of the people (Almond and Verba, 1965; Putnam, 1993). It is that even today Brazilian democratic institutions have not been able to develop the kind of political culture which involves a widespread adherence to democratic or civic values and to the correspondent institutions. Democratic transition in Brazil generated much disillusionment owing to the disproportion between expectations and the poor results offered by democratic state institutions and politics. And yet in this current atmosphere of disenchantment with democratic politics, a substantial proportion of Brazilians have nevertheless followed a tendency of gradual adherence to democratic values. There is a 'reservoir' of legitimacy for democracy to prosper, although one cannot rely on its indefinite continuance (Moisés: 1993). The fact remains, however, that one cannot say that a civic or democratic culture has been established in the country. In such a context, an investigation of determinants of this culture remains an important topic for social research, thus justifying the focus of this chapter on the attitudes that ultimately may result in the assertion of a broad democratic or civic culture. These attitudes, we assume, are embraced by the concept of active citizenship. The less privileged are only likely to lend recognition to the polity if they take part in or struggle to influence decision-making.

2 THE BASIC RESEARCH QUERY

The alternative model of industrial relations has been proposed as the best way to address the changes required by the Brazilian system. On the one hand, it would suit the needs of a modernising and complex economy. The terms of the employment relation would be left to market forces – in economic and political terms – instead of being objects of state arbitration. On the other hand, the model would contribute to improving the citizenship of workers in that they would participate more actively in every sphere affecting their interests – ranging from the workplace to the wider political institutions.

The basic research query of this chapter is restricted to the second type of alleged effects of the alternative conception of labour relations. Citizenship has been identified as social participation deriving from full membership of individuals in a given society. We accept certain insights of participatory theorists concerned with industrial democracy and related themes who have stressed the 'goal of increasing the level of labour participation' as a means to achieve a condition of full citizenship for all (Steenbergen, 1994b: 5).

Thus, our research query has focused on the effects of the alternative model of labour relation developed by the new unionism on the citizenship of workers. To look at this sort of effect we shall concentrate on the participatory aspect of the concept of citizenship. Or, if one prefers, on the conception of citizenship more concerned with participation and involvement, that is, the idea of active citizenship deriving from the so-called republican tradition. This approach suggests that the impact of the alternative model of labour relations on the workers' attitudes proper to a culture of active citizenship may repay study.

In short, we will attempt to identify the prominent features of the alternative model as it is practised by new unionism. Then we will study its consequences for a particular type of political culture and related attitudes: that of an active citizen. The basic research query of this investigation, therefore, may be formulated in the following terms: what effects do the alternative model practised by the new unionism have on the citizenship of workers? More specifically, does the alternative model contribute to enhancing the attitude of active citizenship of workers? Needless to say, we do not assume that the model of industrial relations espoused by a given union is the only factor to influence their members' active citizenship. We do not even argue that it is the main factor. But if the model adopted by the union is a factor, and we suspect it is not a negligible one, the purposes of the research seem justified.

In addressing such a question, this chapter follows one of the major streams of recent research in the field of industrial relations, focusing on workers rather than on institutions and abstract parties such as trade unions, employers' associations, enterprises and the State (Edwards, 1995b). The same need for studies on 'workers as individuals' has been identified by Ranis (1992) in the justification of his seminal study on Argentine workers' ideology, values, beliefs, and attitudes. The present work likewise investigates the process of changes in popular political culture, particularly that of workers, in order to gauge the impact that the alternative practices of Brazilian new unionism have had on it. The more general argument that 'social movements are successful in changing popular perceptions, institutional cultures and political practices', have been presented by Foweraker (1995) on the basis of his research findings on recent Spanish and Mexican social movements. Similarly, the following survey looks into the effects of a particular social movement, the Brazilian new unionism, on workers' popular 'perceptions'.

3   BASIC HYPOTHESIS

The literature on the changing system of Brazilian labour relations and unionism in Brazil analysed in Chapters 2 and 3, as well as our personal observation of the last decade's developments, inclines us to accept the possibility of a positive impact of alternative practices on both the terms of workers' participation in Brazilian society and their political culture.

Industrial relations in Brazil are changing both in practical and institutional terms. The 1988 Constitution allowed for some relaxation of state control, as we have previously discussed, but the institutional framework adopted still enforces certain corporatist aspects. Consequently, unions which have already started practising the so-called alternative model are forced to compromise with certain institutions of the corporatist framework that still exist. Hence, in order to test the influence of the alternative model on workers' citizenship and their attitude, we have to be aware of such an impediment to the new unionism to follow the model in full. In each union or occupational category studied we identified certain characteristics of the model already being put into practice. The empirical test, as a matter of logic, focuses only on those characteristics susceptible to measuring. We have good reasons, however, to assume that further application of the model leads to increasing the effects eventually found in the research. These conceptual analyses will be the object of detailed treatment in Chapters 6 and 7.

Aware of this methodological consideration, our basic hypothesis could be expressed as follows: the alternative conceptions of industrial relations adopted by certain Brazilian unions help to develop the attitude of active citizenship of their members. Or, in another reading: members of unions practising the CUT's model develop a stronger active-citizenship attitude than members affiliated to traditional unions, as a result of their exposure to the alternative model. Two assumptions underly such a hypothesis. Firstly, the new unionism model implies differences from the traditional corporatist union that encompasses union arrangements and practices. Secondly, the alternative conceptions of labour relations practised by the 'new unions' contain a number of features that ultimately influence values and workers' attitudes.

The possible influence of a union model on workers' attitudes was conceived alongside many other variables such as education, familial backgrounds, sex, age, income, size of enterprise, occupation, etc. The union model is just one of the possible factors shaping one of the social groups which affect the day-to-day life of workers alongside the family, the neighbourhood, etc.[2] As Goldthorpe *et al.* (1971) stress, working-class politics are explained rather by workers' group attachments than by workers' income. Such an observation is in line with our contention that the union model affects workers' culture and their stances on politics and related matters. If a given union manages to practise at least partially a different model from the traditional one, it should be expected to generate a distinct impact on its membership's attitudes.

Regarding the dependent variable of the basic hypothesis of this survey – the attitude of active citizenship – for the time being let us state our awareness of the complexity of such a construct and the inherent difficulty to measured it. Nevertheless, several authors have measured what they term 'a civic culture' (e.g., Almond and Verba, 1963; Putnam,

1993). We have dared to build our own attitude scale designed to measure active citizenship, drawing on survey design techniques. Because we are interested in measuring workers' attitudes, our idea of active citizenship is concerned with attitudes about four objects: unions, control at work, associative life, and politics. The assumption is that a worker who shows a critical and participatory stance on such matters may be deemed to have embodied attitudes of active citizenship.

An obvious proviso concerning our dependent variable is related to the fact that people are not easily classifiable as bearing only one type of attitude, nor will they always express a coherent attitude to the question we are investigating. Although such an important remark is well identifiable in the literature (cf. Becker, 1993; and Fosh, 1993, for example) our attitude scale was built in an encompassing way that considered not only workers' attitudes towards their unions but also the active attitude towards unions in general, work, politics and associations. Such a broad range of indicators helps to identify certain basic attitudes displayed by respondents. In short, despite the lack of 'purity' in individuals' attitudes, we assume that some patterns are identifiable.[3]

4   THE SURVEY

4.1   Introduction

From the basic hypothesis outlined above, we have worked deductively towards empirical observations in order to test it. We confronted the basic research query with empirically observed data of unions and workers gathered in a survey of urban workers and unions in the state of Pernambuco, in northeast Brazil. Such a choice was grounded on the consideration that we have lived in that state for a long time and have observed the development of labour relations from the privileged position of legal adviser for a score of urban unions in the city of Recife, the capital of Pernambuco. Some of those unions have a jurisdiction which stretches well beyond the city of Recife, sometimes reaching the whole of the state of Pernambuco. In addition, we have worked as a legal adviser for the 'Central Unica dos Trabalhadores – CUT' in Pernambuco during the 1980s and early 1990s.

True, the sectors of the labour movement most concerned with practices which aim at surmounting the corporatist framework, the new unionism grouped in CUT, were initially developed in the southeastern state of São Paulo. Nevertheless, Pernambuco, being a leading state in the northeast region and already counting a sizeable industrial base, has witnessed a strong advance of the new unionism of the CUT since 1978. In the urban labour movement of Recife, those unions in the CUT are already the hegemonic forces in the most important economic branches. The local research setting was described in Chapter 4.

4.2   Construct Validity

We are testing a claim put forward by new unionism activists and theorists, and present in the literature as well, according to which the new unionism model helps in developing workers' citizenship. Therefore, the hypothesis formulated in Section 3 has the model of labour relations practised by unions as the independent variable. The attitude of active citizenship of workers, in turn, is the dependent variable. Considering that our variables are 'theoretical constructs' which represent abstractions from social reality, we have to understand how they are concretely represented in the survey's hypothesis. In other words, the first task is to examine how these constructs may be identified. What are the variables which integrate them and allow us to identify them?

Let us start with our independent variable. Since the new unionism current of the labour movement is almost totally integrated in the CUT, we have worked with an independent variable which assumes only two possible types of union model. One, from now on termed 'the alternative model', is identified as the practices and theoretical formulations elaborated among unions affiliated to the CUT. The other is the model still practised by the more traditional sectors of the labour movement, which tend to be less critical of the current institutional and cultural features of the Brazilian industrial relations system.

Of course such a research strategy involves a simplification of reality in that different unions display distinctive levels of adherence to the alternative model. Leaving a systematic treatment to another opportunity we think that among the relevant features of the alternative model, we can list (a) diminishing reliance on corporatist organisational inducements (e.g. monopoly of representation and union tax); (b) search for higher levels of voluntary membership; (c) reliance on collective bargaining rather than on labour courts; (d) distinctiveness (from corporatism) of methods of vertical and horizontal organisation; (e) emphasis on organisation of workers within the workplace; (f) search for improving union democracy.

The incidence of these indicators in the real life of each union of our sample varies widely. Such a variation is visible even among unions affiliated to the CUT. Because the institutional features of the traditional model are still enforced by Constitution and labour laws, it is not possible to measure degrees of adoption of alternative practices by given unions. Differences are generated in a comprehensive way that implies leadership attitudes, cultural environment, internal practices and theoretical conceptions. Such a difficulty in constructing scales to measure degrees of adoption of the alternative model forced the option for the dichotomic strategy. That is, we assumed that the differences between the 'CUT model' and the traditional one are real, it being justifiable to compare their different impacts on membership attitudes.

Now let us turn to the dependent variable, the attitude of active citizenship of union members. We are already aware of the difficulties of measuring successfully such a theoretical construct. For attitude we shall employ Almond and Verba's definition: 'an attitude is a propensity in an individual to perceive, interpret, and act toward a particular object in particular ways' (1980b: 13). Although aware of a number of others conceptualisations of attitudes more recently put forward by psychologists, methodologists and social scientists (Oppenheim, 1992: 174: 'a state of readiness, a tendency to respond in a certain manner when confronted with certain stimuli'; Richardson and Wanderley, 1985: 35: 'an emotional and volitive orientation towards a certain object as integrating the world of reference of the individual'; Broughton, 1995: 202: 'a relative stable system of beliefs concerning an object and resulting in an evaluation of that object'), we have adopted Almond and Verba's definition because the behavioural reactions of individuals, comprising the phases of perception, feeling and action, are more explicitly stated. This study focuses on the development of a particular type of political culture which is to be assessed on the grounds of both opinion and behaviour. For this reason we shall retain the broader concept of attitude in that it emphasises the way individuals tend to act in accordance with their system of beliefs.

The point is that we are not considering the set of rights enjoyed by a particular group of workers, that is, their rights of citizenship in a general sense. Rather, we are interested in measuring a more restricted concept – the one of active citizen. Borrowing from Almond and Verba again (1963: 164), an active citizen is so to 'the extent to which [he or she] considers themselves to have some sort of responsibility to be active in the community'. We shall seek to elicit workers' attitude towards both the work community and the wider society, that is, the practice and perception of workers as citizens. This research will assess attitudes of workers towards certain objects that show involvement in and responsibility for collective and public affairs, that is, attitudes proper to an active citizen. Accordingly, we may identify some variables by which the abstract construct 'attitude of active citizenship' could be taken into account in a concrete context: (a) attitude towards unions; (b) attitude towards control at work; (c) attitude towards associative life; and (d) attitude towards politics and the sense of political efficacy. Depending on attitudes shown by the interviewee regarding each of those variables, we shall be in a position to evaluate attitude scores in terms of active citizenship.

4.3 The Survey Design

An investigation may infer different degrees of relationship between two variables, ranging from mere association to causality. In the search for causal links, we have made the methodological choice for the survey design referred to above. By surveying workers belonging to certain occupational categories we aimed to measure certain attitudes that are proper to an active citizen. Data collected through the mentioned survey were submitted to a multiple regression statistical test. The main goal of such a test was the controlling of other possible factors affecting workers' attitudes. We have always been aware of the obvious fact that a union model is not the chief factor to explain variations in workers' attitudes. But this statistical technique is strong enough to yield results (different scores on the scale of 'active citizenship') that are explained only by the chosen independent variable, that is, by the model adopted by the union to which the worker is affiliated.

Bearing in mind such a methodological choice, we carried out a survey with workers belonging to categories of two basic types: those which follow the alternative model and those which fit into the more traditional pattern of industrial relations. We were aware of the fact that unions are not bound to apply the alternative model in full. But as long as the alternative model is a theoretical and practical elaboration developed in the CUT, we could conceive of our independent variable – alternative conceptions of unionism and industrial relations as formed of two basic levels: those unions affiliated to the CUT, which tends to adhere and practise it, and those not affiliated to it. In turn, the dependent variables of our hypothesis are individual characteristics of workers – certain attitudes. Then we set out to assess the degree to which such characteristics are affected by workers' exposure to the prevalent model in their respective occupational categories. Other factors influencing them were controlled by raising individual data from the questionnaire's answers and submitting them to the regression analysis.

The workers forming the sample were purposely selected from seven occupational categories: metalworkers, telecommunication workers, bank employees, data processing employees, textile workers, commerce employees and pharmaceutical industry workers. We focused on rank-and-file union members rather than on their leaders so as to achieve

a better understanding of common workers' attitudes.[4] All
the selected occupational categories are spread around the
Metropolitan Region of Recife. Measured differences in the
dependent variables through the 'active citizenship scale'
were compared with the exposure of workers to the alternative model. Since the questionnaires gathered data on
the other independent variables – such as sex, education,
marital status, age and income – we could control their
influence on workers in order to assess the factor we are
interested in measuring – the practice of alternative
conceptions.

When we referred to other factors influencing the
dependent variable, we could have mentioned the problem of reverse causality. Rather than the attitudes of an
occupational category being shaped by a particular model
of industrial relations, one could argue that workers of a
category who decide to adopt such a model made this choice
because they already displayed certain characteristics. Thus,
the rapid growth of the CUT – where the alternative practices are to be found – would have occurred mainly in
categories which had a tradition of mobilisation, whose members were prone to participate, and located in strategic sectors
of economic activity. In other words, the citizenship and
correspondent attitude of those workers, being previously
more developed, would have led to the adoption of the
alternative model of industrial relations. Certainly this is
the case to a certain extent in that the presence of the
CUT is larger in stronger economic branches such as manufacturing and banking. But it does not exclude the effect
that the model itself has helped to improve workers'
consciousnesss. For instance, the former president of the
CUT in Pernambuco and currently a member of its national
executive board, Jairo Cabral, recognises that previous features of occupational categories do influence adherence.
But, after the onset, the model acts as a sort of independent motor. This causal arrow from the new unionism model
towards increasing mobilisation is assumed by the great
number of 'new unions' or new leadership which have applied
to the CUT in order to affiliate to it, the federal police-
men being just one of the most visible instances (interview
no. 19).

4.4   The Scale of Attitudes of Active Citizenship

4.4.1   *Assumptions and Theoretical Precedents*

Aiming at shedding light on the role of the labour question in the extension of citizenship to the lower social 'strata', we have dealt with a particular conception of citizenship: that concerned with active involvement of citizens in society. This conception of 'an active citizen' might be traced back to the classical political thought and its revival by republican theorists, as we briefly discussed in the introduction. Republicans argue that the willingness to take part in public affairs is at the same time an expression and a condition of citizenship. Bringing this insight to bear on the question of extending workers' citizenship, we believe that there exist some social attitudes identifiable with that 'civic virtue' so dear to the republican or civic humanists. At this point it is worth noting that we are not discussing the normative aspect of the republican approach to citizenship. We are restricting ourselves to recognising such a conception within social thought and then turning our attention to empirical research appropriate to identify the presence in social reality of the elements that, acccording to the republican tradition, constitute the concept of (active) citizenship.

Drawing on the referred literature, a proper scale to measure workers' attitudes was built up.[5] As suggested, we were interested in looking at a particular type of political culture: the active citizenship one, understood as a public-spirited orientation and an inclination to participate in collective efforts. The related attitudes displayed by workers are therefore taken as necessary preconditions to enable them to pursue citizenship entitlements as full members of community. In short, we have termed 'active citizenship attitudes' those related to the above seen political culture.

Dealing with measurement of workers' attitudes of active citizenship, this survey design aimed to elicit both attitudes towards work and towards community at large. Critical and participatory stances were considered as constitutive elements of a culture of active citizenship that spread over job and union matters, as well as over societal and political life. Thus we departed from previous studies that concentrated either on the political aspect of a 'civic culture'

(Almond and Verba, 1965; Putnam, 1993) or on attitudes towards work and unions (Goldthorpe *et al.*, 1970; Fosh, 1981; Fosh and Heery, 1990; Fantasia, 1989; Mann, 1973; Hill, 1981; Heery and Kelly, 1994). Such an approach is justified by the contention that commitment to unionism does not arise independently of other spheres of social life. There exists some underlying basis informing attitudes. Individuals' attitudes in regard to work matters tend to come up in combination with attitudes towards political concerns because of 'a tendency towards the formation of relatively coherent systems of values and beliefs' (Fosh, 1990: 117). Bearing in mind this strategy we built an attitude scale divided into four dimensions, each of them making up a module: unions, control at work, associative life, and politics and sense of political efficacy. This way of grouping questions closer to a common dimension does not imply disregard of the methodological assumption that the four chosen dimensions are an integral part of the workers' active citizenship culture we are studying.

Therefore, the critical, participative and committed attitude proper to a culture of active citizenship is pervasive to the whole scale. Commenting on the cross-country survey reported in Almond and Verba's *Civic Culture* (1963), Lijphart (1980: 42) noted that they failed to present a 'composite index to measure the degree of civic culture'. Bearing in mind this criticism, our survey design tried to provide a single index produced out of a unidimensional variable: the active-citizen attitude. Relating to this search for unidimensionality, we followed Judd *et al.*'s (1991: 148) advice to use a multiple-item scaling procedure. So the respondents were questioned on several items all of which attempt to measure active citizenship. Thus other influences were presumed to be cancelled out as long as the other factors would not be present in every item. Such spurious influences tend to vary randomly. In sum, although our scale gathered several indicators in its multiplicity of items, there was just one underlying construct whose measurement we shall set out to establish. The items integrating each module are mere aspects of the areas in which the attitude may be revealed.[6]

The division of the items into four modules, in turn, is

explained by two practical reasons: firstly, the fact that grouping questions which address a common object is a procedure that helps identify their theoretical roots and, hence, their justification; secondly – a more prosaic motive – such a division embodies practical advantages regarding pilot tests, application of the questionnaire, manipulation of data and analysis of results (Oppenheim, 1992). This procedure of grouping similar items is also recommended by Richardson and Wanderley (1985: 183), having also being employed, among others, by Epstein and McParthland (1975).

Having said that, let us present the structure of the scale.[7] Each module consists of two parts: one gathering questions on the behaviour of the respondent about the measured dimension, and the other targeting at his/her attitudes in *sensu stricto*. In the second part of each module we employed a pool of items built up according to the so-called Linkert procedure (Oppenheim, 1992: 195–200). We provided a statement followed by an ordered sequence of agreement and disagreement with possible answers.[8]

4.4.2   The First Module: Dependent Variables Related to Attitudes Towards Unions

The first module addressed workers' attitudes on union matters. Both the section on behaviour and the one on attitudes *sensu stricto* sought to measure participation and commitment to unions in a general sense rather than on the particular union to which the respondent was affiliated. We tried to evaluate respondents' attitudes regarding motives for affiliation, attendance at union headquarters, intensity of participation in union affairs, participation in strikes, frequency of talking on union matters, participation as candidate in union elections, search for information from union representatives, voting on union elections, reading of the union journal, preference for union channels in solving problems, regard for union's viewpoint while taking own decisions on politics or work, role of unions (on handing out of welfare provisions and struggling for control over work processes and/or distribution) and readiness to act collectively on union calls (Pateman, 1970; Fosh, 1993).

The scale of attitudes towards unions was built upon the two axes of underlying dimensions most often employed by the literature, namely, the ideological/instrumental and the solidaristic/individualistic attitudes (Fosh, 1993; Goldthorpe *et al.*, 1970). As conventionally accepted, the former dimension involves the perception of the union as a bearer of 'social and political goals' or as capable of addressing wider issues of worker control in contradistinction to the attitudes which envisage the union as a mere instrument for the achievement of individuals' goals, often strictly economicist in nature. The solidarististic/individualistic dichotomy, in turn, has to do with the presence or absence of a positive evaluation and readiness to engage in collective actions which presuppose solidaristic ties among workers. The stress on such a predisposition to solidary collective undertaking has been highlighted as a relevant potentiality of trade unions to counteract tendencies of individualism and acquiescence by the workers to the ethos and rules of capitalist production. In his *Cultures of Solidarity*, a book clearly at odds with the major currents of American industrial sociology, Fantasia (1989) presents three case studies of certain unconventional collective initiatives of American workers at the shop floor and in local communities, all of them interpreted as challenging the pattern of acquiescence prevalent in the contemporary US labour movement and too readily taken for granted by most of the literature. What he terms a 'culture of solidarity' relates to workers' tendencies to act collectively on impulses which go beyond the reckoning of cost and benefits emphasised by 'resource mobilisation theories' (Olson, 1971; Zald and McCarthy, 1979). While these solidaristic endeavours are likely to arise only in particular contexts, at times preceded by long periods of passivity and routine, they are not unconnected with the character of the union itself.

The present research aims to appreciate the diverse impacts on workers' attitudes which stem from different types of union approaches (union models) towards workers' organisation and action. As already highlighted, the workers' attitudes being compared are focused under the perspective of the development of a culture of active citizenship, that is, of involvement with work-related and broader societal issues as well. As a corollary, the scale designed to measure workers' attitudes could not fail to address the solidaristic and non-instrumental dimensions of such attitudes, for their very concept entails the type of workers' initiatives deemed to integrate the notion of active citizenship. Such is the underlying assumption of the items inserted in this module.

4.4.3   The Second Module: Dependent Variables Related to Attitudes Towards Control at Work

The employment relationship has a singular nature. The worker hands over his labour power to the employer and from then on he loses control over the way it is used in the work process and over the surplus it generates. The antagonism stemming from this fact displays a double nature. On one hand there is the more apparent dispute over distribution of the results. But a deeper conflict is also latent about the way the productive process is organised. That is the conflict over the organisation of production (Edwards, 1986), which involves both control over processes and over people (Hill, 1981). Matters such as rhythm of working, authority at the workplace, workers' rights and definition of tasks provide firm grounds for conflicting interest on possible arrangements. Such an antagonism over control at work has not been disregarded by the literature (Hill, 1981).

Management's position on the productive process endows it with a prominent power to impose decisions upon workers about work-control matters. But the history of labour insurgence has always been permeated by its struggle for having a say on decisions regarding the organisation of work. A long-standing concern of the British trade unions, the question of authority and power within industry, may be said to be present on the agenda of most labour movements although to varying extents. Moreover, the topic has been addressed by the European Union's directives on industrial democracy (Ferner and Hyman, 1992: 46).

Workers' endeavours to have a say in the management of the shop floor and the enterprise as a whole gives rise to what has been termed 'politics of production' (Burawoy, 1985), or 'shop-floor politics' (Mangabeira, 1993). Such concepts pertain to the understanding of the process of production not merely in its economic aspects but also in its political moment, since there is an apparent dispute of power between labour and management. Any degree of workers' control over shop floor decisions requires both awareness of the existing conflict and participation to enable them to have a say. However, the understanding that the workplace is a field of power dispute, and thus, is politically defined, is not shared by everybody. In the *Civic Culture*, Almond and Verba (1963) consider participation in the workplace as a non-political stance, as a space for acquiring the abilities necessary for a citizen to be involved in politics. But the fact is that participation in the workplace is about the issue of control at work. If such participation entails dispute of power, we may reasonably construe it as a political space. From these considerations there follows the contention that one of the aspects of people's disenfranchisement is precisely the lack of control over their working conditions (Poole: 1986). If assertion of citizenship implies overcoming disenfranchisement, and also that related to deprivation of control at work, an active citizen should be critical and participative on that matter as well.

Focusing this question in the light of the analysis of the Brazilian new unionism concerns, it has been stressed that one of its contributions was the search for explicitation of workplace conflicts. For some authors the new unionism managed to turn such conflicts into 'shop-floor politics'. For others, the alternative model of the new unionism places emphasis on the organised participation of workers in the day-to-day administration of the labour process (Siqueira, 1994a: 24). So far we have asserted that an active attitude towards conflict at workplace is one of the dimensions which make up a culture of an active citizenry. We have also noticed that some analysts claim that the new unionism has contributed to the development of workers' concern with the 'politics of production'. Then, measuring the impact of the alternative model of the new unionism on workers' attitude as active citizens could not fail to include such an indicator, provided that this study attempts to test some of the effects of the new unionism.

In the light of these remarks, we designed our second module with questions on workers' attitude about control at work. We drew on the literature above discussed, linking the identification of conflicts on the organisation of work with the critical and participative stance proper to the attitude of an active citizen. Questions on both conflict over distribution and organisation of work were included. The assumption was that the more a worker is aware of the distinctiveness of employee and employer interests on both order of conflicts, the more he/she will be ready to act on behalf of collective claims.

The selected items targeted at measuring interviewees' attitudes on the following issues: reaction to bosses' unfair decisions at work, frequency of own initiative to improve work processes, availability to take part in committees or groups designed to improve organisation of work, participation in negotiations with the firm as representative of workers, willingness to get more participation in decisions taken by the firm, acceptance of management exclusiveness in decision-taking processes, awareness of the 'structured antagonism' (Edwards, 1995b: 15) between employers and workers in the employment relationship, and participation of workers in decisions regarding distribution of results.

4.4.4   The Third Module: Dependent Variables Related to Associative Life

The third module was inspired by the emphasis on the intensity of associational life as an indicator of a civic culture (e.g. Putnam, 1993: 89–92). Individuals who take part in associations of any kind are easily recognisable active citizens. By participating in associations, individuals develop their capacity to envisage collective goals and to co-operate. Thus, the more an individual is involved in associations and has positive attitudes towards them, the more he or she may be regarded as an active citizen. Although within the limits of this work we are just concerned with the strengthening of an active-citizen culture, it is worth noting that the literature has pointed out that the flourishing of voluntary associations of all kinds is a dimension of a 'civic culture' which has played an important role in fostering economic, social and political development of society in a broad sense. Recent social analysts, writing on Latin America and Southern Europe, respectively, Hirschman (1984) and Putnam (1993), have stressed that the regions with strong traditions of civic engagement tend to experience higher levels of institutional and socio-economic development.

Our module on associational life was formed by questions on respondents' actual participation in several types of associations such as residents' groups, political parties, church groups, leisure clubs and social movement organisations. We probe further through questions about participation in directive bodies of associations, membership campaigns, intensity of readiness to affiliate to associations, perceptions about the need for the poor to act together, fund-raising campaigns and collective actions undertaken by such associations. Because unions and political parties were addressed in other modules, this module concentrated on the other variants of voluntary associations.

4.4.5   The Fourth Module: Dependent Variables Related to Politics and the Sense of Subjective Competence

This module pays tribute to the well-stablished idea that a full citizen should take at least a vigilant stance on politics (Dahrendorf, 1988;Pocock, 1971). This idea belongs to the 'civic humanism' tradition which emphasises the civic virtues of participation and public responsibility. The ability to participate, stemming from both ancient Greece and the Italian city-republics, is deemed to be a very important condition for the self-fulfilment of a citizen.

This module includes items on both interest in political affairs and the respondent's feeling of subjective political competence. As Almond and Verba (1965, 1980b) and Pateman (1970) have argued, a full citizen is one that feels confident in understanding and influencing political decisions that ultimately affect his/her day-to-day life. One's self-confidence in his/her political competence was even said to constitute the most important component of the civic culture envisaged by Almond and Verba (Lijphart, 1980: 41). Since we are concerned with measuring attitudes that form a culture of an active citizen, this sense of personal ability to count on the decision-taking process could not be left aside.

Bearing in mind such theoretical assumptions, this module included items connected with the respondent's interest in politics and his/her feelings of capacity to influence it. Thus the module was provided with items on reaction to threats or violation of rights, talking about politics in everyday life, attempts at influencing other people's voting choices, participation in electoral campaigns, reading of political news, exposure to political programmes on TV or radio, perception of common citizens' chances of influencing public affairs, adherence to democracy, disposition towards collective action, participation in rallies, readiness to vote in case of introduction of facultative voting, support for political parties, and perception of differentiation of interests according to social groups (Almond and Verba, 1963: 116; Moisés, 1993; Oppenheim, 1992: 245).

4.4.6 Questions on Other Factors Affecting Workers' Attitudes: Building Up the Model

A final group of questions relates to independent variables other than the union model. Those questions were included in the two last modules of the interview schedule. Module Five grouped the following questions:

- size of the enterprise;
- type of ownership: whether private or public;
- sector of economic activity: whether industry or service.

Module Six comprised classifying questions on personal characteristics of respondents, allowing for the following variables:

- number of dependents living together with the respondent;
- gender;
- educational level of the respondent;
- age;
- occupation;
- type of job; whether bureaucratic (white collar) or production (blue collar);
- time in the current job;
- interaction at work;
- solidarity at work;
- length of time of affiliation to the union;
- union militancy;
- income;

The relevant literature has stipulated a number of factors to explain differences in workers' attitudes. Most of the variables introduced into our model draw heavily on such previous work, after considering the particular features of our sample. Let us start with the *size of the enterprise*. The large enterprise grouping huge numbers of workers tends to generate depersonalised relations of employment. A common sense of identity arising out of similar situations and grievances is likely to foster solidary attitudes. In addition, the employer is perceived in a more 'institutionalised way', differently from the small or familial firm where either a paternalistic or an authoritarian stance of the employer tends to make individual employees at the same time more vulnerable and more easily influenced by the former. It is not by chance that the industrial relations literature on the so-called 'unitary conception' usually found it in the latter type of firms (Baglioni, 1990; Jackson, 1985; Farnham and Pimlot, 1979; Ubeku, 1983; Barros, 1991). Moreover, the nature of the work experience obviously is distinct in large and small firms. In addition, some non-economic rewards are also linked to the dimension of enterprises and closeness of personal interaction between workers and employer. All those conditions explain the widespread consensus about the relevance of the size of the enterprise. Goldthorpe *et al.*, for instance, recognise the strong links between size of firm, degree of unionisation and left-wing voting (1969), a relationship that has now been documented by subsequent studies (e.g. Marginson, 1984). Other authors such as Mann (1973: 23) make the similar point that class consciousness is positively related to size of plant in that the greater control of work by large enterprises through more rigid routines tends to arouse worker resistance in a higher degree.

A group of independent variables included in our model alongside the one we are interested in testing closely – the alternative union model – were those directly or indirectly connected to the question of labour processes and technology. In fact, this is one of the most common factors present in theories which deal with unionism and workers' attitudes. As Fosh (1981: 10) puts it, attitudes at work and towards unions are often tied to the 'type of productive technology' in operation at the workplace, comprising the labour process and the tasks performed by working people. In the already-quoted investigation on industrial attitudes of the workers in the autocar industry at Luton, Goldthorpe *et al.* (1970: 44–9) refer to it as 'technological constraints', thus recognising the importance of such factors and high-lighting the fact that they also influence shop-floor rela-tions. In the same trend, Seidman's study on the labour movements of South Africa and Brazil (1994: 96) stresses the independent effect of labour processes on the complex causal chain that shapes attitudes of both employers and employees. Likewise, for Edwards, in his study of strikes and industrial conflict in Britain (1995b: 434–60), the reasons why dockers and miners figure among the most strike-prone unions in Britain lie in work group solidarity which arises from certain types of technology.

One could question the absence of a direct item on the technological processes in which the respondent is engaged. But, as we shall observe in the section dealing with the explanation of the statistical test, it would not be practi-cable to quantify the wide range of distinct types of labour processes practised by the 58 enterprises where our sample was scattered. Thus, the sounder methodological solution available seemed to be the reliance on a handful of di-chotomous variables related to the item.

That explains the selection of the following variables, all of them expected to bring some effects originated from labour processes and technology to the surface: *occupation, sector of economic activity of the enterprise, type of ownership, solidarity at work and interaction at work.* The nature of occu-pation was roughly classified in two basic types so as to enable its inclusion as a dichotomous or truncated vari-able in the model. Accordingly, the respondents were categorised as holding, on the one hand, administrative, non-manual or white-collar jobs; and, on the other, pro-duction-related, manual or blue-collar ones. This variable – *occupation* – has been singled out by the literature, not least in the study by Moisés on the Brazilian political cul-ture (1993: 177). While analysing levels of cognition of political values and institutions (what he termed levels of political sophistication), he controls for the variable 'position on the occupation structure' by classifying interviewees on the two categories, whether holding manual or non-manual jobs.

The question on the *sector of activity of the firm* also allows for the 'technical constraint' variable. Take the example of a shop assistant belonging to the 'commerce employees' as described in Chapter 4. He/she was classified as working in the service sector. Such a job is strongly linked to a particular type of work, certainly very different from labour processes likely to be found in the alternative category to this item: industry. *The question on the type of ownership*, in turn, was also regarded as at least indirectly tied to the work processes in that the rhythm of work, pressures and tensions in the private sector are tougher than in the less constrained work environments of the public sector. In addition we advanced two other connected variables – *interaction at work and solidarity at work* – again drawing from Goldthorpe *et al.* (1970: 48–55). They note that the technical organisation of work fosters or hinders the formation of solidary work groups through positive and negative factors. Among the former they list interdependence of the tasks, control over work processes, freedom of movement and direct contact with workmates; as for the latter they cite spatial constraints, noise of machines and changes in work location. Although they strongly emphasise that those technical constraints are not the only or the main factor explaining formation of primary solidary groups, they also suggest certain questions that ultimately turned out to be useful for our quantitative model. Those questions attempted to identify degrees of contact between workers and their sense of attachment to the work groups, as accounted for by questions 74 and 75 of our interview schedule. By probing how often the respondents talk to their peers and how they would feel about being transferred away from the current workplace, we sought to encompass some effects of both interaction and the feeling of solidarity at work, which ultimately have to do with technological processes at least to a certain extent.

Turning to the demographic variables or the particular attributes of interviewees, one need hardly justify them as they have long been established as independent factors shaping human behaviour. Thus, *gender, age, level of education* and *income* were selected in line with a long tradition of social research (e.g., Goldthorpe, 1968a; Mangabeira, 1993; Fosh, 1990). Let us take the question of gender, for instance. By now it is sufficently established that inequalities of reward and type of job have continued to penalise the female workforce. As authors like Rubery and Fagan (1995), Sinclair (1995) and Price and Bain (1983) put it, low pay, part-time jobs and other forms of precarious employment have a strong female face. Such differences of position in the labour market, added to the housework burden on women's shoulders, affect their attitudes towards society and work matters. Similar reasoning applies to age and number of dependents, which gives rise to differences of jobs and social perceptions. Admittedly, a young bachelor living alone will have fewer reasons to be cautious in his or her political stances than, say, a middle-age person committed to providing for his or her family, including the elderly parents.

Education turns out to be a major factor since the illiterate or very low skilled tend to be more passive in regard to both the employer and societal power structures (Mangabeira, 1993: 60). Although the two factors are logically and empirically distinct, in our research perspective, low skill may be taken to imply low educational level. The effect of both was found, for example, in Seidman's study on the new unionisms in Brazil and South Africa (1994: 36) where she perceived a move towards militancy when both black Africans and Brazilian metalworkers became more skilled and educated than workers in rural areas or the informal sector. For the purpose of understanding such an independent variable, we shall cast aside the problem of a rigorous definition of skills. We will limit ourselves to accepting Humphrey's (1982) and Seidman's (1994: 66) suggestion that the criteria for distinguishing unskilled from semi-skilled is the previous factory experience, and from semi-skilled to skilled is special vocational training. Although the issue of skills is also related to power within the labour market (higher costs of replacement of trained workers, a point made by Seidman, 1994: 36), the chief question here is the effect that higher educational and skill levels might have on the self-confidence and availability of instruments to understand and take an interest in public or collective affairs. The process of maturing the sort of political culture that we have termed the 'culture of active citizenship' obviously depends on individual acquisition of certain basic preconditions, or 'tools', if you like. Some of these 'tools', such as information and openness to societal matters, are further dependent on educational attainments. Such links have been stressed by the literature, as exemplified by the finding that social groups deprived of 'intellectual or informational resources' are much more likely to fall in the sector classified as 'apathetic' or 'inactive' (Moisés, 1993: 173).[9]

Still focusing on the particular attributes of our population, let us turn our attention to income. It has been stated that high income workers have a stronger control of their personal careers and other means to get power and economic access to resources. Consequently, they are more prone to develop the self-confidence inherent to the active citizen. Conversely, extremely low income strata often lack all the basic conditions to acquire an active attitude.

Two of our independent variables concern what the literature on methodology usually terms 'maturation', that is, the effect of exposure on a certain factor during a period of time. On the one hand, the *length of time of the interviewee in his/her current job* enables us to assume a stability likely to foster the sense of 'subjective competence' mentioned by Almond and Verba. On the other, the length of time of membership of the union implies the maturation of effects derived from intrinsic culture and practices of the unions. Until now we took those effects in a broad sense, independently of their intensity which, of course, varies according to different union models (or patterns of relationship between leaders and members). As Goldthorpe *et al.* put it, 'mobilisation and active attitudes tend to be more apparent as a result of longer exposure to unions' influence' (1970: 64).

Still directly concerning unions we managed to incorporate a question on whether the respondent regarded him/herself as a *union militant*. The assumption is that the member who has already become an activist is much more likely to hold attitudes proper to a 'culture of active citizenship'. As our investigation seeks to document the effect of one particular factor – the union model – on the attitudes of union members, the personal attribute of being an activist had to be identified and controlled. Otherwise we would end up in a circularity: a union member adopts active attitudes because he/she is a militant; he/she is a militant because of holding active attitudes.

4.5   The Field Research

4.5.1   *Working Out the Schedule Through the Pilot Test*

The previous sections aimed to provide a justification for the schedule and variables selected to make up our 'model of active citizenship'. The next step was to test the first draft of the schedule through a pilot test. Following Richardson and Wanderley (1985), we decided to review the items and their wording after each interview. The procedure was suitable because the ambiguities or misunderstandings were easily identified.

Accordingly, the original schedule was submitted to a number of modifications from the first pilot submission until the last one. Altogether we listened to thirty respondents in this phase of piloting. Individuals were selected on the grounds of similarity with the definitive population envisaged in the survey, so as to cover a range of different educational levels and social backgrounds.

This 'heuristic' procedure led to the definitive schedule presented in Appendices 1 and 2. As we have already noted, the questions were divided into six modules, the initial four relating to the attitudes investigated and the final ones concerning independent variables other than the 'alternative proposals or union model'.

4.5.2   *Choosing the Population for the Survey*

Chapter 4 presented the research setting and the reasons why we set out to make a survey whose population was the workers of the Metropolitan Region of Recife, an area which includes another 11 'municípios' besides Recife.[10] Recife itself is an urban agglomerate of 1,296,995 inhabitants, according to the 1991 census carried out by the 'Fundaçao Instituto Brasileiro de Geografia e Estatística – IBGE' and published in 1994; such a population stretches to 2,871,261 if one considers the whole metropolitan region (IBGE, 1994). In Brazil, workers in the formal sector, which means working under an official and properly registered contract of employment, comprise just half of the occupied population. The other half works in the informal sector, with no labour law protection whatsoever. But Recife is in the core of the poor Northeast Region and has displayed some of the country's worst social records in terms of unemployment, proportion of its inhabitants living in slums, etc. Aiming at quantifying our population, initially we got data compiled for 1992 by the economist Alexandre Rands Barros, from the Federal University of Pernambuco, on the basis of the monthly employment research ('Pesquisa Mensal do Emprego') and the National Households Research ('Pesquisa Nacional por Amostra de Domicílios'), both carried out by the IBGE. Accordingly, the Metropolitan Region of Recife had an estimated 546,000 workers in the formal sector as against 526,500 in the informal sector (297,000 self-employed workers and 229,500 employees without registration). The informal economy comprises in addition to these 526,500 workers, 115,000 entrepreneurs, and thus one may conclude that the majority of the economic active population lacks labour law and social security protection. From the list of employees per economic sector, as compiled by FIEPE ('Federação das Indústrias no Estado de Pernambuco'), we came to the conclusion that the registered worker population was very scattered both in economic branches and in the geographical areas of the Metropolitan Region of Recife. Furthermore, it was apparent that large numbers of such a workforce were not organised in any union at all.

Those circumstances prevented us from employing a stratified random sample procedure according to occupational categories. If it had been possible, we would have divided the population into as many workers' occupational categories as there were present in the research setting; and subsequently, we would have selected a random sample within each strata, in this case, the occupational categories. Leaving aside the ideal design of the stratified random sample, we proceeded to the selection of the sample in two steps. As for the first step, we chose a purposive sample of occupational categories regarded as representative of the labour movement in Pernambuco. Previous studies on the new unionism in Pernambuco have investigated roughly similar samples of occupational categories and their respective unions. In a pioneer study presented to the London School of Economics, Morais (1992) concentrated on the following occupational categories, all of them deemed to be well representative of new unionism in the state: data-processing employees, bank employees, metalworkers, urban workers, private school teachers and state school teachers. Medeiros (1992) paid special attention to the process of emergence of the new unionism in the occupational categories of data-processing workers and telecommunication workers, the latter having also been studied by Barbosa and Silva (1993).

The statistical test employed was a multiple regression that is powerful enough to tell us if the selected independent variables contribute to the attained levels of the investigated dependent variable in each individual. Thus, strictly, there was no need for great similarities in the two groups of workers (members of 'new unions' and of 'traditional' ones), since comparison was undertaken on an individual basis. But, to prevent any possible alleged bias, we picked up two groups of workers that integrate roughly similar occupational categories. In so doing, we tried to get both traditional and 'new unions' from the private and public sectors, and from both the industry and the service sector.

Bearing in mind such remarks, for what could be called the 'experimental' group – members of 'new unions' – we selected the following: telecommunication workers, bank employees, data-processing employees and metalworkers. Apart from the latter, all of them represent persons who work for private and public sectors. Although the first three concentrated more workers in service activities rather than in production, the metalworkers are located mainly in the line of production. Other reasons for selecting such unions have to do with the historical fact that they have played a prominent role in the construction of the CUT in the state of Pernambuco, as already noted in Chapter 4. Most of the resources and militants of the CUT have stemmed from the ranks of those unions. Not surprisingly, they have already served as the object of the previous studies above-mentioned. As for the so-called 'control group' we included unions from Força Sindical and CGT. From the former, the Commerce Employees' Union was chosen mainly because the current co-ordinator of the Força Sindical in the state of Pernambuco is at the same time its president, this union having had a decisive role in the establishment of the 'central' in the state. Its members work in the private service sector. On the grounds of its crucial role in the setting up of the CGT in Pernambuco, we picked the Textile Industry Workers' Union, which groups the weavers in the private sector industry. And, allowing for the need to include workers in the public sector in the 'control group', we managed to select the Pharmaceutical Industry Workers' Union, which represents the workforce of a state-owned laboratory whose majority of workers are in the point of production. This latter union is also affiliated to the CGT.

The second step, in turn, departed from the occupational categories which were chosen according to the above justified purposeful method. Once having selected those occupational categories, we extracted a random sample varying between 18 and 37 workers within each occupational category. Those respondents were randomly selected from the list of union members offered by firms, which, in turn, were randomly picked out. Regarding the choice of firms, it is worth noting that we decided to concentrate on a small number per each occupational category, apart from the case of the commerce workers. This latter comprises a very scattered category by its very nature since there are hundreds of small firms in the trade of retail commerce. Had we interviewed workers from merely a handful of enterprises, it would imply a bias which we tried to avoid. Sometimes the chosen interviewee was on leave of absence and was immediately replaced by another name from the firm's payroll.

4.5.3   Carrying Out the Interviews

Because our survey population gathered individuals with widely different educational levels, we were prevented from merely applying a written questionnaire. Hence, the schedule (see Appendix 2) was orally submitted by a research team formed by myself and four social sciences students. The first step was always the contact with the firms' representatives whose suspicion had to be overcome. Except for two refusals,[11] the firms, to the research team's surprise, always agreed to allow the undertaking of interviews during working time and inside their premises, even though, in certain cases, we had to be very persistent in contacting several hierarchical ranks in the firm. The purely academic purpose of the research, the prestige of the university to which the work was destined, as well as personal previously existing contact, were altogether important factors explaining the success in terms of access to workers. In certain cases we had to persist tenaciously not to be forced to hold some interviews in places and times other than the firm's premises and working time. Differences in this respect could have led to spurious interferences that had to be prevented.

The interviews were carried out by the research team already mentioned, after careful explaining of the objectives of the research and the technical requirements of such an enterprise, which was facilitated by the fact that the group had previous experience with survey, even though not with measuring attitudes. The period of submission lasted from February to June 1994. Each interview had an average duration ranging from thirty to forty-five minutes. In the case of the less-educated respondents, interviewers were allowed to spend more time explaining the meaning of the questions. Invariably the interviewed started with assurance of confidentiality, particularly in relation to the employer, and a reminder of the merely academic purpose. In general terms, we realised that the sample managed to feel confident in the research team's discretion. The number of selected workers who refused to co-operate was insignificant.

4.5.4 The Statistical Test[12]

A multiple regression with each individual as a sample was the statistical procedure used to test the major hypothesis raised. More particularly, the following equation was the starting point:

$$Y_i = \alpha 0 + \alpha_1 Fne_i + \alpha_2 Ow_i + \alpha_3 Fs_i + \alpha_4 Nd_i + \alpha_5 Sex_i$$
$$+ \alpha_6 Ed_i + \alpha_7 Ag_i + \alpha_8 TJ_i + \alpha_9 Ex_i + \alpha_{10} Int_i + \alpha_{11} So_i$$
$$+ \alpha_{12} Tum_i + \alpha_{13} Ac_i + \alpha_{14} Inc_i + \alpha_{15} Um_i + e_i \qquad (1)$$

where:

Fne is the number of employees of the company in which the respondent works;

Ow is a dummy variable with (1) for employees working in government-owned companies and (0) for those in private enterprises;

Fs is another dummy variable with (1) for employees working in industrial companies and (0) for those in firms engaged in services;

Nd is the number of dependents which the employee has;

Sex is the sex of the employee;

Ed is the number of years in formal education of the employee;

Ag is his/her age;

TJ is a dummy variable for his/her position in the company, whether a white-collar (1) or a blue-collar (0);

Ex measures the years of experience in the current occupation;

Int measures the amount of interaction of the respondent with his/her fellows at work;

So is a subjective measure of the existing solidarity in the workplace;

Tum measures the length of time of union membership;

Ac is a dummy variable with (1) for activists and (0) otherwise;

Inc is the income of the employee, measured in number of minimum wages perceived;

Um measures the number of years of exposure of the union of the respondent to the CUT model, varying alongside a continuum which starts with (0) for the unions of the traditional sector.

The dependent variable was defined as a score, which was a non-weighted average of the scores in all questions included in the questionnaire to measure the active citizenship of the employees. All questions were re-ordered so that they were in ascending order and this average could be calculated. All questions are defined from 1 to 5 so that this average will not give higher weight to any question. Some questions are certainly more relevant than others in measuring the active citizenship. Nevertheless, we have tried to overcome the arbitrariness of any weighting system which could be defined by expanding the number of questions as much as possible. This device reduces the weight of individual questions, so that the existence of outliers with a relatively much higher relevance to explain the unobservable variable than the others is considerably reduced, and the unweighted average becomes a reasonable way to obtain a proxy for the unobservable variable.

The errors in equation (1) are represented by e_i and are supposed to be normally distributed with mean zero $e_i \sim N(0, \sigma i)$. To ensure that its average is zero we also introduced a constant in the model, which is represented in equation (1) by αO. The variance of the errors was not forced to be the same for all employees. Estimations were made by ordinary least square, with the t-tests for the null hypothesis that the coefficient is zero calculated through the use of White's (1980) method to correct for heteroskedasticity. No test to confirm the existence of heteroskedasticity was made. The use of this correction is justified mainly on the grounds of generality. This procedure also makes the test more robust to errors in measurement of the independent variables, although there is no strong reason to believe that there are such errors, since the independent variables are all simple to measure, with the exception of So.

This estimation procedure is asymptotically unbiased and consistent, under the assumptions that the errors behave as assumed above and $E(Xe) = 0$, where X is the vector of all independent variables.[13] Since all components of X, except So, are objective variables, not dependent on the subjective views of the individual, while the dependent variable depends highly on his or her subjective view of the world, the independence of the independent variables from the error term of equation (1) is bound to hold. Special attention was subsequently paid to So, since it is the most probable variable to depend on e_i. In Chapter 6 the regression excluding this variable was also presented to check for the robustness of our hypothesis to the possible bias caused by its inclusion.

The natural logarithms of all variables which did not have zeros, including the dependent variable, were obtained before estimations, so that their coefficients could represent elasticities. The most relevant variable for the purpose of this dissertation is *Um*, which represents the union model. The central hypothesis of this book is that its coefficient is positive, so that the longer the respondent's union is affiliated to the CUT the higher his or her citizenship score, as the union is expected to promote attitudes which raise this score.

4.5.5 The Qualitative Data

Our field research was complemented by data collected directly from the unions themselves. We visited personally all the unions included in the sample and gathered data from archives, staffs and officials. Regarding the historical and general features of the occupational categories represented by each union, we submitted an apposite questionnaire. With the exception of the Commerce Employees' Union, all of them returned the questionnaire. Necessary data on this union was attained through interviews nos 13 and 26, respectively the legal adviser of the Watchmen's Union and its president, which is itself an affiliate to the Força Sindical and, therefore, allows the officials to be in intense day-to-day contact with the Commerce Workers' Union. In addition, before the union's refusal to fill in the questionnaire, we made a visit to the union and had the opportunity to talk to both its president and other officials. Moreover, we got information from rank-and-file workers who had been involved with the opposition group in the past (e.g., interview no. 11). In addition to these data, we followed the main facts related to the sampled unions in the press during the year of 1994.

The bulk of the survey data were finally complemented by personal unstructured interviews undertaken with union militants, lawyers, judges, Ministry of Labour representatives and politicians, all of them listed as primary sources. The process of data-collecting in the field made us well aware of the scarcity of systematic material on labour matters in the Northeast region of Brazil. The daily pressures and challenges with which activists have to deal combine with the lack of resources to explain the absence of a systematic endeavour to register the labour movement history and to intensify knowledge of its reality and environment. Such limitations are a further incentive for continuing investigation on the matter. Nevertheless we believe that our research made a contribution, even if a very modest one, to both the recent history of labour in Pernambuco and the understanding of the impact of unions on workers' perceptions. Chapter 6 discusses the research findings, arrived at both from the quantitative data whose analysis was provided by the multiple regression test and from qualitative data and observation made in the field.

6 Survey Findings: New Unionism Fostering the Attitude of Active Citizenship

1 INTRODUCTION

Chapter 5 detailed the research design of this survey and both the theoretical and methodological assumptions of the statistical test constructed to elicit the attitudes of the population survey. This chapter aims to discuss the survey findings in the light of previous research on the Brazilian labour movement and more general theoretical insights for the study of labour and political culture. We start by comparing the results achieved by workers belonging to the two types of unions involved in the survey – the new unionism and the 'traditional' ones. Such a comparison was carried out in accordance with certain selected indicators picked up from the attitude scale on the grounds of both their significance as components of a culture of active citizenship and their recurrent utilisation in previous studies of workers' attitudes and political culture. Still in view of those selected indicators, we then narrow the focus to look at the workers representing two sub-samples – metalworkers from 'Microlite' and textile industry workers from 'Lipasa'. Such an approach seemed appropriate because both sub-samples display very similar general characteristics despite different union affiliations. Subsequently, we discuss aggregate scores of both the entire sample and each of its occupational categories. Next, we present the complete model of the attitudes of active citizenship by discussing the results on every one of the independent variables supposed to influence workers' attitudes. We seek in particular to analyse the effect of the factor included in our basic hypothesis, that is, the workers' exposure to distinctive union models. Finally, we close the

190

chapter by pointing out that the statistical treatment of the survey data on that variable – union models – leads to the conclusion that the alternative model practised by the CUT unions does contribute to the explanation of the higher levels of attitudes of active citizenship held by their members as compared with those affiliated to traditional unions.

2   A PRELIMINARY GLANCE AT THE SAMPLE: SCORES ON SELECTED INDICATORS

The foregoing chapter presented the scale we conceived in order to measure union members' attitudes. We called it 'the active-citizen attitudes scale'. Each respondent was given a final score, constituted of the average of all the scores attained in each item. Such a score is obviously influenced by several factors, many of which we managed to account for in our model. The level of the 'active-citizen attitudes' of each union member is a function of the different factors acting simultaneously. Many of those independent variables are entangled with one another. That is the reason for opting for the multiple regression statistical test. It provides the analysis of the specific effect of each independent variable on the measured level of our attitudes scale.

Through the regression, when examining a given independent variable, we are able to assess whether it has influenced the score attained by the respondent as if all the other things were equal. In this way we managed to control out the other factors that certainly contribute to a great extent to shaping workers' attitudes. By the same token, we place ourselves in the position to assess the particular factor we are investigating: the alternative labour relations practised by the new unionism.

One needs to note that scores have a strictly individual meaning. For each interviewee, different factors shape his/ her attitudes. A high score may be caused by high educational levels, high income, the feeling of job security derived from the firm's features and so on. Conversely, a low score may be caused by the influence of similar factors, but at the same time the one we are particularly concerned with may play an important relative role in the explanation of the respondent's 'active-citizen attitudes'. It follows that observations undertaken without the 'disentangling power' of the statistical test may be misleading, for different measures of the dependent variable may be explained by the influence of other characteristics of respondents and not just their exposure to our two types of unionism.

Nevertheless, as we explained in Section 4.4 of Chapter 5, our overall sample was relatively balanced in terms of general characteristics of the chosen occupational categories. The two basic levels of our main independent variable – the model of the 'new unions' and the model of the 'traditional unions' – gathered workers both skilled and semi-skilled, engaged in both public and private sectors, industrial and service firms alike. Bearing this in mind, we started the analysis of data by comparing scores attained by the sub-samples formed by each occupational category surveyed. It was a cautious, 'naked eye observation' that might prove to be illustrative of our argument.

We should stress that the criteria for selection of special items or indicators from the scale were twofold. We accounted, on the one hand, for their putative relevance to the shaping of what we have termed the 'active-citizen' attitudes and, on the other, for their widespread use in previous studies on workers' attitudes and political culture. We hoped thereby to obviate any personal bias in selection of pertinent indicators. Accordingly, the following indicators were picked out:

1. Motives for affiliating to the union;
2. Search for information from the union representatives;
3. The role of unions;
4. Participation in collective actions;
5. Talking about politics;
6. Trying to persuade voters;
7. Reading of political news;
8. Watching or listening to political programmes;
9. Feelings of political competence;
10. Readiness to vote.

The average scores of respondents by occupational categories are shown in the following tables. Some items are worded in a positive way, that is, a positive reply meaning a high level of the dependent variable 'active-citizen attitudes'. Others are presented in negative wording, that is a 'yes' answer means a low presence of the measured variable. To extract the average per occupational category, of course, we added up all the scores of their individual members after having reversed the negative scores.

Before turning our attention to the tables that summarise the average scores obtained from the respondents affiliated to the seven unions focused by our survey, it is useful to remind ourselves of their respective distribution in the two basic levels of our independent variable.

Accordingly, the unions practising the alternative model are the following:

• The Telecommunication Workers
• Data Processing Employees
• Metalworkers
• Bank Employees.

As described in Chapter 4, these occupational categories have played a prominent role in the building of the new unionism in the State of Pernambuco, having provided the basis for the establishment of the regional branch of the CUT. The unions assumed not to be concerned with the alternative proposals and practices are those affiliated either to the CGT or Força Sindical (FS). Thus, both the Textile Industry Workers and the Pharmaceutical Industry Workers are affiliated to the CGT; the Commerce Employees, in turn, are affiliated to Força Sindical (FS).

Having said that, let us have a look in the summary tables.

The question on the *motives for affiliating to the union* is almost obligatory in every study about workers and unions. Authors like Goldthorpe *et al.* (1969; 1970), Fosh (1981) and Korpi (1978) have employed such an item in their researches on workers' attitudes. The alternatives provided as pre-coded answers were mainly drawn from those employed by Korpi to assess the Swedish workers' attitudes towards their unions. The scores ascribed to each answer assumed that the more the respondent departs from the view of the union as a mere source of individual benefit,

Table 6.1   Motives for affiliating to the union: 'Which of the
following motives was the most important for you to become a union
member?'[1]

Occupational category and CUT/non-CUT	Average
Telecommunications Workers (CUT)	3.94
Data Processing Employees (CUT)	3.91
Metalworkers (CUT)	3.81
Bank Employees (CUT)	3.72
Textile Industry Workers (CGT)	3.28
Pharmaceutical Industry Workers (CGT)	3.70
Commerce Employees (FS)	2.54
CUT	3.86
Non-CUT	3.14
Whole sample	3.51

Average range: 1 to 5.[2]

the higher his or her participatory attitudes are likely to
be. Thus, a respondent who joins the union with the purpose of strengthening general collective interests scored
the highest in this item.

The averages scored by each occupational category as
displayed in Table 6.1 are, without exception, higher among
the respondents affiliated to CUT unions. When we split
the entire sample into two groups according to affiliation
or non-affiliation to the CUT we come across results that
again point to more developed attitudes of active citizenship among the respondents under the new unionism influence. Such findings are in line with the hypothesis that
the new unionism helps to develop certain attitudes proper
to the culture of active citizenship even though no definitive
conclusion may be drawn owing to the existence of other
possible factors in operation.

As Fosh stresses, participation in the union's life has to
be understood in both the formal and informal variants.
Among the former she includes those more direct involve-
ments in union organisations such as voting in elections
and frequency to meetings; among the latter, those indirect
ways of relating to unions such as talk with union representatives and reading of union newspapers (1993: 578).
The variable singled out in Table 6.2, *Interaction with shop
stewards and other union representatives*, is therefore a good
indicator of the informal aspect of participation. This variable

Table 6.2   Search for information from the union representatives:
'Do you seek to obtain information from union representatives?'

Occupational category and CUT/non-CUT	Average
Telecommunications Workers (CUT)	3.52
Data Processing Employees (CUT)	3.66
Metalworkers (CUT)	3.74
Bank Employees (CUT)	3.11
Textile Industry Workers (CGT)	2.58
Pharmaceutical Industry Workers (CGT)	3.00
Commerce Employees (FS)	2.41
CUT	3.55
Non-CUT	2.64
Whole sample	3.10

Average range: 1 to 5.

was also included in the already mentioned research carried out by Goldthorpe *et al.* on the affluent workers of Luton (1970: 106). We took it for granted that a good score on this indicator was linked to an active attitude towards the union aspect of the worker's citizenship.

Here again the sub-sample compounded by the occupational categories affiliated to the CUT revealed better results both in the aggregate and the analytical versions. Among the CUT-affiliated unions, even the one which scored lowest – the bank employees – was slightly above the average elicited from the whole sample.

Table 6.3   The role of unions: 'The main function of unions is providing facilities for their members (medical care, lab tests, lawyers, dentists, etc.)'

Occupational category and CUT/non-CUT	Average
Telecommunications Workers (CUT)	3.42
Data Processing Employees (CUT)	3.81
Metalworkers (CUT)	3.19
Bank Employees (CUT)	3.89
Textile Industry Workers (CGT)	2.61
Pharmaceutical Industry Workers (CGT)	2.90
Commerce Employees (FS)	2.32
CUT	3.56
Non-CUT	2.59
Whole sample	3.09

Average range: 1 to 5.

The variable regarding the *role of unions* has to do with deep-rooted assumptions of the corporative framework entrenched in the country's labour relations. Accordingly, the unions are assigned with a mere 'assistential' role, that is, are charged with the handing out of welfare provisions to their members. Such a union role was strengthened by the constraints imposed by the military. Many unions, officials and membership alike, ended up embodying related views. Of course, if a union member breaks away from this traditional stand, it may be said that he or she has developed different attitudes towards unions that, ultimately, are related to the 'active-citizen' culture.

Table 6.3 shows that members affiliated to unions belonging to the new unionism scored invariably higher averages than those belonging to the 'traditional' sector of the labour movement. It is noteworthy that among the CUT's unions the data-processing employees displayed stronger conviction against the conception of a union as mere purveyor of welfare provisions. One should remember that this union has never provided many individual services to membership, since it was founded in the 1980s by activists already committed to the more militant stances of the new unionism. The three other CUT's unions, on the contrary, were taken over by the new unionism activists through electoral disputes against traditional officials who had developed a vast apparatus to provide facilities to members. Arguably, the memory of that long-established role of unions might have played a part in the slight variation of the metalworkers, telecommunications workers, and bank employees on this item compared with the data-processing employees. Particularly in the case of the metalworkers, the attitudes displayed are much in line with the fact that metalworkers in Pernambuco have a strong need of extra social services as a consequence of their very low wages. According to Morais (1993: 68), although its leaders' new unionism approach emphasises mobilisation and struggle for workers' rights, they decided not to discontinue the 'assistential' services in the light of the findings of a survey they had commissioned in 1981 about the option of restricting certain services, the grassroots response being in favour of combining militancy with continued provision of facilities.

Table 6.4   Participation in collective actions: 'How often do you attend the association's initiatives and campaigns such as demonstrations, collective signature of petitions and other kind of pressures?'

Occupational category and CUT/non-CUT	Average
Telecommunications Workers (CUT)	2.32
Data Processing Employees (CUT)	2.25
Metalworkers (CUT)	2.37
Bank Employees (CUT)	1.83
Textile Industry Workers (CGT)	1.81
Pharmaceutical Industry Workers (CGT)	1.77
Commerce Employees (FS)	1.57
CUT	2.23
Non-CUT	1.71
Whole sample	1.98

Average range: 1 to 5.

The lowest scores on this item, in turn, were those of the commerce employees, a finding which dovetails well, consistent with the decisive emphasis put by the union's officials on the supply of welfare provisions to members.

Participation in collective action is an obvious indicator of a civic culture. Almond and Verba, in *The Civic Culture* (1963: 529), included a related question in their interviewee schedule with the purpose of assessing levels of development of civic culture. The same item may be found in the national survey on the Brazilian political culture carried out in the late 1980s by Moisés (1993: 167).

In comparison with the averages elicited from the questions presented in the prior tables, the overall pattern in this item in Table 6.4 is rather lower. Nevertheless, since in all countries the number of people who actually take part in street demonstrations is normally small, high scores in this question would be a little surprising. Such results therefore contribute to reassuring the validity of our scale in that it confirms established patterns of social behaviour. However, it seems relevant to highlight the comparison among the sub-samples of our survey. Once again the data reinforce the plausibility of the hypothesis that the alternative union model makes a difference to workers' attitudes of active citizenship. Both the aggregate scores (CUT and

Table 6.5   Talking about politics: 'What about talking about politics to other people? [How often] do you do that?'

Occupational category and CUT/non-CUT	Average
Telecommunications Workers (CUT)	3.06
Data Processing Employees (CUT)	3.25
Metalworkers (CUT)	3.67
Bank Employees (CUT)	3.44
Textile Industry Workers (CGT)	2.72
Pharmaceutical Industry Workers (CGT)	2.67
Commerce Employees (FS)	2.54
CUT	3.33
Non-CUT	2.64
Whole sample	3.00

Average range: 1 to 5.

non-CUT) and the individual category ones testify to higher levels of our dependent variable being held by new-unionism-linked respondents.

Most surveys on both workers' attitudes and political culture in general have dealt with the variable *talking about politics* (e.g., Goldthorpe *et al.*, 1969: 222; Fosh, 1981: 108; Almond and Verba, 1963: 116, 527; and Moisés, 1993: 166). An active citizen regards politics as a natural part of his or her day-to-day concerns. Not surprisingly, the findings again indicate (Table 6.5) that the workers exposed to the alternative model reported a stronger interest in politics, both at the aggregate and at the levels of the occupational categories.

A similar assumption underlies the variable *trying to persuade voters*. An individual who takes the initiative of campaigning and trying to persuade voters is easily identifiable as an active citizen. With such reasoning in mind, authors like Korpi (1978: 364) and Moisés (1993:167) benefited from that sort of an item in their surveys. The scores displayed in Table 6.6, like those of Table 6.5, confirmed expectations that not many people usually bother to attempt to interfere with voters' decisions. But what matters for the objectives of this research are the comparisons of the sub-samples of the survey population. Without exception, the respondents linked to the 'new unions' were found to hold more active attitudes in regard to endeavouring to influence other people's votes.

Table 6.6   Trying to persuade voters: 'Have you ever tried to persuade other people to vote in a certain way?'

Occupational category and CUT/non-CUT	Average
Telecommunications Workers (CUT)	2.35
Data Processing Employees (CUT)	2.69
Metalworkers (CUT)	2.89
Bank Employees (CUT)	2.61
Textile Industry Workers (CGT)	1.78
Pharmaceutical Industry Workers (CGT)	2.07
Commerce Employees (FS)	1.95
CUT	2.63
Non-CUT	1.92
Whole sample	2.28

Average range: 1 to 5.

Reading of political news is another recurrent indicator addressed by the literature. Interest in political news is an essential element of an active political culture. Putnam (1993), for example, made use of such a variable as one of the four indicators of his index of 'civic-ness' of Italian communities in his study of the Italian political culture, where he discovered differences in the previously existing civic culture across a variety of regions to be the key factor explaining the successful performance of local governments and institutions. While underscoring the importance of *reading of newspaper*, he invokes Tocqueville, who in his *Democracy in America*, praised newspapers as an indispensable means of allowing individuals to communicate in order to build up democratic associations. For Putnam, newspaper readership remains a mark of citizen interest in community affairs.

The pattern of scores we came across (Table 6.7) was fairly consistent with the basic hypothesis being tested in this work. Members of unions operating in accordance with the alternative model scored higher than those of the 'control group'. The exception was the case of metalworkers, who ranked slightly below the pharmaceutical workers; these, in turn, registered the highest scores among the traditional unions. Certainly, newspaper readership is a variable that goes hand in hand with individuals' concrete conditions for reading, both in terms of time and educational levels.

Table 6.7   Reading of political news: 'Do you read political news in magazines and newspapers?'

Occupational category and CUT/non-Cut	Average
Telecommunications Workers (CUT)	3.48
Data Processing Employees (CUT)	3.72
Metalworkers (CUT)	2.96
Bank Employees (CUT)	3.50
Textile Industry Workers (CGT)	2.36
Pharmaceutical Industry Workers (CGT)	3.03
Commerce Employees (FS)	2.62
CUT	3.43
Non-CUT	2.65
Whole sample	3.05

Average range: 1 to 5.

On this specific point, it is notable that among the whole sample, the metalworkers are probably the most exposed to the tiring pressures of the 'production line'. Within the control group, the textile workers match closely the metalworkers' conditions and, nevertheless, score significantly lower on the item.

Watching or listening to political programmes is a variable based on the same theoretical reasons applied to newspaper readership. Interest in public life is congenial to the political culture of active citizenship. Accordingly, most empirical studies on political culture single out this indicator in their respective survey questionnaires (Almond 1963: 527; Moisés, 1993: 185). It must be added that the easier access to radio and TV may compensate for specific structural difficulties experienced by certain individuals due to occupation and educational level. The findings on such an item (Table 6.8) confirm the stereotype that popular strata are more inclined towards the electronic media. Particularly, low-income people tend to listen to the radio throughout the day. Although the overall pattern of higher scores attained by individuals affiliated to the CUT sub-sample was maintained, the case of the textile workers came up as an exception. They were joined by the metalworkers in their significant rise in scores in comparison with the variable newspaper readership of political affairs. Interestingly, both categories are the ones with the higher percentage of blue-

Table 6.8   Watching or listening to political programmes: 'How often do you watch political programmes or news on the TV or listen to them on the radio?'

Occupational category and CUT/non-CUT	Average
Telecommunications Workers (CUT)	3.87
Data Processing Employees (CUT)	3.94
Metalworkers (CUT)	4.07
Bank Employees (CUT)	3.61
Textile Industry Workers (CGT)	3.67
Pharmaceutical Industry Workers (CGT)	3.40
Commerce Employees (FS)	3.32
CUT	3.90
Non-CUT	3.47
Whole sample	3.69

Average range: 1 to 5.

collar workers in industrial production, submitted to excessive working pressures and probably with lower educational levels.

This item, *the sense of civic competence,* was regarded by Almond and Verba as one of the core elements of the civic culture. They dedicated three chapters of *The Civic Culture* to the task of providing a theoretical analysis of data based on the individual's sense of their ability to influence public affairs: 'the self-confident citizen is likely to be the active citizen: to follow politics, to discuss politics, to be a more active partisan' (1963: 257). Following their remarks we included a handful of items in our own scale of active citizenship with the aim of eliciting our sample's attitudes related to that sense of political competence. Data provided in Table 6.9 refer to just one of the items designed to address the issue.

The general scores are not that high, probably reflecting the respondents' evaluation of the course of Brazilian politics, in the belief that the incipient democracy has allowed the powerful to retain a great deal of control over the political process. In any case, the respondents whose unions apply the alternative model attained clearly higher averages than their counterpart. Such data suggest that they feel more confident to intervene in public affairs, and may therefore be more active citizens.

The assumption underlying the item about *readiness to*

Table 6.9   Feelings of political competence: 'The common citizen can hardly do anything to protect his/her interest because things are decided by the powerful'

Occupational category and CUT/non-CUT	Average
Telecommunications Workers (CUT)	2.61
Data Processing Employees (CUT)	2.78
Metalworkers (CUT)	2.85
Bank Employees (CUT)	3.00
Textile Industry Workers (CGT)	2.36
Pharmaceutical Industry Workers 12 – (CGT)	2.50
Commerce Employees (FS)	2.24
CUT	2.79
Non-CUT	2.36
Whole sample	2.58

Average range: 1 to 5.

vote is self-evident. A citizen prepared to vote even under the facultative voting system is much more likely to be an active participant in both the wider polity and in smaller collectivities. As authors like Moisés have stressed (1993: 180), the willingness to take part in elections, even in the case of introduction of facultative voting in the Brazilian political system, is a good indicator of the development of a democratic or civic culture (or as evidence of 'attachment to political values', as he puts it). A high score in this item has consequences for the assessment of an active-citizen culture, particularly because nowadays Brazilians have become markedly disillusioned with politics and politicians. If a respondent's score is high in spite of such a widespread atmosphere, it is a clear sign of attachment to the values of active citizenship. The results presented in Table 6.10 indicate a consistently higher score for those sub-samples whose unions espouse the alternative model. The deviant case on this issue is the one of the metalworkers who, surprisingly, ranked almost at the same level as two of the unions of the 'control group'. We are unable to account for this deviation.

In sum, this preliminary look at some measured attitudes of our survey population reveals a general tendency for the members of unions affiliated to the CUT to embody more active attitudes towards the selected indicators. Higher

Table 6.10   Readiness to vote: 'Would you vote in elections even if it was not mandatory?'

Occupational category and CUT/non-CUT	Average
Telecommunications Workers (CUT)	3.68
Data Processing Employees (CUT)	3.69
Metalworkers (CUT)	3.41
Bank Employees (CUT)	3.72
Textile Industry Workers (CUT)	3.14
Pharmaceutical Industry Workers (CUT)	3.43
Commerce Employees (CUT)	3.43
CUT	3.62
Non-CUT	3.33
Whole sample	3.48

Average range: 1 to 5.

scores were attained by those workers both on attitudes towards unions and towards politics. Because of the reasons discussed above, the few deviant cases are not relevant enough to refute the hypothesis that the alternative union model has fostered the development of what we have termed the active-citizen culture.

However, the association between higher scores in certain indicators and workers' affiliation to 'new unions' is insufficient to support a claim for direct causality. There exists the obvious limitation of mere associations which by no means imply causality. Of course, other factors may be at work in the complex causal chain that produces more developed active-citizen attitudes. Such methodological caution impels us to deepen our analyses by sounder inferences, which may be provided by the multiple regressions necessary to cancel out other possible factors capable of affecting the dependent variable. Therefore, we may provisionally assume that our hypothesis has not been refuted by the 'naked-eye' observation outlined above. Still, prior to presenting the results of the statistical tests, let us have yet another shot at two specific sub-samples of our population. This is the aim of the following section.

3 THE MODEL OF ACTIVE CITIZENSHIP – AGGREGATE SCORES

Now let us turn to considerations on the entire model. We managed to establish a score for each of the 211 respondents. As is well established in the literature on surveys, attitude measuring is not limited to estimating what proportion of the survey population say they subscribe to a given opinion. This is the task of the so-called opinion poll. Instead, measuring attitudes impels the researcher to go 'further and [try] to measure the strength of the opinions held' (Moser, 1958: 221). Thus, the informant's score implies a given level on the measured attitudes, which displays the strength of his or her adherence to the opinions embedded in those attitudes. These scores consist of an average calculated from all the responses to each question of our ordinary attitudes scale. Since each item offers five possible answers (steps of a scale of the ordinary type), this average may range from 1 to 5.

3.1 The Scores of the CUT and Non-CUT Sub-Samples: General and Module Averages

Sections 2 and 3 highlighted the aggregate averages scores by occupational categories on certain selected items of scale. This section, in turn, presents the results elicited from both the 'experimental' group (CUT-affiliated union members) and the 'control' group (non-CUT-affiliated union members) in regard to both the entire scale of active citizenship and each of the four modules that constitute it. As discussed in Chapter 5, the four modules of our scale are the following:

• Module 1: Attitudes towards unions;
• Module 2: Attitudes towards the issue of 'control at work';
• Module 3: Attitudes towards associative life in general;
• Module 4: Attitudes towards politics and the sense of subjective civic competence.

The final score is a composite index that aims to encompass the workers' attitudes in relation to the four issues. The underlying assumption is that a culture of active

Table 6.11   CUT and non-CUT sub-samples: general and modules averages

	General average	*Module 1*	*Module 2*	*Module 3*	*Module 4*
CUT	3.24	3.54	3.56	2.47	3.41
Non-CUT	2.89	3.04	3.30	2.24	3.02
Whole sample	3.07	3.30	3.43	2.35	3.22

citizenship should be assessed on both work-related and political matters. Hence, we extend the analysis of the scores of the sub-samples to each particular module in order to assess their overall consistency in regard to the measured attitudes. Such an analytical procedure has the further advantage of reinforcing the validity of the complete model to measure the envisaged attitudes, inasmuch as we can observe whether the respondents (and aggregates such as the occupational categories) reveal compatible attitudes in each of the modules. Table 6.11 introduces such data.

Table 6.11 reveals the average scores elicited from our two major groups: the respondents whose unions are affiliated to the CUT and those whose unions belong to other sectors of the Brazilian labour movement. The scores of the CUT-affiliated informants, that is, the 'experimental' group, were higher in both the entire model and each of its four modules. In other words, such data suggest that the members of the CUT unions as a whole hold more positive attitudes towards unions, control at work, general associative life and politics. In all these areas they show greater propensity to be informed, critical and participatory.

3.2   The Scores of the Occupational Category Sub-samples: General and Module Averages

Table 6.12 presents a more analytical version of both the general averages and those of the modules by focusing on the occupational categories of our sample.

To begin with the average valid for the complete scale, we observe that on those scores the picture is a straightforward one. The measures taken from the CUT-affiliated occupational categories without exception yielded higher indices of attitudes of active citizenship. Among the 'control

Table 6.12   Occupational categories: general and module average

Categories	General average	Module 1	Module 2	Module 3	Module 4
Telecommunication Workers (CUT)	3.18	3.55	3.48	2.39	3.33
Data Processing Employees (CUT)	3.33	3.58	3.64	2.57	3.51
Metalworkers (CUT)	3.30	3.69	3.63	2.55	3.39
Bank Employees (CUT)	3.11	3.25	3.46	2.28	3.40
Textile Industry Workers (CGT)	2.89	2.99	3.36	2.27	3.01
Pharmaceutical Industry Workers (CGT)	3.08	3.43	3.54	2.30	3.16
Commerce Employees (FS)	2.72	2.77	3.04	2.15	2.92
Whole sample	3.07	3.30	3.43	2.35	3.22

group' categories, it is notable that the pharmaceutical industry workers scored slightly higher than the average of the complete sample even though still below the 'experimental group' categories. One possible factor at work is the circumstance that the pharmaceutical sub-sample was exposed to the public sector's less adverse industrial atmosphere since the respective workers are employed by a publicly owned laboratory, 'Lafepe'.

As for the Module 1, covering attitudes towards unions, the averages of the CUT-linked union members are invariably higher than of those affiliated to other sectors of the labour movement. The remarkable figures in this module are those for the metalworkers whose scores reached the top of the entire sample. Although the wording of the questions here were intended to target the union issue in general, we cannot dismiss the influence of the specific union to which the metalworkers are affiliated. This observation is consistent with the overall performance of such a union since the new unionism activists seized control of it in 1981, as described in Chapter 4. As for Module 2, concerned with the issue of 'control at work', the figures fail to indicate a clear tendency as in the preceding module. Despite the tendency of the CUT-affiliated categories generally to score higher in this module as well, the pharmaceutical workers, who are affiliated to the CGT, attained higher scores than both the telecommunication workers and the bank employees, two categories within the CUT sub-sample. The findings on Module 3, related to overall associative life, reproduce the pattern for the previous one, where the general trend of CUT members' higher scores is rather blurred by the better average attained by the pharmaceutical workers. In this case, the CUT category superseded was the bank employees who scored even lower than the average for the entire sample. Finally, the module on the sense of civic competence yields results which show unequivocal higher indices of the attitudes of active citizenship achieved by the respondents of the control group.

4 THE MODEL OF ACTIVE CITIZENSHIP – REGRESSION ANALYSIS

4.1 Looking at the Results on Each Independent Variable

Having presented the 'naked-eye' provisional observation of the survey results, we proceeded to analyse the same data with the help of the regression statistical tests. As described in Section 2, the respondents' replies to the interview schedule produced scores which vary along the levels of our dependent variable, the attitudes of active citizenship. Such a dependent variable thus formed by each interviewee's average was then submitted to the multiple regressions as a way of analysing the explanatory power of the factors included in the model. This facilitated an assessment as to whether each of the single factors has explanatory power, if any, to the level attained by the respondent in the scale of the attitudes of active citizenship, that is, in the measuring of the dependent variable.

Table 6.13 presents the results of the complete model, including a number of independent variables thought likely to influence the individuals' measured attitudes.

Before concentrating on the analysis of the results on the independent variable of the basic research query – union model – we shall briefly focus on the other factors that make up the model. Let us start with *the firm's number of employees*. As observed in Section 4.4.6 of Chapter 5, this is

Table 6.13   The active-citizen model: the complete version of the multiple regression test

Independent variables	Coefficient	T-statistics	Significance level
1. Constant	1.0831	6.4879	0.0000
2. Firm's number of employees	–0.0077	–1.1078	0.2680
3. Firm's sector: public (1), private (0)	0.0518	2.3176	0.0205
4. Firm's activ.: industry (1), services (0)	0.0988	4.1509	0.0000
5. Number of dependants	0.0045	0.6976	0.4854
6. Gender: male (0), female (1)	–0.0523	–4.3362	0.0000
7. Years of study	0.0159	5.6336	0.0000
8. Age	–0.0896	–1.9841	0.0472
9. Occupation: non-manual/admin/white-coll. (0); manual/product/blue-collar (1)	0.0131	0.7429	0.4576
10. Time in job	0.0101	0.6908	0.4897
11. Interaction at work: high (1); low (3)	–0.1023	–1.9838	0.0473
12. Solidarity at work: low (1); high (4)	0.0551	2.7371	0.0062
13. Time of union membership	0.0449	3.4493	0.0006
14. Income	0.0026	0.9039	0.3661
15. Time of exposure to the CUT model: CUT (number of years); non-CUT (0)	0.0092	4.5290	0.0000

R^2 = 0.436935; total of observations: 211.

a well-established factor affecting unions and workers' behaviour. Features related to the size of the enterprise such as the extent of depersonalisation of the employment relationship, the institutionalisation of perceptions of the employer by employees, the propensity to forge new identities ensuing from common experiences and grievances,[3] are factors believed to exert direct influence on workers' attitudes. Although we had strong theoretical reasons to include such a variable in our model, Table 6.13 shows no statistically significant results in terms of explaining interviewees' scores in our attitudes scale. More precisely, the hypothesis that the number of employees in the firm is not relevant in explaining active citizenship is not rejected at the 10 per cent significance level.

The second variable of the model – *the sector of the enterprise, whether public or private* – produced results statistically significant at 2 per cent. Generally speaking, public sector enterprises are much less likely to dimiss their employees; pressures put on workers in terms of rhythm of work are lighter, whilst the hierarchical relationships are less authoritarian than in the private sector. Hence, public employees might be expected to be more self-confident and more prone to engage in collective actions – a theoretical conjecture which is entirely confirmed by our data. The positive coefficient on Item 2 of Table 6.13 indicates that, as a result of such a condition, the scores in the dependent variable – attitudes of active citizenship – were higher for public sector employees.

The third variable likewise displays statistical significant results at 1 per cent. *Whether the respondents work in the industrial, or service sectors,* was expected to yield different levels in attitudes of active citizenship since traditionally the former has provided the context for more widespread mobilisation. In Brazil, the new unionism itself was born in the industrial ABC region of Sao Paulo. Data on this variable produced a positive coefficient confirming the hypothesis that industrial respondents' attitudes of active citizenship are higher than those of the service sector employees.

The variable *number of dependants* was included on the assumption that a worker with many people living under his or her responsibility is apt to be more cautious in becoming involved with collective initiatives both in relation to the job and to public affairs. According to the positive coefficient presented in Table 6.13, the aforementioned hypothesis was not confirmed, in that it reflects a higher score on the attitudes scale when the number of the interviewee's dependants increases. But as we may infer from the significance level column, the results we came across failed to fulfil the standard significance level requirement (at least 10 per cent).

Regarding the variable *gender*, it has been argued that in general women tend to be more conservative than men regarding political and social endeavours, as Foweraker has argued for the case of Chile (1995: 59, 110). Taking women's specific attitudes towards unionisation, however, the literature has been more controversial. In Britain, as early as 1957, in his classic study on the class-consciousness of clerks, Lockwood concluded that gender was not a factor playing a noticeable part either for or against the unionisation of white-collar workers. After quoting Bernard Shaw's assertion that clerks and women were the most resistant social categories to unionism, Lockwood demonstrated that his data failed to validate such a contention about a supposed inherent characteristic. In fact, he found only slight differences between the proportions of women employed in the firm or trade sector represented by the union and those actually unionised (Lockwood [1958] 1989: 151). Nonetheless, he acknowledges that on the whole female workers tend to earn lower salaries, experience fewer opportunities for promotion, find work in smaller establishments and hold part-time jobs. Lockwood observes that differences in union membership caused by gender are better explained by factors related to the opportunity to join a union and the part-time type of employment (1989: 256). Identical hampering obstacles for the women in the labour market were underlined by Humphrey (1987) in his study of the gender divisions of the Brazilian industrial labour force carried out in the early 1980s. He challenges the neo-classical economic formulations which see the sexual cleavages of the labour market as being shaped outside it, particularly by household decisions that affect the quantity and quality of the labour power the woman is able to offer in the labour market. The relations of gender in society as a whole penetrate the employment situation and structure the roles, division of labour and the distinctive identities of workers as either 'male workers' or 'female workers'. The social sexual divisions are thus reproduced and reinforced within the factory or firm. In consequence, women are allocated to low-paid functions and experience reduced employment opportunities. Such formidable hindrances faced by women are thus important factors determining a lower likelihood of developing participatory and critical attitudes, leading them to assume a more conservative outlook on a variety of socio-political matters. In Brazil, stratified opinion polls have regularly demonstrated that the female electorate normally endorse more conservative candidates in successive elections. In line with such a pattern, our female sample ranked lower in the scale of the attitudes of active citizenship. Female was given number one, and male, number zero. Thus the negative coefficient implies a reversed relation in the score: the higher the independent variable – female – the lower the score on the measured attitudes. Again, this result complied with the basic requirement of statistical significance.

The variable related to the educational level of the informants, *years of study,* exerts an obvious influence in the individual ability to muster all the skills and other enabling conditions to take a stand in both work-related and political issues. The figures displayed in item 7 of Table 6.13 signal that the theoretical assumptions about the positive effect of education were fully validated by our sample. The positive coefficient and the fulfilment of the standard requisit of statistical significance imply that higher educational attainments lead to more developed attitudes of active citizenship.

Variable number 8, *informant's age,* was stipulated on the grounds that elderly people tend to be more cautious in their critical and participatory stances. Diminishing perspectives of finding other jobs and growing inclination for accommodation may underlie such a generally accepted tendency. The statistically significant results (see third column in Table 6.13) on the age variable underscore the strength of the hypothesis that elderly individuals tend to hold less active attitudes. As occurred with the variable *gender,* the reversed relation means that the higher the age of individuals the lower their score in our attitudes scale. Such findings parallel those of Peter Ranis's survey of Argentine workers held in 1985–6[4] (1992: 144–5). His sample encompassed workers in Greater Buenos Aires belonging to seven occupational categories, some of them coinciding with those of the present study, such as telecommunications workers, bank employees, metalworkers and textile workers. In addition to other convergent results on this variable, it is noteworthy that in his study, too, conservatism increased along the age continuum. Elderly workers

were found to have a greater propensity to describe themselves as 'centre-right' while the youngest were more inclined to a 'centre-left' self-description.

The incorporation of the dichotomous variable on the
type of occupation (manual, production or blue-collar, on the
one hand; and non-manual, administrative, or white-collar,
on the other) into the model sprang from the widespread
contention in the literature that production workers (generally
in industry) have the stronger records of industrial action
and mobilisation. Although the encountered results were
not statistically significant by standard patterns, the positive coefficient may suggest that manual workers in production scored higher. The assessment concerning the greater
propensity of workers in production to engage in collective action has long been put forward in the literature.
Lockwood's (1989) investigation on the class-consciousness
of the 'blackcoated' was set up as a departure of the once
common idea that 'white collar' workers held 'false consciousness'. After dismissing the adequacy and validity of
the very notion of 'false consciousness', he points out that
the peculiarity of the white-collar class position or social
situation inevitably affected their class-consciousness and
preparedness for concerted action. Typically, white-collar
employees enjoyed different market situation, working conditions and social status from manual workers. Contrasting with their counterparts, the non-manual tended to be
better paid, enjoying more job security and greater prospects
of occupational mobility. Such a differentiation among the
propertyless sellers of labour power in the market undermined the notion of the homogeneous interests that according to classical Marxism moved the entire labour force
to join in common efforts to transform the social order.
Drawing on data for the specific situation of the clerks, as
outlined above, Lockwood explained their more amenable
attitudes towards collective action and other features commonly displayed by the manual wage-earners as deriving
from those peculiarities. With all the necessary caution stemming from the failure of our sample to yield a statistically
significant result on this variable, the positive coefficient
would indicate that those assumptions were not gainsaid.
Such a line of reasoning conflicts, however, with other studies

addressing the question of differentiation among manual and non-manual labour. The national survey on Brazilian political culture carried out by Moisés in 1989–90 (1993: 177), for example, found that non-manual workers displayed higher degrees of political awareness than manuals. Similar findings were again reached by Ranis's survey on the workers of Greater Buenos Aires. His data unveiled a much stronger involvement of white-collar employees both with union and political party activism (cf. pp. 116–18). Given such contradictory interpretations, our provisional data intends to provide no conclusive account of the influence of this variable on workers' attitudes. For the time being we restrict ourselves to calling attention to the need for further research on the issue.

The following independent variable in the model is the one dealing with *time in job*, that is, the time the informant has held his or her current job. Underlying such a variable is the idea that a worker with a lasting job is likely to feel more confident initially and then adopt more critical and participatory stances. He or she is thought to become more 'subjectively competent' in the sense of the already quoted literature (Almond and Verba, 1963; Pateman, 1970). By analogy, Lockood envisages the feelings of stability as one of the factors of the distinctive market situation of the white-collar employees capable of affecting their attitudes (1989: 204). The findings on that variable also necessitate caution due to its lack of statistical significance. Nevertheless, there is a case for suggesting that the longer the worker has been in the current job, the higher his or her measure on the scale of active citizenship. Such a pattern would be consistent with the assumptions already referred to.

Variable number 11, *interaction at work*, as has been spelled out in Section 4.4.6 of Chapter 5, draws on Goldthorpe *et al.*'s (1970: 49–50) analysis of the factors, among them the technological constraints, which affect the shop-floor relations and the formation of work groups. Although the amount of conversation during work cannot be regarded as the only determinant of a variable like 'interaction at work', presumably workers who often talk to each other are more likely to be integrated at their respective work groups. This integration is an important element to enable them to get involved in collective and active undertakings. Hence, to assess degrees of interaction at work, we followed the mentioned authors by asking the respondents about the frequency of their talking to working mates during work. The replies were classified in three levels; reported frequent conversations were given score 1; 'now and then', score 2; and 'almost never', score 3. Therefore the measured 'interaction at work' decreases in the direction from score 1 to 3. Item 11 of Table 6.13 reveals a negative coefficient, that is, the higher the figure attributed to the independent variable, the lower the level of the dependent variable. Since a high figure in the independent variable means a low level of 'interaction at work', the results imply that workers with lower 'interaction at work' scored lower in the scale of attitudes of active citizenship. Such findings evidently complied with the statistical significance requirement and this may be regarded as consistent with the theoretical assumption put forward above.

The variable on *solidarity at work*, as it was made clear in the prior paragraph, was also borrowed from Goldthorpe *et al.*'s (1970: 49–50) research on industrial attitudes of workers in the motorvehicle industry at Luton, in Britain. The assumption is that a worker well integrated with his or her working group will be more disposed to engage in collective action and hold values that we are defining as integrating a culture of active citizenship. The possible levels of attachment were conceived in relation to the respondent's feeling in the event of being forced away from the current working group even though to perform identical tasks under the same wage or salary. Score 1 in the scale of 'active citizenship' means that the worker would not mind being transferred and consequently is considered to experience less solidarity at work. Score 2 means 'minding a bit'; score 3, 'being upset'; and score 4, 'being very upset'. The presence of the variable therefore is assumed to increase in the direction from 'not mind' to 'very upset'. As it emerges from item 12 of Table 6.13, the finding confirmed the theoretical contention as long as the positive coefficient implies that the more upset the worker feels about the idea of being transferred (and then, the higher his or her solidarity), the higher he or she scores on the dependent variable. Such a correlation was also found to be statistically significant under standard significance levels.

Time of union membership, in turn, has to do with the notion that a worker tends to become more critical, participatory and self-confident the longer he or she stays in the union, which suggests that the impact of union membership is cumulative with time. Again, the results were statistically significant as is shown in the third column of item 13. The positive coefficient signifies that workers' scores on the dependent variable are higher as a consequence of increasing length of union membership.

Before analysing the variable involved in the basic research query of this survey, a task we undertake in Section 4.4, let us direct our attention to the last co-factor included in the model: *the respondent's income*. Particularly in a context like the Brazilian, higher incomes are connected with the access to resources that ultimately work as necessary preconditions to the embracing of active-citizen attitudes. To start with, education is highly associated with income. Better-educated people almost invariably attain better-paid jobs, subsequently feeling more confident to develop independent and critical attitudes. They can also afford to acquire the facilities necessary to gain access to information. Further, being better educated and more affluent, they are placed in a privileged position to understand and manipulate information, and so on. All these circumstances combine to make the income variable a major factor shaping workers' attitudes. Whilst one might expect lower-paid workers to have greater incentives to mobilise against deprivation, in effect it is the better remunerated who tend to be more militant because they are also better educated and possess more resources to act. The regression presented in Table 6.13, however, produced results that justify a cautious approach to any inferences as long as they do not meet the standard requirement of statistical significance. The positive coefficient would suggest that the scores elicited from our sample are in line with the contention put forward above. This means that higher wages and salaries would cause higher attitudes of 'active citizenship' as long as the multiple regression allows the assumption that the 'other factors' have been maintained 'equal'.

In the foregoing paragraph we alluded to the solid association between *education* and *income*. This observation calls for a close examination of the possible influence mutually exerted on each other. Both the literature and our statistical test provide apparent grounds for the understanding of such a correlation. In the already invoked study on the contemporary Brazilian political culture, Moisés (1993: 176) underlines how *education* and *income* are bound together in the country's society:

> It would be fanciful to think that the 'conservative modernisation' put into practice by the military governments in Brazil would have profoundly altered the pattern of inequality which lies at the root of the paradigm in which those with higher incomes are those with better education and with non-manual jobs, and who at the same time are those who participate more in public life.

Occupation, income and education, according to the same author, form the 'tripod of political participation'. Such a strong link between the variables *education* and *income* implies that the potential impact of the latter on the respondent's attitudes has already been captured by the former. This interpretation is ratified by Table 6.14, where we restrict ourselves to looking at the explanatory contribution of education to income measures. Self-evidently, in Table 6.14, the variable income is turned into the dependent variable.

The indice for R^2, the coefficient of determination, means that the variable *years of study* (education) alone accounts for 27.47 per cent of the explanation of the measures of the variable *income*. Moreover, they are correlated in a positive direction. The better educated the respondent, the higher he or she scores on income. Typically, their correlation leads to a phenomenon of 'multicollinearity'[5] in the original model when the two variables are included.

Bearing in mind such theoretical and statistical remarks, in Table 6.15 we present the figures of our model without the variable *years of study* with the chief aim of examining the effect of its absence on the results of the variable *income*.

Table 6.15 invites some remarks. Firstly, the figures for the variable *income* became statistically significant when

Table 6.14   The effect of education on income

Independent variables	Coefficient	T-Statistic	Significance level
Constant	0.3338	2.2689	0.0233
Years of study	0.0987	6.8877	0.5670

R^2 = 0.2747; total of observations: 211.

Table 6.15   The complete model excluding the variable 'education'

Independent variables	Coefficient	T-statistics	Significance level
1. Constant	1.5280	10.6723	0.0000
2. Firm's number of employees	−0.0054	−0.7475	0.4547
3. Firm's sector: public (1); private (0)	0.0751	3.0831	0.0020
4. Firm's activ.: industry (1); services (0)	0.0704	2.6798	0.0074
5. Number of dependants	0.0021	0.2979	0.7657
6. Gender: male (0), female (1)	−0.0370	−2.9038	0.0037
7. Age	−0.1848	−4.4803	0.0000
8. Type of occupation: non-manual/bureauc-admin/ white-collar (0), manual/prod/ blue-collar (1)	−0.0026	−0.1341	0.8933
9. Time in job	0.0203	1.4458	0.1482
10. Interaction at work: high (1); low (3)	−0.1178	−2.1501	0.0316
11. Solidarity at work: low (1); high (4)	0.0556	2.6394	0.0083
12. Time of union membership	0.0511	3.7356	0.0002
13. Income	0.0075	2.6871	0.0072
14. Union model: CUT (no. of years); non-CUT (0)	0.0090	4.1590	0.0000

R^2 = 0.366414; total of observations: 211.

education ceased to be inserted into the model. Moreover, the positive coefficient indicates that higher scores in the attitudes scale were achieved by better-paid interviewees. The hypothesis that links positively the attitudes of active citizenship to *income* levels was thus fully confirmed by the survey data.

A comparison between Tables 6.13 and 6.15 unveils a general pattern of similar results. Nevertheless, there were two exceptions formed by the items which altered either the significance level or the direction of the coefficient. It is safe to argue that such an occurrence is caused by certain variables capturing effects otherwise conveyed by others. Besides the already described case of the variable *income*, the item on *the type of occupation* also presented changes from one version of the model to the other. This independent variable was conceived to encompass two basic levels: the manual or production workers and the non-manual or administrative ones. Despite being regarded by the literature as important factors in the shaping of workers' attitudes, as already noted in Chapter 5, both measures failed to yield statistically significant scores. In Table 6.13 the manual workers scored higher levels in the focused attitudes. By contrast, in Table 6.15, the non-manual workers scored higher. Notwithstanding the lack of significance this is another issue inviting further research. But leaving aside the two mentioned exceptions, all the other variables continued in the same position of significance in both tables and identical direction of causality, whether positive or negative. Accordingly to methodology developed by Lerner and used by Levine and Renelt (1992), the results concerning these variables are deemed really robust.

4.2   The Variable 'Union Model'

Now is the time to scrutinise the independent variable that was conceived with our general hypothesis. As already discussed in Chapter 5, we set out to investigate the claim that the alternative union model practised by the Brazilian new unionism has fostered certain workers' attitudes definable as the attitudes of active citizenship. Instead of inquiring into whether those unions have expanded their members' citizenship in terms of winning rights (extensions of entitlements, in Dahrendorf's expression), we concentrate on the more basic stage of the development of a political culture envisaged as a necessary precondition to the attainment of those entitlements.

Moreover, we departed from previous studies that had

looked into the Brazilian new unionism, aiming to test its claim to have developed a more democratic model of unionism. Particularly the work by Morais (1992) on seven 'new unions' in the state of Pernambuco provided the framework of what we envisaged as a promising research programme: the investigation of the new unionism in the light of testing their chief claims to be more democratic than the traditional union model and at the same time to extend workers' citizenship. Drawing on extensive empirical data gathered from Pernambuco's urban 'new unions', Morais' study validated the hypothesis that those unions are more accountable and responsive towards their membership, and therefore, are more legitimate than the other models of unionism still existing in the Brazilian labour relations panorama.

Our hypothesis goes beyond Morais' findings in the sense that once the democratic character of Brazilian new unionism is granted, a further step towards its understanding is concerned with its effect on the political culture of its constituency. In other words, what are the effects of democratic leadership and practices of the new unionism on the political culture of the rank-and-file? As discussed in Chapter 5, we advanced a general hypothesis identified both from reality (the new unionism's claim to develop workers' citizenship) and theory alike (the contention that the new unionism, being more democratic, has contributed to asserting the workers' citizenship).

The multiple regression statistical test measures the explanatory contribution of different independent variables believed to cause variations in the levels of the dependent variable. As already advanced, the latter was comprised by the attitudes of active citizenship of union members. To facilitate comparison of different models of unionism with regard to differences in the political culture of union members we conceived of two basic categories. Accordingly, unions affiliated to the CUT and having had a role in its development were assumed to practise the alternative union model, despite the continuance of clear differences of level even among themselves. Unions not affiliated to the CUT, and hence not committed to the alternative union model, were conceived to provide the 'control group'.

With the inclusion of the independent variable 'union model', therefore, we aimed to measure levels of exposure to the alternative model practised by the CUT unions. Such different levels of exposure were measured by the number of years the sample unions had been under the control of leadership committed to the alternative model. The longer a union was under the CUT model, the longer the time its members had been exposed to its effects. Accordingly, while the unions not concerned with the alternative model were given score 0, the 'experimental group' constituted by the CUT unions were attributed the following levels:

- Metalworkers: 14 years
- Telecommunication Workers: 11 years
- Data Processing Employees: 10 years
- Bank Employees: 8 years

In order to find out if the union model had explanatory power in the scores on the measured attitudes attained by our survey population, the results needed to meet the requirements of both significance (the third column in Tables 6.13 and 6.15) and positivity of the coefficient. In fact, as is easily noticeable from the scores for this item, both the statistical significance and the positivity of its coefficient indicate that the longer the respondents have been exposed to the CUT model, the higher they score in the scale of attitudes of active citizenship. Moreover, the compliance of the statistical significance requirement at standard levels in the two versions of the complete model (Tables 6.13 and 6.15) attests that this result is robust.

The employed type of multivariate analysis – multiple regression – works as though 'everything else was constant' (Oppenheim, 1992: 27). To put it another way, such a positive coefficient implies the controlling of all the other factors included in the model. Of course these other factors are not expected to respond to all the conceivable variables shaping workers' attitudes. As we see from the coefficient of determination (R^2) of both Tables 6.13 and 6.15, the model accounts for almost 50 per cent of the variance of the dependent variable. This means that the selected independent variables can explain almost half the variations of our sample's attitudes. Given the natural difficulties of asserting causal relations in the social sciences, a model accounting for something between 40 per cent and 50 per cent of the 'explanation' of the dependent variable is generally accepted (Oppenheim, 1992: 28). Granted that within the social sciences the kind of measures we attempt – measures of attitudes – raise more complex issues than measures concerned only with demographic characteristics, or even opinions, we have good reasons to think that the 'explanatory' power of our model was satisfactory enough.

That said, to finish this section we reassert that the higher attitudes of active citizenship held by workers of our sample who are affiliated to 'new unions' proved to rest upon the model adopted by their unions. Even though such a factor is not the only one at work in the explanation of the variation within our attitudes scale, it was found to be a factor endowed with individual (and disentangled) explanatory power. One could therefore claim that within our sample the workers affiliated to the CUT's unions adopt more developed attitudes of active citizenship as a consequence of increasing exposure to the alternative model of labour relations espoused by those unions. Furthermore, as the following chapter discusses, qualitative data and theoretical assumptions incline us to accept the generalisation of those findings to larger settings than that of our sample.

5   THE PROBLEM OF CAUSAL DIRECTION

In Section 4.2 we put forward a strong conclusion drawn from the application of the multiple regression statistical test to the survey data. We saw that such a test works as if the other independent variables were controlled altogether, that is, if other things were equal. The controlling out of other factors implies that the independent variables being focused might bear a relationship of causation to the measured dependent variable. In this study, the member's exposure to the alternative model practised by his or her union explains to a certain degree the score he or she attained in the attitudes scale. In other words, the alternative model of unionism causes members' attitudes, although not alone.

Obviously, any talk of attitudes being shaped by certain union models rests on an underlying assumption about a causal direction at work. This causal relation goes *from* the practice of the union model *towards* political culture. A union model such as we are referring to entails both organisational arrangements and practices. On the one hand, the way the union organises, its deliberative bodies (general assembly, directorate, workplace organisations) and the facilities it affords, are all aspects that might arguably be encompassed by the union organisational arrangements. On the other, the way the union bargains with employers, its relationship to the State, the links between members and officials and its general leadership style are factors which make up what we are terming 'union practices'.[6] Thus, union organisational structures and practices combine to shape members' political culture.

This general pattern of causal direction has been identified in the literature. Putnam (1993: 89), for instance, in his seminal research on civic culture and institutional performance in Italy, accepts that social structures and practices influence political culture. As he puts it 'the norms and values of the civic community are embodied in, and reinforced by, distinctive social structures and practices'. The reference to reinforcement suggests that the other direction is also at work in the shaping of the 'civic culture'. What then emerges is a picture of a complex causal network where both structure and culture are concomitantly and mutually influencing each other.

This issue was the object of an interesting debate on the Almond and Verba's *Civic Culture* (1965). One of the major criticisms of that work – perhaps even the chief bone of contention for critics such as Barry (1970) – was that the imputation of a causal direction from political culture towards political structure (democratic stable institutions) is both threoretically and empirically unsatisfactory, even implausible. In reply to their critics, in the opening chapter of the *Civic Culture Revisited* (1980), Almond and Verba emphasised that 'cultural patterns' in the sampled countries were not absolute givens but were themselves explained by reference to particular historical experiences, such as the sequence of Reform Acts in Britain, the American heritage of British institutions, the Mexican Revolution, and Nazism and defeat in World War II for Germany. In short, he acknowledges the weight of 'socialisation experiences' (through which structure acts) in shaping 'beliefs, feelings and values' (culture). Thus, for these authors, 'it is quite clear that political culture is treated as both an independent and a dependent variable, as causing structure and as being caused by it' (1980: 28–9). Allowing for the existence of both causal directions implies the recognition that each of them constitutes an analytical moment of explanation of social causal networks. As Lijphart (1980: 47) puts it, the analytical nature of such a distinction does not warrant any conclusion about definitive positions of variables as cause and effect.

In the present research design, we recognise such a double causal direction between structures and practices (union models) and culture (members' attitudes). But for analytical purposes we confine ourselves to the study of one of the directions of causality, namely, the effect of the union model on workers' attitudes. As pointed out in Chapter 5, such a choice is grounded on the objective of testing a claim put forward by the new unionism according to which the alternative practices bolster workers' citizenship. The close focus on this analytical causal relationship attempts to move the study of the new unionism from rhetorical claims towards a close scrutiny of empirical and quantitative data. As we have argued, the sample surveyed permits a positive inference about the effect of the new unionism on the development of attitudes conducive to citizenship.

The other direction of causality, that is, from workers' attitudes and political culture towards the union organisational arrangements and practices, albeit not being the focus of this study, is an issue that needs to be addressed for the sake of the clarification of the argument. Once this other possible direction of causality is recognised, the problem of 'reverse causality' surfaces. One could argue that the occupational categories affiliate to the alternative unions because of certain already held characteristics, among them, certain prior attitudes of their members. Yet the argument fails to hold for two basic reasons. Firstly, the attitudes of the members of occupational categories which are capable of determining their model of union need to be attitudes held by the whole category or, at least, an expressive majority. In the statistical test undertaken in this study, however, each individual is a sample in itself. Hence, the measured attitudes are individually held rather than being attributes of the whole category. Of course, the attitudes of any one member alone *does not* affect the adoption of the union model by the entire occupational category. Secondly, even if an indirect mediation – the individual's attitudes determining the model followed by the category – was feasible at all, the design of the statistical test would provide further assurance about the validity of the causal direction focused in this study. As noted above, the test attempted to capture the effect of a continued exposition to the alternative model on workers' attitudes. This is true because the independent variable *union model* was measured in levels related to the years of exposure to it. *Thus, even if a given category had adopted the alternative model because of previously held characteristics of the rank and file, the effect of the model would be captured anyway by the positive relation found between the longer exposure to the model and the higher levels of the dependent variable.*

Still bearing in mind this problem, one could argue that the variable *solidarity at work*, which was used as one of the independent variables of this study's model, would introduce reverse causality because it represents personal attitudes of individual respondents. Moreover, it could be thought that such a variable would be biased in that it would constitute an intrinsic element of the alternative conceptions. Although the reasons provided in the precedent paragraph also seem sufficient to overcome such a way of reasoning in relation to this specific variable, in Tables 6.16 and 6.17 we present two other versions of the regression proceeding without *solidarity at work*, one including the variable *years of study* and the other excluding it.

Comparing the version of the model presented in the Table 6.16 with that of Table 6.13 what emerges is the confirmation of virtually all the previous results. None of the variables changed either the direction of the coefficient or the compliance with the standard significance levels. Whether one accepts the methodological soundness of the variable *solidarity at work* or not, identical results were reached

Table 6.16   The complete model excluding 'solidarity at work'

Independent variables	Coefficient	T-statistics	Significance level
1. Constant	1.0987	6.2373	0.0000
2. Firm's number of employees	−0.0096	−1.3264	0.1847
3. Firm's sector: public (1); private (0)	0.0607	2.7061	0.0068
4. Firm's activ.: industry (1); services (0)	0.1061	4.3206	0.0000
5. Number of dependants	0.0028	0.4381	0.6613
6. Gender: male (0), female (1)	−0.0497	−4.0465	0.0001
7. Years of study	0.0159	5.4819	0.0000
8. Age	−0.0856	−1.8131	0.0698
9. Occupation: non-manual/ admin/white-collar (0); manual/product/ blue-collar (1)	0.0101	0.5707	0.5682
10. Time in job	0.0118	0.7950	0.4266
11. Interaction at work: high (1); low (3)	−0.1202	−2.2541	0.0242
12. Time of union membership	0.0485	3.5919	0.0003
13. Income	0.0015	0.5200	0.6031
14. Time of exposure to the CUT model: CUT (no. of years); non-CUT (0)	0.0097	4.7005	0.0000

R^2 = 0.415996; total of observations: 211.

in its presence or absence. As a consequence, the survey findings gain further evidence of robustness.

In this version of the test (Table 6.17) where we dropped the variables *solidarity at work* and *years of study*, once again the general pattern of relationships is maintained. If one compares this table with the preceding one the only important variation is the acquired statistical significance of the variable *income*. Due to the solid correlation of the latter with *years of study*, the effect of the former becomes apparent when both variable are 'disentangled'. The same evidence had arisen from the comparison of Tables 6.13 and 6.15, where the variable *solidarity at work* had been included in both versions and the one concerned with *years of study* had been dropped in the second variant.

Table 6.17   The model without both 'solidarity at work' and 'years of study'

Independent variables	Coefficient	T-statistics	Significance level
1. Constant	1.5449	10.3788	0.0000
2. Firm's number of employees	−0.0072	−0.9817	0.3262
3. Firm's sector: public (1); private (0)	0.0841	3.4735	0.0005
4. Firm's activ.: industry (1); services (0)	0.0778	2.8863	0.0039
5. Number of dependants	0.0004	0.0573	0.9543
6. Gender: male (0), female (1)	−0.0344	−2.6781	0.0074
7. Age	−0.1810	−4.2677	0.0000
8. Type of occupation: non-manual/bureauc-admin/ white-collar (0), manual/ prod/blue-collar (1)	−0.0057	−0.2958	0.7674
9. Time in job	0.0221	1.5630	0.1181
10. Interaction at work	−0.1358	−2.3755	0.0175
11. Time of union membership	0.0547	3.9004	0.0001
12. Income	0.0064	2.2954	0.0217
13. Union model: CUT (years); non-CUT (0)	0.0096	4.3403	0.0000

R^2 = 0.345107; total of observations: 211.

6   THE REGRESSIONS TAKING THE MODULES AS DEPENDENT VARIABLES

The scale of attitudes of active citizenship employed in this work is formed by four modules. Each of them attempts to elicit the sample's attitudes in a particular domain, namely, in respect of unions, the issue of control at work, general associative life, and politics. Attitudes towards these four domains were brought together in a single scale on the assumption that the kind of attitudes being measured are likely to emerge in relation to all of them. Hence, the general hypothesis that the alternative union model boosts attitudes of active citizenship was assumed to hold true in relation to every one of the single modules that make up the entire scale. To check the validity of this assumption it is necessary to cast a look at the regressions which take the sample's

Table 6.18   Regression for the Module 1: attitudes towards unions

Independent variables	Coefficient	T-statistics	Significance level
1. Constant	0.7770	3.7994	0.0001
2. Firm's number of employees	−0.0102	−1.2350	0.2168
3. Firm's sector: public (1); private (0)	0.1096	4.3152	0.0000
4. Firm's activ.: industry (1); services (0)	0.1219	4.0032	0.0000
5. Number of dependants	0.0019	0.2453	0.8062
6. Gender: male (0); female (1)	−0.0439	−3.1795	0.0015
7. Years of study	0.0172	4.7619	0.0000
8. Age	−0.0265	−0.4770	0.6333
9. Occupation: non-manual/ admin/white-collar (0); manual/product/ blue-collar (1)	0.04498	1.98340	0.0473
10. Time in job	0.0152	0.8418	0.3999
11. Interaction at work: high (1); low (3)	−0.1166	−1.7314	0.0834
12. Solidarity at work: low (1); high (4)	0.0756	3.1340	0.0017
13. Time of union membership	0.0605	3.6275	0.0003
14. Income	−0.0009	−0.3254	0.7449
15. Time of exposure to the CUT model: CUT (number of years); non-CUT (0)	0.01397	5.4981	0.0000

R^2 = 0.473068; total of observations: 211.

replies given to each module. In those regressions, therefore, the dependent variable *workers' attitudes* is considered only in relation to each specific module. To begin with, let us present in Table 6.18 the regression with the sample's scores attained in the questions of Module 1, those concerning attitudes towards unions.

The figures for Table 6.18, although mirroring the active attitudes concerning the narrower domain of *union matters*, are very consistent with those valid for the entire scale presented in Table 6.13. The minor exceptions are *age*, *type of occupation* and *income*. In the two former cases, the standard statistically significant situation is altered. In the

Table 6.19   Regression for the Module 2: attitudes towards 'control at work'

Independent variables	Coefficient	T-statistics	Significance level
1. Constant	1.2683	6.7254	0.0000
2. Firm's number of employees	−0.0061	−0.6934	0.4881
3. Firm's sector: public (1); private (0)	0.0547	2.4224	0.0154
4. Firm's activ.: industry (1); services (0)	0.0994	3.3997	0.0007
5. Number of dependants	0.0109	1.6847	0.0921
6. Gender: male (0); female (1)	−0.0493	−3.5232	0.0004
7. Years of study	0.0125	3.7475	0.0002
8. Age	−0.0952	−1.8595	0.0630
9. Occupation: non-manual/ admin/white-collar (0); manual/product/ blue-collar (1)	0.0105	0.5153	0.6063
10. Time in job	0.0004	0.0243	0.9806
11. Interaction at work: high (1); low (3)	−0.0978	−1.6119	0.1070
12. Solidarity at work: low (1); high (4)	0.0375	1.8496	0.0644
13. Time of union membership	0.0421	2.3115	0.0208
14. Income	0.0039	1.4330	0.1519
15. Time of exposure to the CUT model: CUT (no. of years); non-CUT (0)	0.0062	2.7320	0.0063

R2 = 0.473068; total of observations: 211.

case of *age*, the numbers found are not statistically significant any more, while with *type of occupation* the findings become statistically significant by standard levels. With *income*, once again, the results are apparently influenced by its highly correlated variable *years of study*. As already analysed in Section 4.1, Table 6.14 the hypothesis that the *income*'s effect is captured by the *years of study*'s was confirmed by a variant of this regression carried without the latter (Table 6.15). In that case, the positive coefficient of *income* (0.0075) became statistically significant as one may infer from the third column (0.007). Because a similar variation of Table 6.18 practically repeated the same procedure and results of Table 6.15 (where we dropped the variable *years of study* in the regression of the entire model) we abstained from presenting all the figures we came across. But what seems worth remarking on from Table 6.18 is the consistency of the findings in respect to the variable *union model*, the main focus of this study. The positive coefficient and the compliance with the standard levels of statistical significance imply that the interviewees' attitudes of active citizenship in relation to union matters are higher when they are exposed to higher levels of the independent variable, namely, the alternative union model.

The regression presented in Table 6.19, concerning attitudes towards *the issue of 'control at work'*, unveils only slight variations in comparison with that valid for the entire model. The findings for the variable *number of dependants* now are imbued with statistical significance and, hence, rebut the hypothesis that a higher number of dependants hinders the development of active attitudes. But once more the general hypothesis about the influence exerted on workers' attitudes by continuing exposure to the CUT's union model is well confirmed in this narrowly focused domain of conflicts at work.

Table 6.20 introduces the figures for the regression for the module on attitudes towards *associative life in general*. Among the four modules this is the one which manifests more variations in relation to the complete model whose regression was conveyed by Table 6.13. Although those variations do not affect the independent variable of the basic hypothesis of this work, it may be illustrative to have a glance at those numbers. The variables *firm's sector, age, interaction at work* and *solidarity at work* cease to produce statistically significant results; the variables *number of dependants* and *time in job*, in turn, change direction though continuing to miss the standard levels of statistical significance. In regard to the variable union model, the results persist, corroborating the hypothesis that longer exposure to the CUT's model leads to an increase in workers' attitudes of active citizenship. This time the hypothesis is confirmed within the narrower scope of the questions addressing the attitudes towards associative life.

Table 6.20   Regression for the Module 3: attitudes towards associative life

Independent variables	Coefficient	T-statistics	Significance level
1. Constant	0.5708	2.4056	0.0161
2. Firm's number of employees	−0.0059	−0.5504	0.5821
3. Firm's sector: public (1); private (0)	0.0128	0.3683	0.7126
4. Firm's activ.: industry (1); services (0)	0.1105	3.3212	0.0009
5. Number of dependants	−0.0052	−0.5207	0.6026
6. Gender: male (0); female (1)	−0.0462	−2.2168	0.0266
7. Years of study	0.0175	4.1263	0.0000
8. Age	−0.0199	−0.3024	0.7624
9. Occupation: non-manual/ admin/white-collar (0); manual/product/ blue-collar (1)	0.0064	0.2282	0.8195
10. Time in job	−0.0085	−0.4287	0.6681
11. Interaction at work: high (1); low (3)	−0.0305	−0.4379	0.6615
12. Solidarity at work: low (1); high (4)	0.0351	1.1619	0.2453
13. Time of union membership	0.0466	2.4504	0.0142
14. Income	0.0011	0.2176	0.8277
15. Time of exposure to the CUT model: CUT (no. of years); non-CUT (0)	0.0090	3.1407	0.0017

R^2 = 0.191861; total of observations: 211

The module addressed by the regression displayed in Table 6.21 gathered the questions on attitudes towards politics and the feeling of subjective competence. Its results are very close to those of the complete model presented in Table 6.13. Minor variations are detected in the following variables: *firm's sector*, whose results are no longer statistically significant; *type of occupation*, where the coefficient changes direction but remains without statistical significance; and, finally, *income*. The results for the latter in this module comply with the standard levels of statistical significance even if we fail to account for the variable *years of study*. In conformity with the overall pattern of the other modules, the findings for

Table 6.21   Regression for Module 4: attitudes towards politics and sense of civic competence

Independent variables	Coefficient	T-statistics	Significance level
1. Constant	1.4262	6.9464	0.0000
2. Firm's number of employees	−0.0083	−1.0172	0.3090
3. Firm's sector: public (1); private (0)	0.0340	1.2635	0.2064
4. Firm's activ.: industry (1); services (0)	0.0795	2.9662	0.0030
5. Number of dependants	0.0078	1.0639	0.2874
6. Gender: male (0), female (1)	−0.0621	−4.3915	0.0000
7. Years of study	0.0157	4.5201	0.0000
8. Age	−0.1626	−2.9379	0.0033
9. Occupation: non-manual/ admin/white-collar (0); manual/product/ blue-collar (1)	−0.0005	−0.0225	0.9821
10. Time in job	0.0197	1.3147	0.1886
11. Interaction at work: high (1); low (3)	−0.1352	−2.5154	0.0119
12. Solidarity at work: low (1); high (4)	0.0585	2.48846	0.0128
13. Time of union membership	0.0370	2.7318	0.0063
14. Income	0.0049	1.4401	0.1498
15. Time of exposure to the CUT model: CUT (number of years); non-CUT (0)	0.0079	3.5510	0.0004

R^2 = 0.389013; total of observations: 211.

the variable *union model* remain yielding a positive coefficient at levels of statistical significance. Hence, it is safe to infer that the longer a worker is exposed to the alternative union model the higher are his or her feelings of civic competence.

7   CONCLUSIONS

This chapter presented the survey data collected in order to measure attitudes of urban workers of Recife, in the state of Pernambuco. For analytical purposes the sample was split up into two basic groups according to the union's affiliation to the CUT or to the other sectors of the labour movement. The presentation of the findings followed a two-step procedure. Firstly, we provided the aggregate scores for the sub-samples formed by both the occupational categories and the CUT and non-CUT groups. Scores elicited on both certain selected indicators and the entire scale were explored. The close focus on some indicators, all of which were employed in other related studies, served also to enable the reader to have a more concrete idea of the way the scale was conceived. Secondly, the average scores were submitted to regression analysis taking both the entire scale and each of its constituent modules.

The results reached through such procedures lead to a number of conclusions:

1. The figures elicited from the occupational category sub-samples on some selected indicators unveils a pattern of responses where the respondents affiliated to CUT unions scored regularly higher than their counterpart. Among the ten highlighted indicators, there were exceptions to that pattern in merely two cases: listening to or watching political programmes, where textile workers scored better than bank employees; and readiness to vote, where metalworkers rated lower than pharmaceutical and commerce employees. Notwithstanding these few localised variations, even in those situations, the overall score of the sub-sample formed by all the CUT-affiliated respondents was always higher.

2. When one looks at the scores for the aggregates formed by CUT and non-CUT-linked respondents, the picture is not a dissimilar one. As we can see from the tables of Section 4.1 both the scores in the whole scale and in each of its four modules were higher for the CUT-affiliated sub-set.

3. The figures presented in Section 4.2 reflect the averages elicited from each of the occupational categories in respect of the whole scale and its modules. As for the general average in the entire scale, all the occupational categories exposed to the CUT model ranked above their counterparts. As for the averages on each of the

four modules, the trend is repeated but with two individual exceptions. In fact, in the Modules 2 and 3, which deal respectively with the issues of *control at work* and *associative life*, one of the traditional-sector categories, the pharmaceutical workers outperformed the telecommunications workers and the bank employees in the former module, and just the bank employees in the latter.

4. The multiple regressions performed with the sample's responses to the complete model, as a rule lived up to theoretical expectations about the nature of the effect of the selected factors on workers' attitudes. This was true of almost all the fourteen independent variables accounted for in the model, with a few exceptions where the standard levels of significance were not achieved. When we replicated the regressions both with slight variations on the independent variables and with each of the scale's four modules the results tended to persist in terms of both coefficient and significance levels.

5. The regressions presented in the previous sections, with no deviant occurrences, uncovered a positive coefficient for the independent variable *union model* which integrates the basic hypothesis of this work. In all the cases the positivity of the coefficient was matched by the achievement of statistical significance at the level of at least 10 per cent and more often even lower than that, as is generally accepted for similar samples. As already noted, the higher measures on the independent variable were ascribed to longer time of exposure to the CUT union model. Therefore, the positive coefficient on this variable means that the worker's attitudes of active citizenship go up as a function of a longer exposure to the alternative model embraced by his or her union.

6. Although this study does not fail to recognise the existence of causal networks in both directions from structure to culture and vice versa, its main aim is to test a hypothesis concerning the former direction of causality. The union organisational arrangements and practices which form the union models – structure – were then taken as the independent variable; the workers' attitudes of active citizenship – culture – as the dependent variable. Neither the 'naked-eye' observation of the results nor the regressions

failed to lend support to the hypothesis that the union model adopted by the CUT unions helps to explain the higher levels of active citizenship held by their members in comparison with those belonging to unions affiliated to other sectors of the labour movement.

7 Conclusion

1 THE ALTERNATIVE MODEL AND CITIZENSHIP: STRUGGLING BEYOND THE FACTORIES

This research has found evidence to support the thesis that the revived Brazilian labour movement, particularly the new unionism grouped in the CUT, has contributed to giving the popular sectors a voice in the public arena. At the same time it has undermined the corporatist framework of industrial relations and forged new workers' identities which we have described as the 'culture of active citizenship'. This and the following sections address these three spheres of the contribution of the more dynamic sector of the labour movement.

Starting such analysis this section explores one of the leading features of the new unionism alternative model: its effort to set out a broad agenda capable of going beyond the particular economic interest of organised labour. As the former president of the new unionism's central confederation Jair Meneguelli once put it, the CUT is at the same time a body that represents class interests and a centre of developing popular aspirations (interview no. 18). In practice, the CUT has acted in the Brazilian scene as a sort of mouthpiece for the articulation of a broad range of concerns of the popular movement, as it has been recognised by the literature (Rodrigues and Cardoso, 1993).[1] The platform of the CUT, updated in each of its six congresses, has always embraced general demands going beyond the system of industrial relations such as land reform, popular-oriented economic policies, improvement of retired workers' pensions, urban reform, gender equality, minority rights, and so on (see particularly the summary of its congresses in Table 3.4 in Chapter 3).

Concern for the demands of all the popular sectors is commonly reinforced by the overlapping of militants of the labour and community movements. The community leader holding a position in directive bodies of unions is a very common occurrence throughout the country and also in the 'new unions' which made up the sample of the survey carried out in this research. The world famous case of Chico Mendes, the leader of the Amazonian rubber tappers, is just a more visible example of the combination of the union struggle with broader issues affecting people's life. Throughout his militant life, Mendes conjoined the presidency of the Rural Workers' Union of Xapuri (the CUT-affiliated union representing all the workers in agriculture in the region of Xapuri, Acre) with a key role in the foundation of the National Council of Rubber Tappers ('Conselho Nacional dos Seringueiros – CNS') in 1985, a civil society organisation committed to defending the Amazon forest, raising people's educational level and knowledge about the forest, and advancing the popular alternative development proposals for the Amazon forest based in co-operatives and extractive reserves. A member of the CNS since its foundation in 1985, Mendes and other militants of the Xapuri and Basiléia Rural Workers' Union have been active in cementing a broad alliance of the 'people of the forest', devoted to defending the forest and improving living standards, as exemplified by the educational 'Rubber Tapper Project' ('Projeto Seringueiro') run by the CNS and by the successful involvement of the Indian people of the region in the CNS organising grassroots commissions (Mendes, 1989).

In regard to the setting of this study, the Metropolitan Region of Recife, some of the oral testimonies we obtained through in-depth interviews were personal stories of combination of the militancy in the 'popular' movement with that in unions. Deputy João Paulo (interview no. 23), for example, was elected as member of the state parliament for the Workers' Party in 1994 with the largest number of votes of all the candidates after taking part in both the birth of the 'new unionism' in Pernambuco (as president of the Metalworkers' Union – 1984–7, president of the state branch of the CUT – 1983–9, member of the national directorate of the CUT – 1983–9) and in the articulation of the popular struggles of the neighbourhood association of 'UR-6, Ibura' (as activist and member of the directorate of the association). João Batista Filho (interview no. 21) has also conjoined involvement in the communitarian struggles (as secretary-general of the residents' association of 'Rio Doce – 4a. Etapa' in 1983–5 and as an activist in the association of 'Rio Doce – 5a. Etapa' since 1988) with that in the union movement (as member of the directorate of Sinttel since 1984, of the state branch of the CUT in 1984–8 and of the National Federation of the Telecommunications Workers – Fittel in 1992–3). Florindo Morais de Lima ('Rui') (interview no. 12) became a union militant as an aide of Sinttel in 1985 after active participation in the residents' association of 'Morro da Conceição' (from 1978 onwards) and in the squatters' movement known as 'Terras de Ninguém' (1982–3). In their testimonies all these 'double militants' recalled that the 'new unionism' activists have provided logistical support (such as printing and distribution of leaflets, transport, loud speakers, etc.) to the communities' struggles. They recalled also that a number of urban improvements in neighbourhoods such as 'Totó', 'Colina', 'Brasília Teimosa',[2] 'Morro da Conceição', 'Várzea', 'Brasilit', 'UR-5', 'UR-10', 'Rio Doce – 4a. Etapa', 'Rio Doce – 5a. Etapa', 'Vila das Aeromoças' and 'Minha Deusa' were made possible because the struggles of the local residents received the political and material help of the new unionism activists. As a result, those communities secured urban improvements such as housing, school, public health centres, garbage collection, new public transport services, reduction of public transport fares, and so on.

It is not only union officials who have engaged in community campaigns but also union advisers. In several instances, union lawyers have made a contribution to struggles for urban plot titles and in electoral disputes for the control of community associations. In our local research setting the same pattern is no less frequent. The trajectories of some union lawyers in Pernambuco such as João Batista Pinheiro de Freitas, Morse Lyra Neto and Ricardo Estêvao are good instances of such a 'double militancy' (interviews nos. 22, 28 and 29).

The combining of union and community militancy is likewise apparent from the recurrence of community support for various union industrial actions. Within our research setting we have already alluded to the famous 1981 strike in the 'Cia. Hidroelétrica do São Francisco', when the military repression and invasion of the union headquarters in the town of Paulo Afonso[3] was resisted thanks to the solidarity of the town inhabitants (see Subsection 1.2, Chapter 4). Similarly, the first metalworkers' strikes in the ABC region of Sao Paulo, where the military government intervened in the union and removed its leadership, could only last as long as they did because of the decisive support of the population's fundraising and other solidaristic initiatives (Keck, 1989).

One of the most important features of the new unionism is its capacity to combine with community movements. The comparative study carried out by Seidman (1994) on the Brazilian and South African new unionisms concluded that those labour movements did succeed in constructing a broad-based popular alliance capable of combining demands for improvement of pay with demands for urban services. Such agendas may be interpreted as attempts to raise the historically defined living standards of the working people and to better conditions in working-class neighbourhoods. As she puts it (1995: 197):

> When the new unionism emerged in the late 1970s, activists in both South Africa and Brazil emphasised shop-floor organization and developing workers' capacities to negotiate with employers. By the mid 1980s, however, labor activists in both cases had shifted: rather than concentrating solely on factory-related issues, both labor movements targeted the state as well as employers, seeking to increase the share of the broadly defined working class in the benefits of economic growth. Unionists joined in community-based campaigns, and were as likely to call for *full citizenship* [emphasis mine – MRB] – defined in terms of political inclusion and economic redistribution – as to speak of the right to form independent unions.

Also recognising such links between the two movements, authors such as Foweraker (1995: 86) stress that the combined struggle of social movements and trade unions originates from the shared feelings of deprivation arising out of the 'manifest failure of the state to manage the social questions'. This combination of struggles in the sphere of production with those over the sphere of reproduction (Seidman, 1995) implies a redefinition of citizenship to include not only political rights but also social and economic rights to collective goods and services such as electricity, water supply, sewage disposal, etc. Both sectors of the popular movement in Brazil managed to include a broad range of issues in their agendas, linking work to neighbourhood as two faces of the same demand for the upgrading of living standards. In short, the new unionism stance towards a combined struggle for both work-related and social entitlements provides further evidence of its contribution to the building of Brazilian workers' citizenship. This effect may be said to work at two levels. Firstly, the articulation of the labour movement with popular struggle clearly reinforces their potential success. Although such struggles for entitlements are not always successful, it is safe to assume that even partial achievements amount to increasing the citizenship position of the Brazilian poor. Secondly, the involvement of trade unionists with communitarian struggle contributes to the developing of militant attitudes among the participants of the communitarian movements. This second effect is also stressed by Seidman (1994) when analysing the militant stance of Brazilian and South African social movements. She attributes a rising 'class consciousness' of participants of the popular movements to the example of the new unionism's achievements and its political views.

The cementing of this alliance between labour unions and communitarian struggles, coupled with the embracing of broad popular demands, shows that the CUT unionism has been strongly concerned with expressing workers' stance in the public arena. As emerges from the descriptions offered in Chapters 2 and 3, it managed to turn workers into active players of the socio-political game in Brazil. Since the beginning of the democratisation effort in the late 1970s, it has tried to provide a voice for the popular sectors and include the so-called 'social debt' among the national priorities. Workers' channels of expression have benefited as well from the new unionism participation in the creation of the Workers' Party ('PT') in 1980, an initiative that consolidated the popular sectors' commitment to seek to influence wider political decisions.[4] Such a contribution can hardly be neglected in any assessment of the role played by the alternative unionism in the striving for extending full citizenship to the Brazilian lower classes.

The concerns described in this section were thus depicted by Vicente Paulo da Silva, the president of the CUT since 1994 (interview no. 35):

> In this moment, we are acting on three axes. First, the strengthening of the grassroots organisation ('trabalho de base'). This is vital. A second aspect is the consideration that we have to be accountable to the society; we can't act in a detrimental way to the interests of society.... We don't think of the worker as the guy who merely works with the hammer, we think of him as a person who brings up children, who wants good housing, who has the right to sexual pleasure, happiness, and other pleasures, that is, [*we adopt*] a broad and integral perspective. And another aspect we regard as very important is related to the attitude of not merely saying no. We have to advance concrete proposals... The other day someone told me: 'Pô', Vicentinho, I have never seen a union "central" dealing with slave labour.' We are worried about it, we are campaigning.... Take the informal sector, we have proposals for it. We are holding a congress on this issue the coming year. We are starting a discussion about the youth in this country, that is, we intend to deal with and discuss various aspects of our lives... The CUT is much broader than people usually think. Look, the CUT represents 17 million people today... This campaign that we have launched against slave labour, it yielded international respect. That one in defence of children and youths, another recognition, that is, the CUT has broadened its scope. We advocate a thesis we call the 'unions social subject' [*'sindicato sujeito social'*], that is, [*a type of unionism*] which goes beyond the bread and butter issues. It seeks to discuss the questions of life: against racial discrimination (the other day we carried out a protest march of 227 Km through 11 cities, from November 6 to 11 [*1995*], to protest against racial discrimination), in short, the CUT thinks more broadly. I guess this is important: thinking of citizenship as a 'whole' [*'um todo'*].

2 THE ALTERNATIVE MODEL AND CITIZENSHIP: UNDERMINING STATE CORPORATIST INDUSTRIAL RELATIONS

Having once asserted the effect on citizenship of the new unionism's ability for forging a broad agenda in alliance with other popular sectors, we shall now argue that its attitudes towards the system of industrial relations are also conducive to developing workers' citizenship.

To begin with, membership involvement through a participatory 'leadership style'[5] has meant that rights and benefits have been won as a result of the common endeavour of the grassroots, a practice that shakes the very basis of the bureaucratic nature of the corporatist unions. Old populist behaviour such as the 'leave it to me' approach and that of presenting achievements as being won by the leaders on behalf of membership have been explicitly eschewed. We have already seen how the president of one of the traditional trade unions included in our sample – the Commerce Employees' Union – insisted on being given all the credit for certain facilities and benefits earned on behalf of the occupational category (see Chapter 4, Section 3.7), a practice not so likely to be observed among the new unionism leaders. On the contrary, the participation of the grassroots in the winning of rights among the new unionism of our survey sample is a matter of principle for those practising a different style of leadership, a picture which emerged from various interviews which are cited throughout this work. Indeed, a number of interviewees regularly stressed the CUT-affiliated unions' concern with treating individual grievances in a collective way and trying to involve the membership both during the annual collective bargaining procedure and in day-to-day problem-solving arising at the workplace, as well as in union decisions (e.g. interviews nos 3, 5, 7, 17, 19, 27 and 35). This type of participatory and militant leadership was also found to be the rule for the new unionism urban unions in Pernambuco in the well-documented study by Morais (1993). After analysing data on the militant attitude of the unions concerned and their respective bureaucratic apparatus, he concluded that even those 'new unions' which maintained some sort of 'assistential'

Table 7.1   General meetings per year

Unions	No. of general meetings	Average attendance
Sinttel (CUT)	24	200
Sindpd (CUT)	20	120
Metalworkers (CUT)	40	450
Bank Employees (CUT)	20	100
Pharmaceutical Workers (CGT)	02	300
Textile Industry (CGT)	02	200
Commerce Employees*(FS)	02	30

* Although the Commerce Employees' Union refused to return the questionnaire we sent to all the unions of the sample, data provided by members of the opposition group (interview no. 11) indicate that the union has held two general meetings per year with no more than thirty members attending.

Source: Unions' response to the questionnaire presented in Appendix 3.

benefits for the membership, never failed to stress militancy and involvement of the grassroots. Moreover, where 'assistance' was preserved, as in the case of the metalworkers' decision to keep providing medical care to the membership, this was a response to preferences expressed by membership through formal processes of consultation.

Data displayed in Table 7.1 covering general meetings and attendance illustrate the search for establishing a participatory leadership style on the part of the CUT-affiliated unions of our sample. The first four unions listed in the table are those affiliated to the CUT. Self-evidently, participation cannot be assessed merely by formal channels as general meetings. Union press, dealing with day-to-day grievances through union structures and other union informal activities are likewise expressions of participation. But the contrast in the frequency of general meetings called by the two types of unions we have investigated seems to supply a sound indicator of a 'participatory leadership style' on the part of the 'new unions'.

In addition to defying the bureaucratic corporatist union through its participatory style of leadership, the new unionism has managed to develop a complete alternative model to replace the current 'neo-corporatist framework'. Chapters 2 and 3 described how the emergent new unionism rose up against the main pillars of a legal framework which channelled the conflicts between capital and labour into the state apparatus and exerted strict control over union internal affairs. From the outset, the union monopoly of representation, the vertical structure of categorical federations and confederations, the Ministry of Labour authorisation for creation of fresh unions, the union tax and the Labour Court compulsory arbitration were identified as major hindrances to a pluralistic system of industrial relations. These proposals were synthesised in the slogan 'collective labour contract' as early as in the first half of the 1980s, conceived as an alternative for ensuring union freedom and collective autonomy of the parties to deal with labour conflicts.

The recent evolution of the Brazilian system, as described in Chapter 2, has presented the CUT as perhaps its most creative and decisive protagonist of change. Even when there still existed a relative consensus seeking to reconcile a relaxation of state interference with the maintenance of some key corporatist institutions as had happened in the defeat of more radical proposals in the Constituent Assembly in 1988, the new unionism remained almost isolated in insisting on the full dismantling of the state-sanctioned union structure. The proposal of the 'collective labour contract' was thus consolidated as its official platform for the system of industrial relations earlier than in the case of any other single actor. As it emerged from the examination of the proposals submitted by all the relevant actors of the Brazilian system to the 'Foro do Contrato Coletivo de Trabalho' under the auspices of the Minister of Labour Walter Barelli in 1993, it took time for the other actors to accept some of the elements of the 'collective labour contract' conception. Entrepreneurial organisations such as FIEPE, FEBRABAN and CNI and the non-CUT sectors of the labour movement lagged considerably behind the CUT's pioneer initiatives as is apparent from the very terminology employed to formulate each actor's plan of reforms: following the CUT, 'collective labour contract' has now become an expression equated with the replacement of the current system.

The CUT's contribution to the superseding of the corporatist framework consists also in implementing some of the main elements of the alternative model. The union

structure has been gradually changed through the merging of unions to encompass broader economic branches
and geographical areas, thus surmounting the breaking up
of the occupational category nexus with official unions, as
exemplified by the creation of the Metalworkers' Union of
the ABC Region, the chemical workers and petrochemical
industry workers of Bahia, the plastic and chemical worker
of São Paulo (Chapter 3, Section 5.4). The creation of such
unions implements the CUT policies towards the union
structure as they were adopted in its fifth congress and
seventh 'plenária', held respectively in 1994 and 1995,
according to which the 'CUTist unionism' must create the
so-called 'organic union of the CUT'. As detailed in Section 5.4 of Chapter 3 this seeks to constitute another type
of union, organised by economic branches and submitted
to common dispositions which apply the principles of union autonomy, freedom, accountability to membership and
internal democratic procedures.

As for the union tax, there is an increasing concern of
the 'new unions' to find alternative sources of revenues,
based on voluntary contributions, in order to replace it.
As noted in Section 3.1 of Chapter 3 the first unions to
return such revenues to the workers belong to the CUT
ranks: the metalworkers of São Bernardo, the plastic industry
workers of São Paulo, the chemical industry workers of São
Paulo, the metalworkers of Campinas, the oil workers of
Camaçari and the telecommunication workers of Pernambuco. Not surprisingly, within our research setting, the first
union to initiate such a practice was that of the CUT-affiliated
Telecom Workers.

No less significant seems to be the refusal of the CUT
unions of our sample to resort to the Labour Court settlement of the collective conflict, most of the solutions having
been reached through direct bargaining (Chapter 4). All
this evidence suggests that one cannot dismiss the role of
the CUT model in overcoming the main traits of corporatism,
both at the theoretical level of elaboration of an alternative and at the practical level of its implementation, albeit
at the practical level the process is still quite incipient due
to the enduring enforcement of an adverse legal framework.

The CUT's efforts to replace a framework which inhibits

both expression of conflicts and involvement of workers in their settlement have been directed at the achievement of a pluralist system of industrial relations. Workers' involvement in the decision-making process of industrial life, after all, has been assessed as the great strength of a pluralist system. In Britain, for instance, the model known as 'collective laissez faire' has encouraged workers' participation both in union life and in workplace disputes. In Davies and Freedland's words (1993: 665), 'its [the collective laissez faire model's] main strengths lay in the relatively high degree of worker participation in the setting of terms and conditions of employment, and in the commitment which it embodied to providing decent levels of protection at the workplace'. Our study of the proposals and practices of the Brazilian new unionism allows a similar evaluation of its effect on workers' participation. Through such participation and related arrangements, the workers have attained what the literature has labelled 'industrial citizenship', that is, the rights to form independent and free unions, and bargain with employers and the state over individual rights and working conditions. What is suggested, accordingly, is that the practice, self-confidence and responsibility engendered through participation additionally helps develop a political culture which proves functional in asserting workers' citizenship. The analysis of such a culture is the focus of the following section.

3 NEW IDENTITIES: FORGING THE POLITICAL CULTURE OF ACTIVE CITIZENSHIP

What throughout this work has been labelled the 'political culture of active citizenship' relates to a twofold set of roots. On the one side it is recognised that the process of extension of citizenship rights is intrinsically conflictive: citizenship develops as a result of social struggles of individuals and groups to secure access to its entitlements and thus become full members of societies, as authors like Dahrendorf (1988), Hirschman, (1991) and Turner (1992) have not failed to note. On the other side, this book highlights the republican approach which focuses on the citizen not merely as a bearer of rights but rather as someone co-responsible for the attainment of the common good and in duty bound to join his or her fellows in the collective endeavours directed at such a goal (Pocock, 1971; Skinner, 1984). Rights are intrinsically tied to the 'civic virtues' of participation in the collective affairs and the duty of public service. The worker ready to engage in collective undertakings developed amidst the social struggles is identified as an active citizen whose attitudes may be fostered, among other factors, by the labour movement whereby he or she engages in those struggles.

The potential role of such a culture is apparent if one bears in mind that in industrial systems where union membership is optional, low rates of union members may obtain. Given the fact that non-members may enjoy much the same benefits as union members whilst union members have to pay special costs in dues, effort, strike action, etc., workers may be disinclined to join unions. Such non-participation may be overcome by what Olson calls 'selective incentives' which reward individuals either positively or negatively (Olson, 1971). But in addition to such 'selective incentives' union membership may become attractive or self-sustaining owing to the creation of collective identities capable of replacing the logic of individualistic and purely instrumental action by motives of solidaristic action (Offe and Wisenthal, 1985).

The general contention that unions are at the same time a result and a factor helping to develop the conditions for collective action is a commonplace in the literature. Zapata (1986), for example, points out that unions generate the conditions of cohesion, solidarity and organisation which enable conflicts to become manifest. Lord Wedderburn (1995: 40) makes the same point that 'trade unions ... demonstrate the value of collective action of individuals, [and therefore] cannot adopt the mantle of those who claim they can cure social injustice by the impact of legislation alone'. The preconditions of collective action are strictly tied to the issue of forging identities. Unions play a special part in creating those new identities apt to value the common sharing of grievances and objectives. But of course not all the actual existing unions fulfil such a role to the same extent. Differences in structures and behaviour will impact working people in distinctive ways. As some analysts of workers' consciousness have long emphasised, the '[trade unions'] character does shape consciousness in important ways, and there can be significant variations in its content' (Fantasia, 1989: 240). Assessing the potential variation of the influence of different types of unions on workers' political culture is precisely one of the foremost objectives of this study, what led us to look at the extent the new unionism model has contributed to forging the new identities necessary to impel workers to act as 'active citizens'. Hence a relevant query addressed through the attitudinal survey presented in Chapters 5 and 6 was the assessment of how far the new unionism has differentiated itself from the traditional sectors of the labour movement in shaping rank-and-file political culture.

The results achieved on the scale of active citizenship by the sub-samples in our survey were contrasted in Sections 2 and 3 of Chapter 6. We compared the average scores of respondents exposed to the alternative model of unionism of the CUT (the 'experiment group') with those of the workers affiliated to more 'traditional' unions (the 'control group') although aware of the limits of such a comparison due to the fact that this 'naked-eye' observation might produce scores that are better explained by other factors. In any event, we came across a general pattern where members of the 'experiment group' displayed higher scores in certain items selected on the assumption that they constitute sound indicators of a 'culture of active citizenship'. These higher scores were found when either the occupational categories or the aggregates per the two great groups (CUT/ non-CUT) were scrutinised thus endorsing the view that the workers of our sample who are represented by CUT-affiliated unions have at least started developing fresh identities.

Sections 4, 5 and 6 of Chapter 6, in turn, presented the statistical test where various other factors affecting workers' attitudes were controlled. The type of multiple regression employed took each individual respondent as a sample thus allowing the assessment of whether each independent variable of the model had explanatory power, if any, in the score of 'active citizenship' attained by the respondent. The variable of most interest in testing the basic research query of the undertaken survey, *union model*, yielded positive coefficients at the significance level lower than 1 per cent. Since it was measured through the number of years of exposure of part of the sample to the alternative model of unionism practised by CUT unions, one is entitled to infer that the positive coefficient means that the longer a worker is exposed to the CUT union model, the higher he or she scores on the scale of 'active citizenship'. The same pattern of 'explanatory power' was reproduced when the respondents' scores on each of the individual modules – the specific issues of union, control at work, associative life, and civic competence – were considered. Given that the multiple regression allows the controlling of the other factors which affect the result for a given variable, one can infer that the attitudes of the sampled workers are higher when they are exposed to the alternative new unionism model. This is further evidence that the CUT-affiliated unions are developing new identities among their constituencies which shape a particular culture conducive to asserting their citizenship.

Other evidence on the same direction can be drawn from data presented in Chapter 4 about the Telecommunications Workers' Union – SINTTEL. Probably this union, within our sample, is amongst those which has made more progress in the application of the alternative proposals developed in the CUT's field. To begin with, SINTTEL's union density of 76.5 per cent is in itself a sign that the occupational category values unionism and collective action.[6] Further indication of the forging of new identities can be traced in successive decisions of union members with regard to the union tax, as already reported. After the union decided not to charge it in response to the CUT's proposal of not relying on compulsory contributions, the members resolved to return the resources to the union itself as a voluntary contribution.

This capacity of the new unionism for representing membership and forging new identities through democratic practices has led analysts like Mangabeira (1993: 15) to conclude that such a characteristic provides the 'opportunity for expanding the workers' citizenship', the assertion of worker's citizenship being regarded by her as an element of the very definition of what is conventionally termed new unionism. Morais (1992) has also called attention to the successful experience of the new unionism in developing new identities for union members. Drawing on the same research setting as our study – urban workers of the state of Pernambuco – he argues that the new type of relationship between the new unionism officials and their constituency created novel channels of participation and recognised the interests of rank-and-file. This relationship then forged 'new identities both for the radical union officials and militants and the members themselves'. In short, both the more militant strategies and democratic practices espoused by the 'new unions' of our sample impacted not only the external environment, but also shaped the collective identity of the unionised workers and the way they interpret the issues related to their lives. This double impact has confirmed the contention that social movements shape their members' identities and perceptions (e.g., Foweraker, 1995).

Up to this point we have discussed the research findings in the light of the new unionism's contribution to the building up of workers' new identities through the development of attitudes which are proper to a political culture we are terming 'active citizenship'. Both the quantitative and qualitative analysis we carried out have supplied evidence of the positive impact of the new unionism model in fostering workers attitudes of 'active citizenship'. Let us now concentrate in more detail on some theoretical implications stemming from the introducing of the theme of political culture into the analyses of the changing system of Brazilian labour relations and the specific influence of the CUT unionism.

One of the effects detected by the reggression analysis presented in Chapters 5 and 6 – the impact of the new unionism alternative model on workers' political culture – brings such a discussion to the fore. Political culture, it is generally conceded, has again become an important concern for political scientists (e.g., Street, 1994). This might be credited in part to disillusion with purely individualistic accounts of political processes; and in part to a rejection of structuralist approaches. In any event, it is clear that to claim that political culture may be explanatory is not as unfashionable as it was a decade ago. The underestimation of political culture has been alleged to be a shortcoming of certain analyses of democratic transitions in Latin America which focus chiefly on interactions of the so-called relevant actors. Moisés (1994), for example, has argued for the deploying of more complex analytical models in the theory to allow for the multidimensionality of those democratic transitions. Such an extension of explanation should include the variable related to the changes in the mass political culture as an explanatory factor. This suggestion is congenial to our study, for our findings show that the forging of a new political culture is at the same time a chief effect and a cause of the growth of the new unionism in Brazil.

The concept of political culture has been the object of intense discussion in the literature. In their *The Civic Culture*, Almond and Verba (1965) provide an initial account which has been said to highlight psychological dispositions of individuals. For Almond and Verba, political culture consists of 'attitudes towards the political system and its various parts, and attitudes towards the role of the self in the system' (Almond and Verba, 1965: 13). Those attitudes pertain to individuals' knowledge of the political institutions (cognition), their feelings (affect) and judgment of them (evaluation). A slightly different formulation of the concept is provided by Martin (1987): 'the complex of values, beliefs and emotional attitudes surrounding political institutions'. For Topf (1989), in turn, political culture 'consists of attitudes or stances which citizens adopt and interpret in order to make sense of politics'. Hence we see that there are different emphases on the various aspects that make up the notion of political culture. One can stress either the 'psychological dispositions of individuals' or the way they interpret political matters ('assumptions about the political world', Elkins and Simeon, 1979). Throughout this work we have limited ourselves to employing the notion as a set of attitudes which express individuals' values and perceptions concerning political matters. It should be noted that values can either legitimise authorities and arrangements or 'permit any subordinate group to challenge successfully the hegemony of the dominant group' (Poole, 1986: 25). Thus values are an important aspect of attitudes which help to shape political cultures and may impel 'subordinate groups' to act in pursuit of their demands.

The renewed interest in political culture as a possible explanatory factor of political processes leads to the question of its determinants. In Section 5 of Chapter 6 we stated our assumption about the problem of direction of causality. When we note that both structure and culture affect each other, we rejected the idealist stances which tend to interpret culture as the whole story. Rather, we acknowledge the effects of structures on the shaping of the way social actors value, feel and interpret reality. However, the direction of causality that starts with structural factors entails a number of mediating factors which shape individuals' perceptions, as is the case of the processes of socialisation through the school, the family, the media, the role of intellectuals and the participation in social groups. Naturally, uneven processes of socialisation owing to exposure to distinct mediating factors are likely to yield dissimilar political attitudes. Not infrequently, one comes across situations where quite different meanings are accorded to the same fact by individuals under distinct influences as, say, a conservative Protestant sect or a militant trade union. The importance of such mediating factors has been recognised in recent discussion of the subject as exemplified by the writings of Welch (1993) and Street (1994), the latter explicitly mentioning the role of organised political groupings in the determination of culture.

As it becomes apparent, this research highlights the role of one of the determinants of political culture among a host of others. We contend that one of the traditional 'organised political groupings' – the trade union – even if perhaps too quickly dismissed by some currents of social thought, continues to play a role in the development of mass political culture. The persistence of similar influences was recently highlighted by Moisés (1993: 174), when he suggests that one cannot dismiss the impact of mobilisation of popular sectors on recent changes in the Brazilian political culture. As he puts it:

> It is a notable feature of countries like Brazil, that this [popular experience and involvement in politics] comes partly from the mobilization and organization of the

poorest sectors in pursuit of a less unequal distribution
of the resources (like education) needed for social integration. Now, there is no reason to exclude the possibility
that this experience ... plays some role in shaping the
differentiated patterns of political sophistication among
the less privileged, thereby influencing their political
convictions.

His hypothesis about consequences of popular mobilisation,
among them new unionism, was corroborated by our empirical data. A similar conclusion has also been reached by
Mangabeira (1993) when she argues that the new unionism approach to work conflicts led to the transformation
of a previously existing political culture. Looking at the
Metalworkers' Union which represents the workers of
'Companhia Siderúrgica Nacional – CSN', located in the
city of Volta Redonda in the state of Rio de Janeiro, she
takes account of the changes brought about within the CSN
plant by the new unionism leadership elected in 1983. From
a culture that dealt with grievances on the individual plane,
the union evolved towards a political culture that treats
them as collective claims in need of political mobilisation
and participation. In other words, in line with our research
findings, she maintains that the new unionism has developed a political culture in which workers become active
citizens, capable of acting individually and collectively alike.

  In sum, the analysis of our findings from the perspective
of the discussion on political culture allows us to assert
that the particular political culture shaped with the help
of the new unionism alternative model does have explanatory implications for the way workers identify their interests
and act upon them. It means that the new unionism, through
the attitudes of 'active citizenship' – and therefore a certain
political culture – as an intermediate variable, leads to
developing workers' citizenship as a result of their action
in pursuit of their interests.

4 THE RESEARCH IN CONTEXT

4.1 Generalisability

Given the fact that the alternative conceptions of industrial relations, although originating in the most industrialised state – São Paulo – have spread to several states and regions of the country, one ideally should have carried out a nation-wide survey and gathered quantitative data from the whole country. Obvious material limitations prevented us from embarking upon such a project. However, we have reasons to believe that the panorama of industrial relations in the state of Pernambuco is not too different from that of other regions. More or less industrialised metropolitan regions such as Rio de Janeiro, Belo Horizonte, Porto Alegre, Brasília, Curitiba, Salvador, Recife, Fortaleza, and Belém have seen the adoption of alternative practices by a growing number of unions. As a result, the coexistence of two basic conceptions within the labour movement may be encountered in several geographical regions. Thus, our relatively minuscule sample is not expected to yield significant deviations from the characteristics of other settings. Although we do not assume that all relationships we came across were automatically valid for the whole country, we believe that in general terms the research findings may be common to the settings where the duality of models of industrial relations is present.

4.2 Research Contributions, Limits and Prospects

A doctoral dissertation is a programme of research whose outcomes are scarcely predictable at the outset. The rationale and the state of affairs of the literature on the chosen subject permit only general guidelines to the long journey the student embarks upon. This book was no exception to such uncertainties, a circumstance which was further aggravated by the very nature of one of its major hypotheses brought to empirical scrutiny – the one covering the positive impact of the alternative model practised by the new unionism on the workers' political culture of active citizenship.

The risks involved with such a basic query were twofold.

First, measuring attitudes and political culture is far from problem-free. Difficulties of building up proper scales which actually measured the targeted dimensions combine with shortcomings on the understanding of the items by the respondents. In addition, the survey methodology designed to measure attitudes is not powerful enough to capture the world of people's cultural manifestations in its complex richness. Workers' attitudes are liable to contradictions which stem from their very conflictive position within the relation of employment. The nature of the latter implies that workers' attitudes tend to oscillate as a result of the tensions between the co-operative aspect of work, without which production is infeasible, and the structural conflict with management for control over work and its results. As the literature has acknowledged, survey measurement techniques focus on workers' responses triggered in a single moment, usually under the calmness and routines of daily working life. 'Explosions of consciousness' (Mann, 1973) proper to instants of more visible collective actions are only indirectly captured by attitude measuring. Moreover, such a contradictory workers' consciousness is not static. The dynamism inherent in working life obviously affects workers' attitudes and this evolving state of affairs is not easily caught by surveys. Unsurprisingly, attempts to predict workers' behaviour on the basis of surveys have registered glaring failures, as exemplified by the well-known fate of certain inferences drawn by Goldthorpe and his colleagues about the instrumental attitudes of the motorcar workers of Luton and their acceptance of managerial goals. Indeed, only a couple of months after being surveyed and having expressed their acquiescence in the 'team work' analogy so common in industrial relations research (67 per cent), those workers went on a very aggressive strike against the management of Vauxhall Motors in 1966, a mobilisation which included some episodes of rioting or quasi-rioting. Regarding the specific theme of the political culture which has been gradually developed among the CUT unionism, the insufficiencies of the survey technique surfaced likewise as a result of the complexity of workers' attitudes. Indeed, surviving 'traditional' cultural traits developed in past experiences may often coexist with 'modern' ones. One therefore could not expect the new unionism model to cancel automatically all the remnants of the political culture proper to corporativism. The survival of old practices and of traits of the traditional culture epitomised in populism, paternalism and bureaucratism, even among the workers exposed to the alternative unionism, make the analysis of the workers' present culture a very complex matter. Such contradictions in workers' attitudes of course are not easily captured or explained by surveys. Hence, to cope with these shortcomings of the survey methodology, we pursued a strategy of combining the quantitative analysis with qualitative data gathered through in-depth interviews with union leaders, advisers, labour judges and public servants as well as through consulting union archives for data on meetings, organisation within the workplace, the union press, methods of conflict settlement and other indicators of membership involvement.

Yet, leaving aside the risk outlined above, there was the possibility that the research failed to discern a consistent relationship between the alternative model of labour relations developed by the CUT unions and the attitudes of 'active citizenship' under investigation. At first, there even existed the possibility that correlations eventually found could not be explained by the influence of the alternative union model. That is the reason for our selecting the multiple regression analysis which took each individual as a sample. By looking into the coefficient elicited from each respondent on the variable *exposure to the alternative union model* we managed to assess the particular effect of such a variable on his or her score in the scale of 'active citizenship' as though the other independent variables were held constant.

In addition to the hypothesis on the role of the new unionism in the shaping of the political culture of active citizenship, this research sought to provide evidence for the contention that the alternative CUT union model has further contributed to extend the workers' citizenship by addressing a broader social agenda in conjunction with other sectors of the Brazilian poor and by forging a comprehensive alternative to the corporatist framework of industrial relations. The overall picture emerging from the data and analysis undertaken, although still unsuitable for definitive conclusions, allows a positive assessment of the role played by the new unionism in the long struggle of the Brazilian popular sectors to attain citizenship through processes fundamentally distinct from the pattern of selective handing down of citizenship from above as implicit in the 'regulated citizenship' model hitherto prevalent in the country (Santos, 1979). It might therefore be asserted that, in the process of extension of citizenship to the lower classes, the phase of 'regulated citizenship' has gradually given place to the phase of a 'conquered citizenship' whereby the condition of 'full member of society' is attained by the popular sectors through participation and struggle.

Looking back retrospectively at this journey throughout the itinerary of the construction of the citizenship of Brazilian workers, we consider that this book has made a number of contributions to the related areas of scholarship, though essentially modest in nature. Firstly, the analysis of the country's system of industrial relations provided in this work may facilitate the understanding of its recent evolution, major events and prospects for changes. Secondly, the study of the new unionism is deemed to have advanced the knowledge about its history, characteristics, proposals and the role it has played in the process of extending citizenship to the lower classes; the specific account of the evolution of the new unionism in the research setting of the state of Pernambuco was also meant to fill in an area where the scholarship has been comparatively scarce. Thirdly, the analysis of the promotion of the political culture of active citizenship by the CUT unionism, we believe, has progressed a step further beyond the usual assertion that the latter fulfils the requirements of union democracy (Morais, 1992, 1993; Mangabeira, 1993); thus, once that democratic character is established, the examination of its impact on the political culture of the rank-and-file is deemed yet another stage in its understanding. Last but not least, while assessing the role of this type of unionism and the political culture it generates, this study offers some theoretical insights into both the determinants and the explanatory role of political culture for the analysis of the growth of citizenship; in addition, the attempt at measuring a particular variant of political culture may have contributed to fill in the gap which stems from the inherent difficulty of taking such measures and have been said to constitute one of the obstacles explaining the underestimation of political culture as a causal element shaping societies (Inglehart, 1990).

Aside from the potential deepening – and rectification – of the foregoing lines of research, there are other possible developments related to the same research programme which seem in need of further enquiry. This analysis of Brazilian labour relations and new unionism has departed both from major studies which primarily focus either on the institutions and abstract actors (Erickson, 1977; Keck, 1989; Souza, 1990, 1992a; Boito Jr, 1991a, 1991b; Araújo, 1993; Comin, 1994; Noronha, 1994; Oliveira, 1994) and from those which concentrate on the behaviour and conceptions of the leadership of those actors (Weffort, 1973; Moisés, 1978, 1982; Keller, 1986; Rodrigues, 1990; Antunes, 1991; Medeiros, 1992; Morais, 1992, 1993; Mangabeira, 1993; Seidman, 1994). Researches on political culture tend to focus either on the attitudes of the mass or on the attitudes of relevant elites. While the bulk of work just mentioned may fit in with the latter, this book concentrates on the former by exploring the practices and political culture of the rank-and-file alongside the more general attention to the abstract actors. Considering the relative scarcity of the literature following such a perspective,[7] the widening of such a focus on the rank-and-file remains a promising research programme which may contribute to a better grasp of workers' attitudes and labour movements in general. The attitudes of workers located in some other key sectors of the labour force apart from in the urban setting considered in this book, and exposed to distinct patterns of labour relations or unionism apparently deserve further attention, for they may either confirm or impose qualifications on our findings. The attitudes of the rural workers exposed to either CUT or non-CUT unions, for instance, may extend the research programme embedded in this book so as to assess the effect of the new unionism model in a very different socio-economic context.

Additionally, the scrutiny of the alternative proposals advanced by important organisations of employees and employers that have been gradually replacing the hybrid corporatism still prevalent suggests that the levels and consequences of their partial implementation – in some sectors, by certain actors – would merit further empirical research. These purposes have already served as a rationale for some works in progress on the Brazilian new unionism such as a study being currently undertaken on the actual implementation of the alternative model ('collective labour contract proposal') by the new unionism of the state of Pernambuco, the same setting singled out in this book. Still in regard to the consequences of the alternative model practised by the new unionism, a promising line of research relates to the effect of the CUT unions on the workers' salaries. With such a goal, we have used the data of the survey presented in this book in another empirical study (Barros and Barros, 1995) which focused on the determinants of relative wages. Some theories on labour economics (e.g. Kahneman et al., 1986; Akerlof and Yellen, 1990; Barros, 1991, 1993) which emphasise the factors *wage bargaining* and *ideals of social justice* in the determination of relative wages were tested. Using regression analyses which took *wage* as the dependent variable, we came across results which showed that the higher wages of the urban workers of Recife belonging to CUT-affiliated unions are in part explained by the factor *CUT model*. Such findings suggest that the bargaining power of the workers exposed to the CUT model is higher and thus confirmed the impact of the factor 'bargaining power' in the determination of wages.[8] Another research in progress which fits in with this perspective is a study being carried out in the states of Rio Grande do Sul and Santa Catarina which attempts to assess the impact of direct bargaining on the real wage levels of those workers whose unions have settled their conflict with employers through such a means instead of relying on labour court arbitration, just in accordance with the CUT's alternative proposals. In addition, since we have seen that there are at least three broad groups of proposals advanced by the actors to transform the country's system of labour relations, another line of research worth pursuing is the scrutiny of the evolution of this process of change in order to identify which elements of each set of proposals are prevailing and thus illuminate the road ahead. Still with regard to the study of the changes in the Brazilian system of industrial relations, the analysis undertaken in this book about the latter invites subsequent more detailed enquiries into each of the elements of the system such as the labour court and the Ministry of Labour as exemplified by Barreto's work on the 'classist judges'(1994) and by Buchanan's (1989) analysis of the administration of Almir Pazzianoto in 1986–7.

As for workers' political culture, some already-noticed insufficiencies of this study invite complementary endeavour, an obvious instance being the undertaking of in-depth studies of workers' culture during the so-called 'critical junctures', where mobilisations are likely to give birth to 'explosions of consciousness'. Such a pursuit would fill in the gaps left by the intrinsically static nature of the survey attitude measurements carried out in this book. In addition to the many variables incorporated in our research design, such factors as religion, mass media and neighbourhood may affect workers' political attitudes in varying degrees and therefore remains as a promising field of enquiry. However, in effect we may have captured religious influence to some degree inasmuch as the progressive Catholic Church played an important role in the formation of the new unionism. Finally, still in respect of the theme of political culture, another suggestive line of investigation relates to the degree to which it is able to account for political change. While looking into the new unionism alternative model as a factor explaining the birth of a specific political culture, this work has taken the latter primarily as a dependent variable. Nonetheless, the culture of active citizenship was explicitly recognised as an independent variable crucial to the building of workers' citizenship since it was assumed that the latter can only be achieved if the workers themselves fight for it. In other words, political culture was also taken as an explanatory factor of social change. Such a perspective, too, invites a continuing research effort targeted at following up the effects of the 'culture of active citizenship' on the ensuing social changes which have been labelled the 'conquered citizenship'.

Appendix 1: The Sample

The sample of 211 urban unionised workers of Greater Recife employed in the survey was selected with the chief goal of providing data for the comparison of the different effects of the two basic models of unionism on the attitudes of the workers. As detailed in Chapters 5 and 6, the survey was designed to test the hypothesis that the score attained by the interviewees on the scale of active citizenship would increase as a function of longer exposures to the CUT-model of unionism. The sounder methodological device to test such a hypothesis proved to be the multiple regression statistical test inasmuch it allows the researcher to control for the other determinants of the dependent variable under measuring – the attitudes of active citizenship.

Because the multiple regression allows for other factors which shape individuals' attitudes, the sample had to be sufficiently diversified to encompass the variety of features of each respondent. Initially we purposively selected the occupational categories most representative of both the CUT model and the other sectors of the labour movement. The unions affiliated to the CUT (metalworkers, bank employees, data-processing employees and telecommunications workers) have been widely regarded as constituting the stronghold of the CUT in the state of Pernambuco. In addition, they cover both the private and the public sector, and both the industrial and service activity of the firms whose work they represent. The traditional sector, in turn, was represented by some of the strongest and most representative of the unions of the CGT (Textile workers, pharmaceutical industrial workers) and Força Sindical (commerce employees). They too provided sub-samples with workers from the private and the public services and from industry and service alike.

From these seven occupational categories we drew the sub-samples whose individuals were picked up by the use of random numbers applied to the unionised workers of a number of firms thought to be typical representatives of each occupational category. Accordingly, the respondents belonging to each occupational category were drawn from the following 58 firms thus distributed:

Textile Industry: Cotonifício Moreno, José Rufino, Braspérola, Fábrica Yolanda and Lipasa. All of them are private industrial factories.

Commerce Sector: Livraria e Papelaria Selmovene, Casa das Rendas, Lojas Jurandir Pires Galdino, José Mário de Andrade, Esquisita Calçados, Art-Livre, Esplanada, Casas José Araújo, Girafa Tecidos, Barbosa Móveis e Decoradora, Casa Luxótica, Livro-7, Lojas Cattam, Armarinho São Severino, Sabina Modas, Casa Sloper, Lojas Costa Júnior, Casas Pernambucanas, Casas Raimundo Bastos, Eletrofu, Edições Paulinas,

Mesbla, Sapatomania, Bazar Guarani, Casas Regente. All of them (25) are private commercial shops.

Pharmaceutical Industry: The state-owned pharmaceutical laboratory Laboratório Farmacêutico de Pernambuco – Lafepe.

Telecommunications: Telefônica de Pernambuco – Telpe, Telebrás, Embratel (state owned), Catel, Base Construtora, Montel (private building companies).

Data Processing: Serpro, Fundação Nacional de Saúde, Dataprev, Datamec (federal government-owned), Fisepe (Pernambuco state government owned), Emprel (Recife municipality owned), Procenge, Elógica, Jabur Inormática (private firms).

Metal Industry: Microlite and Noraço (private companies).

Banking: Banco Central do Brasil, Banco do Nordeste do Brasil, Banco do Brasil, Caixa Econômica Federal (federal government owned), Banco do Estado de Pernambuco (Pernambuco state owned), Banco Itaú, Banco Econômico, Banco Mercantil de Pernambuco, Bradesco and Bamerindus (private sector).

The size of the sub-samples and the total number of employees and union members to which they relate are displayed in Table A.1.

As it emerges from the number of respondents by occupational category, they constitute a simple random sample with no stratification. The reasons for such a procedure have to do with the already mentioned circumstance that our statistical method controls the factors which in

Table A.1 The sample by occupational categories

Occupational category	No. of Individuals in the sub-samples	Number of employees	Number of union due-payers
Textile Workers (CGT)	36	4,560	2,100
Commerce Employees (FS)	37	100,000*	8,000
Pharmaceutical Workers (CGT)	30	800	480
Telecom. Workers (CUT)	31	3,644	2,787
Data Proces. Employees (CUT)	32	2,667	2,430
Metalworkers (CUT)	27	7,324	3,500
Bank Employees (CUT)	18	25,000	16,000
Total	211	143,822	34,711

*Estimate provided by the union although it recognises the lack of firm ground for the estimation.

fact are characteristics of the respondents (sex, age, income, size of the firm, sector of the firm, type of occupation, etc.). So we needed a reasonable number of individuals whose features were diversified so as to provide different incidences of those variables, which was attained by the above sub-samples. Although the individuals were randomly selected in the chosen firms within each occupational category, rigorously speaking, the simple frequency of such features does not necessarily correspond to the actual frequencies of the selected occupational categories because of the absence of stratification.

Obviously such a stratification would be very difficult to achieve owing to the large number of companies in the occupational categories. But such a stratification was not necessary because these variables were already accounted for (and controlled) through their inclusion in the equation of the multiple regression. Moreover, the statistical device which controls the other factors shaping the respondents' attitudes assures a weaker probability of errors because it includes factors which would not be easily captured and understood by any stratification.

In Sections 2, 3 and 4 of Chapter 6 we illustrated our argument, so to speak, after having come across differences in the aggregated scores of the respondents by occupational categories which were in accordance with the hypothesis that the CUT union members scored higher in the scale of active citizenship than their counterparts in the union of the other sectors of the Brazilian labour movement. Although those aggregate scores were presented merely to illustrate our argument, since the more reliable statistical inferences were afforded by the regression analysis, the following Tables A.2 to A.9 advance the simple frequency of the main factors inserted into the model by occupational category. The reader thus may have an overview of the distribution of the characteristics of the survey sub-sample.

Table A.2   The sample by gender

Occupational category	No. of individuals in the sub-samples	Female (no.)	%	Male (no.)	(%)
Textile Workers (CGT)	36	5	13.88	31	86.11
Commerce Employees (FS)	37	19	51.35	18	48.64
Pharmaceutical Workers (CGT)	30	15	50.00	15	50.00
Telecom. Workers (CUT)	31	11	35.48	20	64.51
Data Proces. Employees (CUT)	32	11	34.37	21	65.62
Metalworkers (CUT)	27	2	7.40	25	92.59
Bank Employees (CUT)	18	4	22.22	14	77.77
Total	211	67	31.75	144	68.24

Table A.3   The sample by type of ownership of the respondent's firm

Occupational category	No. of individuals in the sub-samples	Public ownership (no.)	(%)	Private ownership (no.)	(%)
Textile Workers (CGT)	36	–	–	36	100.00
Commerce Employees (FS)	37	–	–	37	100.00
Pharmaceutical Workers (CGT)	30	30	100.00	–	100.00
Telecom. Workers (CUT)	31	26	83.87	5	16.12
Data Proces. Employees (CUT)	32	21	65.62	11	34.37
Metalworkers (CUT)	27	–	–	27	100.00
Bank Employees (CUT)	18	5	27.77	13	72.22
Total	211	82	38.86	129	61.13

Table A.4   The sample by type of job

Occupational category	No. of individuals in the sub-samples	Type of job White-collar (no.)	(%)	Blue collar (no.)	(%)
Textile Workers (CGT)	36	06	16.7	30	83.3
Commerce Employees (FS)	37	37	100.0	–	–
Pharmaceutical Workers (CGT)	30	12	40.0	18	60.0
Telecom. Workers (CUT)	31	18	58.1	13	41.9
Data Proces. Employees (CUT)	32	16	50.0	16	50.0
Metalworkers (CUT)	27	04	4.8	23	85.2
Bank Employees (CUT)	18	18	100.0	–	–
Total	211	111	52.6	100	47.4

Table A.5   The sample by the respondent's firm's economic sector

Occupational category	No. of individuals in the sub-samples	Firm's sector Industrial (no.)	(%)	Service (no.)	(%)
Textile Workers (CGT)	36	36	100.00	30	83.3
Commerce Employees (FS)	37	–	–	37	100.0
Pharmaceutical Workers (CGT)	30	30	100.0	–	–
Telecom. Workers (CUT)	31	–	–	31	100.0
Data Proces. Employees (CUT)	32	–	–	32	100.0
Metalworkers (CUT)	27	27	100.0	–	–
Bank Employees (CUT)	18	–	–	18	100.0
Total	211	93	44.1	118	55.9

Table A.6   The sample by years of study

Occupational category	Sub-samples	Years of study							
		0–5 (no.)	(%)	5–10 (no.)	(%)	10–15 (no.)	(%)	15+ (no.)	(%)
Textile Workers (CGT)	36	10	27.8	9	25.0	17	47.2	–	–
Comm. Employees (FS)	37	5	13.5	6	16.2	26	70.3	–	–
Pharmac. Workers (CGT)	30	3	10.0	9	30.0	14	46.7	4	13.3
Telecom. Workers (CUT)	31	4	12.9	3	9.7	15	48.4	9	29
Data Proces. Emp. (CUT)	32	1	3.1	1	3.1	20	62.5	10	31.3
Metalworkers (CUT)	27	10	37.0	11	40.7	6	22.2	–	–
Bank Employees (CUT)	18	–	–	–	–	10	55.6	8	44.5
Total	211	33	15.6	39	18.5	108	51.2	31	14.7

Table A.7   The sample by income: number of minimum wages (1 mw = 1 US$)

Occupational category	Sub-samples	Number of minimum wages							
		0–2 (no.)	(%)	2–5 (no.)	(%)	5–10 (no.)	(%)	10+ (no.)	(%)
Textile Workers (CGT)	36	12	33.3	18	50.0	6	16.7	–	–
Comm. Employees (FS)	37	28	75.7	8	21.6	1	2.7	–	–
Pharmac. Workers (CGT)	30	6	20.0	19	63.3	2	6.7	3	10.0
Telecom. Workers (CUT)	31	4	12.9	7	22.6	10	32.3	10	32.3
Data Proces. Emp. (CUT)	32	3	9.4	10	31.3	13	40.6	6	18.8
Metalworkers (CUT)	27	8	29.6	17	63.0	2	7.4	–	–
Bank Employees (CUT)	18	–	–	3	16.7	9	50.0	6	33.4
Total	211	61	28.9	82	38.9	43	20.4	25	11.8

Table A.8   The sample by age

Occupational category	Sub-samples	Age							
		0–25 (no.)	(%)	26–35 (no.)	(%)	36–45 (no.)	(%)	45+ (no.)	(%)
Textile Workers (CGT)	36	6	16.7	14	38.9	14	38.9	2	5.6
Comm. Employees (FS)	37	2	5.4	18	48.6	12	32.4	5	13.5
Pharmac. Workers (CGT)	30	2	6.7	15	50.0	10	33.3	3	10.0
Telecom. Workers (CUT)	31	1	3.2	4	12.9	17	54.8	9	29.0
Data Proces. Emp. (CUT)	32	–	–	17	53.1	11	34.4	4	12.5
Metalworkers (CUT)	27	1	3.7	13	48.1	8	29.6	5	18.5
Bank Employees (CUT)	18	2	11.1	10	55.6	5	27.8	1	5.6
Total	211	14	6.6	91	43.1	77	36.5	29	13.8

Table A.9(a)   The sample by size of the respondent's firm (under 500 employees)

Occupational category	Sub-samples	Size of the firm: total number of employees							
		1–10		11–50		51–100		101–500	
		(no.)	(%)	(no.)	(%)	(no.)	(%)	(no.)	(%)
Textile Workers (CGT)	36	–	–	–	–	–	–	–	–
Comm. Employees (FS)	37	9	24.3	7	18.9	8	21.6	13	35.1
Pharmac. Workers (CGT)	30	–	–	–	–	–	–	30	100.0
Telecom. Workers (CUT)	31	–	–	3	9.7	2	6.4	3	9.7
Data Proces. Emp. (CUT)	32	1	3.1	5	15.6	4	12.5	11	34.4
Metalworkers (CUT)	27	–	–	–	–	–	–	14	51.9
Bank Employees (CUT)	18	–	–	–	–	–	–	–	–
Total	211	10	4.7	15	7.1	14	6.6	71	33.6

Table A.9(b)   The sample by size of the respondent's firm (over 500 employees)

Occupational category	Sub-samples	Size of the firm: total number of employees			
		501–1,000		1,000+	
		(no.)	(%)	(no.)	(%)
Textile Workers (CGT)	36	25	69.5	11	30.6
Comm. Employees (FS)	37	–	–	–	–
Pharmac. Workers (CGT)	30	–	–	–	–
Telecom. Workers (CUT)	31	–	–	23	74.2
Data Proces. Emp. (CUT)	32	11	34.4	–	–
Metalworkers (CUT)	27	13	48.1	–	–
Bank Employees (CUT)	18	6	33.3	12	66.7
Total	211	55	26.0	46	21.8

Appendix 2: Measuring the Attitude of Active Citizenship – Interview Schedule

We are carrying out a study to be presented to the University of Oxford, England. We are interested in collecting information on workers' opinions, habits and feelings in the Metropolitan Region of Recife in order to assess their attitudes towards citizenship. Your name has been selected alongside two hundred other respondents. The contents of the responses that you will be requested to produce are absolutely confidential. Information identifying the respondent will not be disclosed under any circumstances.

MODULE ONE – UNIONS

I. Factual Questions on Behaviour

1. From the following motives, which one was the most important for you to have become a union member?
( ) some colleagues and\or union representatives asked me to do that [1]
( ) I needed to benefit from the facilities the union offers to its members [2]

( ) I realised that the union has performed a good job in raising our working conditions [3]
( ) strengthening my occupational category or professional group [4]
( ) strengthening workers' power [5]

2. How often do you attend the union headquarters?
( ) does not know   [1]
( ) never   [1]
( ) seldom   [2]
( ) once a month   [3]
( ) once a week   [4]
( ) always   [5]

3. Has your union ever called a strike? **[If the answer is no, please make the respondent go to question 5]**
( ) yes
( ) no

4. Have you ever taken part in the strikes that your union has already called?
( ) no   [1]
( ) yes [5]

5. How often do you talk to your work mates about union matters?
( ) don't know   [1]
( ) never   [2]
( ) seldom   [3]
( ) often   [4]
( ) always   [5]

6. Have you ever stood for elections in the union or workers' representation?
( ) no   [1]
( ) yes   [5]

7. How often do you seek to obtain information from representatives?
( ) never   [1]
( ) don't know   [1]
( ) seldom   [2]
( ) eventually   [3]
( ) often   [4]
( ) always   [5]

8. Did you vote in the last election in your union?
( ) no   [1]
( ) yes   [5]

9. Does your union have a newspaper? **[if yes, make the respondent answer question 10]**
( )   no
( )   yes

10. How often do you read the union's newspaper?
( ) don't get the newspaper   [1]
( ) never   [1]
( ) almost never   [2]
( ) read it sometimes   [3]
( ) read it rather often   [4]
( ) read it every edition   [5]

II. Attitudinal Questions

[Ask the respondent to choose the alternative that better express how he/she feels about the statements].

11. One better protects his/her interests by being a good employee and getting on well with the bosses than taking part in the union life.
( ) strongly agree   [1]
( ) agree   [2]
( ) uncertain   [3]
( ) disagree   [4]
( ) strongly disagree   [5]

12. The worker should take into consideration the union's position when he/she makes a decision about politics or working matters.
( ) strongly agree   [5]
( ) agree   [4]
( ) uncertain   [3]
( ) disagree   [2]
( ) strongly disagree   [1]

13. The main function of unions is providing facilities for their members (medical care, tests, lawyers, dentists etc.).
( ) strongly agree   [1]
( ) agree   [2]
( ) uncertain   [3]
( ) disagree   [4]
( ) strongly disagree   [5]

14. Unions should be concerned with the employer's managerial decisions besides striving to improve wages.
( ) strongly agree   [5]
( ) agree   [4]
( ) uncertain   [3]
( ) disagree   [2]
( ) strongly disagree   [1]

15. Your participation or lack of participation does not affect the union power to attain benefits for the workers.
( ) strongly agree   [1]
( ) agree   [2]
( ) uncertain   [3]
( ) disagree   [4]
( ) strongly disagree   [5]

16. Unions should try to have a say on political matters and governmental decisions.
( ) strongly agree   [5]
( ) agree   [4]

( ) uncertain   [3]
( ) disagree   [2]
( ) strongly disagree [1]

MODULE TWO – CONTROL AT WORK

I. Factual Questions on Behaviour

17. When your hierarchical superior makes an unfair or bad decision, what do you do?
( ) accept it   [1]
( ) don't know   [2]
( ) complain to the working mates only   [3]
( ) express your discordance to the hierarchical superior   [4]
( ) besides complaining to the hierarchical superior or to the working mates, you report it to the union or shop steward   [5]

18. How often do you try to interfere or make suggestions to improve work processes?
( ) never   [1]
( ) don't know   [1]
( ) seldom   [2]
( ) eventually   [3]
( ) often   [4]
( ) very often   [5]

19. Would you like to take part in any committees, seminar or course designed to discuss and improve organisational methods in your work?
( ) no   [1]
( ) yes   [5]

20. Have you participated in any negotiations with the firm as a representative of the union during the last 12 months?
( ) none   [1]
( ) don't know   [2]
( ) less than three [3]
( ) three–four   [4]
( ) five or more   [5]

II. Attitudinal Questions

[Ask the respondent to choose the alternative that better expresses how he/she feels about the statements].

21. You should have more participation in the management of the firm for which you work.
( ) strongly agree   [5]
( ) agree   [4]

( ) uncertain   [3]
( ) disagree   [2]
( ) strongly disagree   [1]

22. Decisions about production should be undertaken by the employer because he/she is the owner of the enterprise.
( ) strongly agree   [1]
( ) agree   [2]
( ) uncertain   [3]
( ) disagree   [4]
( ) strongly disagree   [5]

23. Workers have nothing they can do against a supervisor or boss who is unfair in his/her managerial decisions.
( ) strongly agree   [1]
( ) agree   [2]
( ) uncertain   [3]
( ) disagree   [4]
( ) strongly disagree   [5]

24. Workers should not aspire to workplace control measures because such a matter is up to the employer.
( ) strongly agree   [1]
( ) agree   [2]
( ) uncertain   [3]
( ) disagree   [4]
( ) strongly disagree   [5]

25. The worker should always comply with the employer's decisions because this is what he/she agrees when signing the contract of employment in return for wage.
( ) strongly agree   [1]
( ) agree   [2]
( ) uncertain   [3]
( ) disagree   [4]
( ) strongly disagree   [5]

26. Workers should have a say in the sharing of the firm's profits.
( ) strongly agree   [5]
( ) agree   [4]
( ) uncertain   [3]
( ) disagree   [2]
( ) strongly disagree   [1]

MODULE THREE – ASSOCIATIVE LIFE

I. Factual Questions on Behaviour

27. Are you a member of any neighbourhood association?
( ) no   [1]
( ) yes   [5]

28. Are you an active member of church movements?
( ) no   [1]
( ) yes   [5]

29. Are you affiliated to any political party?
( ) no   [1]
( ) yes   [5]

30. Are you a member of any other civil society bodies such as environmental associations, racial groups, feminist organisations or student unions?
( ) no   [1]
( ) yes   [5]

31. Have you ever participated in the union's affiliation campaigns or other associations of which you are a member?
( ) no   [1]
( ) yes   [5]

32. And in fundraising campaigns?
( ) no   [1]
( ) yes   [5]

33. How often have you been a member of the directive bodies of your association?
( ) never   [1]
( ) one mandate   [2]
( ) two mandates   [3]
( ) three mandates   [4]
( ) four or more mandates   [5]

34. In case you have already taken part in directive boards of your association, have you ever been a member of any executive committees?
( ) no   [1]
( ) yes   [5]

35. How often do you attend the association's promotions and campaigns such as demonstrations, collective signature of petitions and other kind of pressures?
( ) never   [1]
( ) seldom   [2]

( ) eventually   [3]
( ) often   [4]
( ) always   [5]

II. Attitudinal Questions

[Ask the respondent to choose the alternative that better expresses how he/she feels about the statements].

36. On the hypothesis that you had a good salary and good conditions of life, you would still participate in the association of which you are a member. **[skip to question 37 if the respondent is not a member of any association]**
( ) strongly agree   [5]
( ) agree   [4]
( ) uncertain   [3]
( ) disagree   [2]
( ) strongly disagree   [1]

37. Some people say they do not become members of associations because one can more easily protect his/her interests by taking care individually of one's own life. How do you feel about that?
( ) strongly agree   [1]
( ) agree   [2]
( ) uncertain   [3]
( ) disagree   [4]
( ) strongly disagree   [5]

38. The poor need to combine to protect their interests because individually they are not influential enough.
( ) strongly agree   [5]
( ) agree   [4]
( ) uncertain   [3]
( ) disagree   [2]
( ) strongly disagree   [1]

39. Acting in combination through political associations such as unions and parties is an illusion that benefits only the politicians and ideologists.
( ) strongly agree   [1]
( ) agree   [2]
( ) uncertain   [3]
( ) disagree   [4]
( ) strongly disagree   [5]

40. In order to advance the opinions and needs of the common citizen, voting is a necessary step but not sufficient.
( ) strongly agree   [5]
( ) agree   [4]
( ) uncertain   [3]

( ) disagree   [2]
( ) strongly disagree   [1]

MODULE FOUR – POLITICS AND SENSE OF SUBJECTIVE COMPETENCE

I. Factual Questions on Behaviour

41. When your rights are threatened or violated, what course of action do you prefer to undertake?
( ) don't know   [1]
( ) do nothing   [2]
( ) protest at home or with friends   [3]
( ) act alone (directly contact political leaders or administrative officials, appeal to the courts, vote against offending officials at next election)
                                                    [4]
( ) try to enlist aid of others (get people to write letters or to sign a petition, work through a political party, union, church, neighbourhood association or professional entity) [5]

42. What about talking about politics to other people? How often do you that?
( ) never   [1]
( ) seldom   [2]
( ) from time to time [3]
( ) often   [4]
( ) always   [5]

43. Have you ever tried to persuade other people to vote in a certain way?
( ) never   [1]
( ) seldom   [2]
( ) from time to time [3]
( ) often   [4]
( ) always   [5]

44. Would you mind telling us how often you participated in electoral campaigns in the last five years?
( ) none   [1]
( ) only one   [2]
( ) two   [3]
( ) three   [4]
( ) four or more   [5]

45. Do you read political news in magazines and newspaper?
( ) never   [1]
( ) seldom   [2]
( ) once a week   [3]

( ) several times a week   [4]
( ) daily   [5]

46. How often do you watch political programmes or news on the TV or listen to them on the radio?
( ) never   [1]
( ) seldom   [2]
( ) once a week   [3]
( ) several times a week   [4]
( ) daily   [5]

47. Did you vote in the plebiscite on parliamentarianism or presidentialism held in 1993?
( ) don't remember   [1]
( ) no   [1]
( ) yes   [5]

48. Does it happen that you try to interest a fellow worker in reading an editorial or political article in a newspaper?
( ) never   [1]
( ) seldom   [2]
( ) from time to time   [3]
( ) often   [4]
( ) always   [5]

II. Attitudinal Questions

[Ask the respondent to choose the alternative that better expresses how he/she feels about the statements].

49. Some people claim that the ordinary citizen can influence public affairs. What do you think about that?
( ) strongly agree   [5]
( ) agree   [4]
( ) uncertain   [3]
( ) disagree   [2]
( ) strongly disagree   [1]

50. The ordinary citizen can hardly do anything to protect his/her interest because things are decided by the powerful.
( ) strongly agree   [1]
( ) agree   [2]
( ) uncertain   [3]
( ) disagree   [4]
( ) strongly disagree   [5]

51. Democracy is a better form of government than any other.
( ) strongly agree   [5]
( ) agree   [4]

( ) uncertain   [3]
( ) disagree   [2]
( ) strongly disagree   [1]

52. Acting together with other people is too complicated and slow to produce any good results to advance my interests.
( ) strongly agree   [1]
( ) agree   [2]
( ) uncertain   [3]
( ) disagree   [4]
( ) strongly disagree   [5]

53. You feel that you can persuade other people to strengthen your common claims.
( ) strongly agree   [5]
( ) agree   [4]
( ) uncertain   [3]
( ) disagree   [2]
( ) strongly disagree   [1]

54. Mobilisations such as rallies and meetings do not normally yield significant results.
( ) strongly agree   [1]
( ) agree   [2]
( ) uncertain   [3]
( ) disagree   [4]
( ) strongly disagree   [5]

55. You would vote in elections even if it was not mandatory.
( ) strongly agree   [5]
( ) agree   [4]
( ) uncertain   [3]
( ) disagree   [2]
( ) strongly disagree   [1]

56. Under certain circumstances, a dictatorship is better than a democratic regime.
( ) strongly agree   [1]
( ) agree   [2]
( ) uncertain   [3]
( ) disagree   [4]
( ) strongly disagree   [5]

57. The government should be allowed to crack down on certain strikes.
( ) strongly agree   [1]
( ) agree   [2]
( ) uncertain   [3]
( ) disagree   [4]
( ) strongly disagree   [5]

58. The poor should not vote for poor candidates because the latter are prone to become corrupt.
( ) strongly agree   [1]
( ) agree   [2]
( ) uncertain   [3]
( ) disagree   [4]
( ) strongly disagree   [5]

59. A citizen should have a preference for a particular political party.
( ) strongly agree   [5]
( ) agree   [4]
( ) uncertain   [3]
( ) disagree   [2]
( ) strongly disagree   [1]

60. When voting, the elector should only care about the personal characteristics of the chosen candidate instead of their political party affiliation.
( ) strongly agree   [1]
( ) agree   [2]
( ) uncertain   [3]
( ) disagree   [4]
( ) strongly disagree   [5]

MODULE FIVE – DATA ON THE ENTERPRISE

61. Size of the enterprise where you work: _____ employees

62. Type of ownership of the enterprise where you work.
( ) public   [1]
( ) private   [0]

63. Sector of activity of the enterprise where you work.
( ) industry   [1]
( ) services   [0]

64. Employer's attitude. What's the attitude of the enterprise towards the union?
( ) make all possible efforts to eliminate it   [1]
( ) try to prevent the union from growing   [2]
( ) try to co-opt it   [3]
( ) don't worry about it   [4]
( ) respect the union's role   [5]
( ) help within certain limits   [6]
( ) co-operate as much as possible   [7]
( ) don't know   [8]

MODULE SIX – DEMOGRAPHIC CHARACTERISTICS OR CLASSIFYING QUESTIONS

[We are now asking you some questions about personal characteristics in order to classify and analyse the data we are collecting. The information you are requested to give us is confidential].

[Please declare the alternative that corresponds to your situation]

65. Number of dependants: _____

66. Sex
( ) male   [1]
( ) female   [2]

67. Father's occupation:
a) occupation: _____
b) last job: _____

68. Mother's occupation:
a) occupation: _____
b) last job: _____

69. Educational level of the respondent.
( ) illiterate   [0]
( ) less than five years   [2]
( ) five years   [4]
( ) from five to seven years [6.5]
( ) eight years   [9]
( ) from eight to ten   [10.5]
( ) eleven years   [12]
( ) incomplete graduate   [14]
( ) graduate or more   [16]

70. Age: _____ years old

71. Occupation. Your job in the enterprise is: _____

72. Type of job:
( ) bureaucratic or white collar   [0]
( ) production or blue collar   [1]

73. Time in the job: _____ years

74. Interaction at work. How often do you talk to your working mates during work?
( ) often   [1]
( ) seldom   [2]
( ) almost never   [3]

75. Solidarity at work. Suppose you were transferred to another sector of the enterprise, away from the current mates, but keeping current tasks and wage. How would you feel?
( ) you would not mind   [1]
( ) you would mind a bit   [2]
( ) you would be upset   [3]
( ) you would be very upset   [4]

76. How long have you been affiliated to the union? _____ years.

77. Do you regard yourself as a militant unionist?
( ) yes   [1]
( ) no   [0]

78. Your monthly income is worth _____ national minimum wages.

79. Union of affiliation: _____.

80. Name: _____.

CODIFICATION. The alternatives 1 to 60 correspond to the dependent variable – workers' attitudes. The dimension being measured is that which we term 'the attitude of active citizenship'. Each item was given a score from 1 to 5. The higher the score, the stronger is the presence of such a dimension displayed by the respondent in that particular answer. A total score will be elicited from each respondent for questions 1 to 60 (the sum of his or her scores in each item), from which an average will be calculated and used in the multiple regression test. The second parts of each module, concerned with attitudes sensu stricto, are made up of both positive and negative items. The positive ones are scored as follows: SA=5; A=4; U=3; D=2; SD=1. The negative ones, as follows: SA=1; A=2; U=3; D=4; SD=5. The positive items are: 12, 14, 16, 21, 26, 36, 38, 40, 49, 51, 53, 55 and 59. The negative ones are: 11, 13, 15, 22, 23, 24, 25, 37, 39, 50, 52, 54, 56, 57, 58 and 60. The possible variation of the scale ranges from 60 to 300.

Appendix 3: Recorded Strikes in Pernambuco, 1955–64

Start	End	Occupational category	Place	Goals	Worker's organisation	Mediation	Achievements
07.55	–*	Port Workers	Recife	Against threat of intervention in the union	Union	–	–
07.09.55	20.10.55	Port Workers	Recife	Union prerogatives	Union and Commission	–	defeat
10.55	n.a.	rural workers	Goiana	Wage equalisation	Union and Commission	–	–
05.05.56	–	Textile workers	Paulista	Against wage restraint	Worker's Commission	–	–
14.05.56	16.08.56	Textile workers	Moreno	Payment of the legal minimum wage	Union	Ministry of Labour	attainment of demands
29.07.56	16.08.56	Textile workers	Paulista	Readjustment of the minimum wage	Union and Commission	Shop Stewards and employers	attainment of demands
13.08.56	14.09.56	Textile workers	Paulista	Readjustment of the minimum wage	Union and Workers Commission	Shop Stewards and employers	attainment of demands
1957	–	Textile workers	Goiana	Wages overdue	Union	State Government and Regional Office of the Ministry of Labour	–
02.07.57	–	Telegraph Workers	Recife	Wage increase	Union	State Government	attainment of demands
21.01.58	10.03.58	Textile Workers	Recife and Escada	Payment of wage increase ruled by the Labour Court	Commission of Unions	Labour Court	attainment of demands
08.09.58	11.09.58	Railway Workers	Jaboatão	Wage increase	–	–	–
07.03.59	05.04.59	Port Workers	Recife	Wage overdue	Inter-union pact and Union Worker's federation	State Government	attainment of demands
14.12.59	16.12.59	Port Workers	Recife	Wage increase	'Confederação Sindical dos Trabalhadores' (Consintra)	–	–
29.08.61	29.08.61	General	Pernambuco	Against the military manoeuvres not to allow vice-president João Goulart to take office after Jânio Quadros resignation	–	–	–
03.09.61	09.09.61	Port Workers	Recife	For the release of imprisoned workers	–	–	–

continued on page 280

Start	End	Occupational category	Place	Goals	Worker's organisation	Mediation	Achievements
20.10.61	28.10.61	Bank Employees	Recife	Wage increase	Union	Direct bargaining	–
26.05.62	–	Bank Employees	Northeast Region	Wage increases	–	–	–
07.07.62	21.07.62	Oil Workers	Pernambuco	Wage increase	Union and Consintra	–	–
21.09.62	22.09.62	Civil Servants	Pernambuco	Wage increase	State Civil Servants Association	–	–
06.02.63	–	Drivers	Recife	Wage increase	Commission	State Government	demands partially met
13.02.63	20.02.63	Textile Workers	Paulista	Wage increase	'Peasant Leagues'	–	attainment of demands
04.01.63	10.01.63	Rural Workers	Vitória de Santo Antão	Wage increase and working conditions			
18.02.63	02.02.63	Rural Workers	Jaboatão	Wage overdue	'Peasant Leagues' and Union	–	attainment of demands
		Rural Workers	Jaboatão (Usina Tiúma)	Wage overdue	–	–	–
		Rural Workers	Vitória de Santo Antão	Wage increase	'Peasant Leagues'	–	–
14.03.63	15.03.63	Port Workers	Recife	Wage increase	Strike Commission	State Government	attainment of demands
		Paper Industry Workers	Jaboatão	Wage increase and unpaid holidays	–	–	–
18.03.63		Building Industry Workers	Metropolitan Region of Recife	Wage increase	Union and Commissions	State Government and Regional Office of the Labour Ministry	partial attainment of demands
21.03.63	09.04.63	Printing Industry Workers	Recife	Wage increase	Union	–	attainment of demands
		Commerce Employees	Recife	Wage increase	–	–	–
22.04.63	26.04.63	Rural Workers	Trapiche Sugar plant	Wage increase		State government	partial attainment of demands
21.05.63	22.05.63	Rural Workers	Jaboatão	Union recognition by the state		State Government	–
13.07.63		Rural Workers	Catende	Against dismissals and unfair measuring of work tasks by employers	'Peasant Leagues'	–	–
		Rural Workers	Moreno	Against illegal wage discounts for habitation	Union	State Government	attainment of demands
		Rural Workers	Jaboatão	Against illegal wage discount for habitation	'Peasant Leagues' and Union	State Government	attainment of demands
		Cigarettes Industry Workers (Souza Cruz)	Recife	Wage overdue	Union	–	–

06.06.63	07.06.63	Port Workers	Recife	Solidarity with Port Workers of Santos	Union	–	–
18.06.63		Rural Workers	Jaboatão, Vitória, and Goiana	Right to paid weekend rest	'Peasant Leagues' and Union	–	–
15.06.63		Rural Workers	Ipojuca, Igarassu Ribeirão	Wage increase	'Peasant Leagues'	–	–
27.07.63	20.08.63	Rural Workers		Wage overdue and labour law enforcement	Union	Ministry of Labour and State Government	attainment of demands
10.08.63		Rural Workers	També	Protest against the murder of a rural worker	'Peasant Leagues'	–	–
19.09.63	24.09.63	Rural Workers	Jaboatão	Against unemployment and the dismissal of union leader	'Peasant Leagues' and Union	Regional Office of the Labour Ministry	partial attainment of demands
26.09.63	28.09.63	Port Workers	Recife	Wage increase	Union	Regional Office of the Labour Ministry	–
10.11.63	15.11.63	Fishers	Pernambuco	Demand for a regular wage and payment of weekend rest	'Peasant Leagues'	–	–
18.11.63	18.11.63	Rural and Sugar Industry Workers	Pernambuco (general)	Wage increase	Union and 'Peasant Leagues'	Regional Offices of the Labour Ministry and State Government	attainment of demands
	11.12.63	Bank Employees	Pernambuco	Against the violation by banks of the wage increase settled by the labour court	Union	State Government	defeat in the judgement by the labour court
16.02.64		Rural Workers	Vitória and Moreno	Against the dismissal and expelling of peasants by the farm Serra	'Peasant Leagues'	State Government	–
24.02.64	03.03.64	Sugar Industry Workers	Pernambuco	Wage increase	Union	State Government	–
03.03.64	03.03.64	General strike in the state	Pernambuco	Solidarity to the sugar industry workers and to the Government of Miguel Arraes SINTRA	Consintra	–	–
31.03.64	31.03.64	General strike in the state	Pernambuco	Against the threat of military take-over	Consintra	–	–

Note: Instead of the conventional N.A. for unavailable data, we indicate them with (–) for reasons of style.

Source: Soares (1982).

Notes and References

1 Introduction

1. Throughout this book, purely for stylistic reasons, we shall use the expression 'new unionism' without the inverted commas. Likewise, the type of unions identified with the current 'new unionism' will be referred to as 'new unions'.
2. The benefits introduced in the 1930s were made available on the condition of workers' affiliation to the official unions as a means to attract a labour force which up to the early 1940s remained largely reluctant to voluntary affiliation to the state-sponsored unions (Vianna, 1976; Araújo, 1993). The Decree 22,128, of 25.11.32, for example, whilst creating the 'Juntas de Conciliação e Julgamento' (an embryo of the labour courts later organised by Decree-law 1,237 of 02.05.39), stipulated that only union due-payers could have access to it. Similarly, the Decree 23,768 of 18.01.34 granted the right to paid vacations to industrial workers only if they became union members.
3. French's study of the metalworkers of the ABC (Santo André, São Bernarbe, São Caetano) region in São Paulo in the 1940s and 1950s tends to stress the way the leftist militants penetrated the union structure and pressed for a more militant union stance, often trying to gain benefits for labour through electoral politics. Wolfe, in turn, is primarily concerned with informal organisation at the grassroots; an effort which attempts to reconstruct labour history through a 'phenomenological approach' which emphasises the way the workers themselves perceived the relations and institutions in which they were immersed. It may be argued that Wolfe somewhat exaggerates grassroots opposition, for account should be taken also of the attempts by the PCB and left-wing union officials both in the Constituent Assembly and at union level to secure greater autonomy for unions. It should also be noted that in certain moments (e.g. 1945–46) there emerged a gap between the official line of the PCB and their union militants when the latter took further steps towards rank-and-file mobilisation.
4. The presence of contradictions in worker attitudes will be addressed in more detail in Chapter 7.
5. For a further analysis of the assumptions of the 'instrumental authoritarians', see the argument developed by Costa (1992).
6. In this particular, one might recall an often quoted saying by one of the key finance ministers of the military, Antônio Delfim Neto: 'Let's first wait for the growth of the cake; then we will distribute it.'
7. The 'regulated citizenship' instituted by the State may be said to bear an elective affinity to deep-lying factors in the 'national political culture', according to the analyses of a long line of Brazilian scholars

from Oliveira Vianna (1987) to a recent interpretative essay by Sales (1994). The long-standing patterns of dependency of the poor have sustained one or another variety of clientelistic attitudes towards private or public patrons and a 'culture of the gift' ('the obverse of citizenship'). It may be added parenthetically that many other contemporary Brazilian social analysts have coined expressions with a similar connotation such as 'culture of the favours', 'culture of orders' ('mando'), 'culture of subservience', 'culture of bestowal' ('outorga'), 'relational culture' of inequality', etc. In the expression 'culture of the gift', gift is understood in the anthropological *sensu stricto*, implying the obligation to give, the obligation to receive as well as the obligation to repay. This 'culture of the gift' underpins what Sales calls 'granted citizenship' ('cidadania concedida'), where rights (political or social) are solely bestowed by superordinate actors.

Whilst such generalisations have been ably defended by a number of leading Brazilian sociologists and political scientists, there are of course serious conceptual and methodological difficulties with this type of argumentation. First, the overall characterisation of 'national political culture' in terms of a few master traits is always problematical. Second, there are serious difficulties with the attribution of remote causality to long-past historical conjunctures (in this case, one of the most often invoked causal antecedents is the social circumstances of the aftermath of the abolition of slavery). Third, one must disaggregate 'national political cultures' into a more analytically accountable array of sub-cultures, e.g. regional and sectoral variation. In this case, Brandão (1994) has pointed to the legacy of the less dependent relationship in the coffee zone in the Southeast as they emerged in the 1880s and after the abolition of slavery (though this claim is liable to the kinds of objections raised in our second point).

8. Of course, his excessive emphasis on class conflict as the medium for expansion of citizenship tends to overshadow the role of other areas of the social struggle such as that of the 'underclass' or the new social movements. It has been argued that Giddens's approach in fact overlooks the special role of the new social movements in the battle for extension of the frontiers of citizenship (Barbalet, 1988).

9. Some dimensions of labour and work with an important bearing on citizenship theory but not discussed in the present study, such as the 'right' to work as a condition of full participation in society, and the issue of citizenship 'at work' or 'industrial citizenship', have been addressed by authors like Leisink and Coenen (1993b) and Heycock (1993).

2 The Brazilian System of Labour Relations and the Revival of the Labour Movement

1. The literature has identified different modalities of corporatism such as the state or the societal, the inclusionary or the exclusionary variants. Applying such analytical distinctions on the Brazilian case, there are interesting studies which further detail the country's system

of industrial relations such as Schmitter (1971); Mericle (1977); Erickson (1977); and Humphrey (1982).

2. For well-informed studies on the relationship of the Brazilian labour movement with the corporatist framework in the period from the 1930s to the 1950s, see Wolfe (1993), French (1992) and Collier and Collier (1991, 1992). The first provides useful insights on the workers' reaction to coporatism as exemplified by the initial refusal of the influential 'Federação Operária de São Paulo – FOSP', the Metalworkers' Union and the Textile's Union to apply for recognition by the Ministry of Labour (pp. 55, 229).

3. Henceforth references to category will mean occupational category.

4. As we shall see, the 1988 Constitution maintained the union tax and other features of the corporatist model.

5. Up till 1967 Article 482 of the CLT granted workers the right not to be dismissed after ten years in the job, except for certain kinds of conduct.

6. In Britain, Section 60A of the Employment Protection (Consolidation) Act 1978 prohibits dismissal in retaliation against the initiative of the employee either for suing the employer to enforce a statutory right or merely for complaining against its breach. Even the anti-labour legislative programme enacted after 1979 did not fail to acknowledge its importance.

7. Interview with Marcos Sá Correia in *Revista Veja*, 21 June 1995.

8. This right, termed 'procedural substitution by the union', has a precedent in the Italian Statute of Workers of 1970.

9. The 'classist judges' are representatives of the occupational categories chosen by the labour courts from lists presented by unions. Following the parallelism between the occupational categories, each 'junta de conciliação e julgamento' functions with one representative of employers and another of employees. In the higher levels, the courts also comply with such a parallelism. The justification of the institution has been said to lie on the contribution to the fairness of the court decisions provided by the classist judges' knowledge of the reality of the occupational categories' working conditions. Critics argue that in practice decisions are made up by the career judges (who are professionally trained and chosen through public contest) and the institute has merely reinforced the proliferation of bureaucratic 'stamp unions' ('sindicatos de carimbo') created in order to secure access to the highly paid job of 'classist judge'. Being typical of corporatism, such an institute has reinforced union dependence on state apparatuses. For a detailed study of the 'classist representation', see Barreto (1994).

10. Interview in *Revista Veja*, already quoted.

11. Accurate reports on those events connected with the rise of the so-called new unionism are in Moisés (1982), Skidmore (1988), Keck (1989) and Branford and Kucinski (1995).

12. The role of the regional branches of the Brazilian Laywers Association should not be overlooked.

13. According to prevalent usage, 'pelego' refers to the non-militant

unionist whose action deadens the labour conflict and very often acts on behalf of the employers. Henceforth the expression will be employed without inverted commas.

14. Personal communication in Brasília, May 7th 1995 (interview no. 18).

15. CONTAG is the upper-level confederation of rural workers which played an important role in the renascence of the labour movement in the late 1970s. It was a militant sector within the CGT whose leadership did not share certain concepts of the sectors which had founded the CUT, particularly concerning the unity of the movement (interview no. 25, with José Francisco da Silva).

16. See 'Estatutos da CGT', in *Boletim DIEESE*, April 1986, pp. 11–15; and the CGT's 'Plano de Lutas', in *Boletim DIEESE*, May 1986, pp. 25–6.

17. Joaquim dos Santos Andrade resigned as president of the 'Central Geral dos Trabalhadores' in April 1991. His retirement signalled the end of one of the most important and controversial careers of a union official in the country. His successor in the presidency was Antônio Neto, an MR-8's activist. Justifying the reasons for his resignation, 'Joaquinzão' alleged that the 'central' had ceased to be a pluralist organisation, having become a prisoner of certain ideological groups (cf. *O Estado de São Paulo*, issue of 24.04.91).

18. When President Collor came to office in 1990 he appointed Antonio Rogério Magri as his Minister of Labour in a clear move to strengthen the 'unionism of results' branch of the labour movement at the expense of the antagonistic CUT.

19. Força Sindical's programme and the report on the founding congress may be found in *Boletim DIEESE*, April 1991, 11; see also Martins (1991: 154) and Rodrigues and Cardoso (1993).

20. As Rodrigues and Cardoso remark (1993: 164), one of the most important entities in FS is the Federation of Food Workers of São Paulo, whose leader was elected vice-president of FS in the inaugural congress in 1991. Despite representing 28 unions in the sector, this federation has always tended to enter into poor agreements with the Federation of Industries of the State of São Paulo (FIESP) without seeking to strengthen its position through industrial action.

21. Cf. Rodrigues and Cardoso, *Força Sindical* (1993), and interviews nos 26 and 13 with José Inácio Cassiano de Souza and Francisco Fragoso, respectively, the president of the FS-affiliated Watchmen Union of Recife and the lawyer of a number of unions affiliated to FS in the state of Pernambuco. See also the section on the Commerce Employees of Recife presented in Chapter 4.

22. The 'Communist Party of Brazil' originated from a split in the 'Brazilian Communist Party' in the late 1950s, being marked by an orthodox line.

23. Notwithstanding certain divergences with the CUT's proposals against the monopoly of representation, the 'Corrente Sindical Classista' joined the CUT on the basis of agreement on its militancy and concern with the need for changes in the wider society. For details about the principles adopted by such a group, see the report on

the mentioned congress in *Boletim DIEESE*, April 1990, pp. 18–19.
24. According to Brazilian Law, when a civil servant is made redundant ('en disponibilidade') it means that his or her link with the state is either temporarily or definitively suspended.
25. The FGTS is a fund formed by contributions from employees and employers to provide the workers with compensation in the event of dismissal. It was first introduced in 1967 by the military as a substitute for the job stability of 10 years of employment and it was provided by the CLT.
26. This is a fund formed by resources from the PIS-PASEP, which in turn is constituted by a contribution equal to 0.65 per cent of the total enterprises's payroll to the benefit of the employees and civil servants.
27. This is a fund made up by resources from the Treasury whose aim is the financing of social policies in general.
28. A discussion of the origin, assumptions and details of this set of proposals is provided in the following chapter. See also, Ministério do Trabalho (1994a); *Boletim Informacut*, nos 205, 206 and 250; Barros (1994); Medeiros (1994); and Siqueira-Neto (1994b).
29. For details of these proposals, see Pastore (1992 and 1993), Siqueira-Neto (1994, 1994b), *Boletim Informacut* no. 250, Zylberstajn (1993).
30. For the complete name of these employers entities, see the table of abbreviations provided at the outset of this book.
31. According to the report offered by *Revista Veja* (issue of 31.05.95), the decision of the 'Tribunal Superior do Trabalho' had already been announced to the government the day before. One of the judges of that court, Almir Pazzianoto, had talked to the Minister José Serra assuring him that the court would rule against the strike but feared loss of moral authority if the government reached an agreement with the union after its decision.
32. Cf. *The Economist*, 27 May 1995; *Revista Veja*, issue no. 1,394, 31.05.95; *Folha de São Paulo*, issues of 04.05.95, 12.05.95, 13.05.95 and 30.05.95; and *Jornal do Commercio*, 31.05.95.

3 The CUT's Model: Structures, Practices and Proposals

1. For an account of this general strike with reference to the stoppages per sector and states, see *Boletim DIEESE* of February 1987.
2. For details and balance, see Antunes (1991) and *Boletim do DIEESE*, April 1989, 'separata'.
3. Data from *Análise de Conjuntura*, no. 18, July 1990.
4. 'Resoluções do 4o. Congresso', CUT(1991: 5).
5. The research carried out by the 'Núcleo de Estudos de Políticas Públicas da Universidade Estadual de Campinas' rests on data compiled by the 'Departamento Intersindical de Estatística e Estudos Sócio-Econômicos – DIEESE'. Since the DIEESE is linked to the whole labour movement, its data on strikes are more likely to depict a wider range of stoppages than the DESEP's – a body of the CUT which was the source employed in the above tables for the year 1992.

6. Quoted by Keck (1989: 260–61), reporting a personal interview held late in 1978.
7. Interview no. 18, carried out by the author on 7 May 1995.
8. Unionisation ratio in countries like Brazil, which are still based on compulsory union contribution and monopoly of representation, have to be considered with caution in that the survival of the union does not depend on voluntary affiliation.
9. In contrast with the economically active population, occupied population refers to all the people actually working.
10. Data presented in the survey co-ordinated by Rodrigues, 'A Representação Sindical da CUT', reviewed and modified in 1991. In 'Retrato da CUT', São Paulo, published by the CUT, 1991.
11. The influence of the bargaining in big companies on the general standards settled in other sectors of the labour market has been recognised by the literature, as is exemplified by the observation made by Ferner and Hyman (1992: 22) about the impact of bargaining in companies such as Ford on the setting of the 'going-rate' of wages in other agreements in Britain.
12. The acronym OWW will henceforth stand for 'organisation within the work place' in an analogous way to the expression used in the Brazilian context by proponents of the reform of the industrial relations system – 'OLT', an abbreviation for 'organização no local de trabalho'.
13. The main contours of this process of decentralisation of collective bargaining and the birth of the factory commission within the enterprise is accurately described by Keller's study of the factory commissions of the metalmechanic sector in São Paulo (Keller, 1986).
14. See 'Resoluções da 6a. Plenária Nacional' (CUT, 1993). 'Plenária Nacional' is the national meeting called to adopt general deliberations in the meantime between two national congresses, which in turn, are the supreme deliberative body of the CUT.
15. 'CIPA' stands for 'Internal Commission for the Prevention of Accidents', a body introduced by the CLT (Articles 163/165) to oversee health and safety matters at the workplace. Half of the members are appointed by the employer and the other half by the employees, the latter being protected by provisions against unfair dismissal. Such a protection should not be confounded with the job stability stipulated by the former Article 492 of 'CLT' (repealed by the 1988 Constitution), which prohibited the dismissal of the worker who had stayed in a job for ten or more years. The legal protection of the employees elected to the 'CIPA' led the unions to use such a worker's representation as an arm of the union within the enterprise. In practice, most members of the 'CIPA' act as if they were elected shop stewards, as exemplified by the Metalworkers' Union of Pernambuco, one of the unions surveyed in this study. Given the fact that many enterprises do not allow the election of shop stewards, as is the case of the steel producer 'Gerdau', the workers' representation in the 'CIPA' became practically the only outlet for union organisation within the workplace.

16. For the term 'classist' the new unionism militants understand a conception which stresses the workers' autonomy and independence as a social class.

17. When the 'collective labour contract' proposal was advanced as a synthesis of the CUT's approach, its alternative structure of vertical organisations had already been put into practice in some economic branches such as banking and metalmechanic industry.

18. The reference to 'articulation of levels of negotiation' means that the contents of bargaining are distributed among such levels as national, regional, economic branch and enterprise in a co-ordinated way. The competence of the more specific spheres of negotiation is, so to speak, devolved by the more aggregate levels.

19. The text of the 'protocolo' can be found in *Cadernos da CUT*, 1991, no. 5, p. 38.

20. Texts of both agreements are respectively in *Cadernos da CUT*, 1991, no. 5, p. 45, and *Cadernos da CUT*, 1990, no. 3, São Paulo, internal publications.

21. The expression 'collective laissez faire' was coined by Kahn-Freund (1959: 224) to characterise the British system as based on the immunity of the unions from the restriction imposed by the 'common law' under the doctrine (and pretext) of 'restraint of trade'. For this author, the British system rested upon the assumption that regulation of the employment relationship should be left to the parties, the State and the law being assigned with the task of marginal intervention in support of those areas of great imbalance of power between employers and employees.

22. For a sample of the support rights embedded in the Italian 'Statuto' which offers us a good idea of its importance to the development of collective bargaining, see the 'Statuto dei Lavoratori', in Giugni's *Codice di Direito del Lavoro* (1994).

4 Trade Unionism in Pernambuco

1. For more information and analyses of the 'peasants leagues' and rural unions in that period, see Kadt (1970: 24–31, 67–121) and Touraine (1989: 209–10). For an analysis of the rural trade unionism in the period which followed the pre-1964 labour unrest, with a focus on the state of Pernambuco, among others, see Maybury-Lewis (1994).

2. See note 22 in Chapter 3.

3. On 31 August, the Second National Bank Workers' Meeting, gathering 4,000 delegates, defeated the CONCLAT's proposal not to call the national strike on September 11th, thus concurring with the CUT's proposal to call the stoppage (*Boletim da CUT/PE*, October 1985).

4. The members of the Commission Pro-CUT coming from the movement in Pernambuco were José Francisco da Silva (then president of the National Rural Workers Confederation – CONTAG), Edvaldo Gomes de Souza (from the Urban Workers' Union), José Siqueira (from the Metalworkers' Union) and José Rodrigues da Silva (from the Rural Workers' Federation).

5. In the National Congress of Foundation of the CGT held in March 1986 the following trade unions of Pernambuco were elected to form the First National Council of the CGT: Rural Workers' Federation, Industrial Workers' Federation, Textile Workers' Union and Bank Employees' Union (CGT, 1986: 14).

6. The first executive direction of the CUT in Pernambuco, elected in the First Congress held on 27 July 1984, had the following composition: President – João Paulo (Metalworkers' Union), Secretary – Vera Gomes (Private Schools Teachers' Union), Finances – José Alves de Siqueira (Metalworkers' Union) and Nélson Viana Pecly (Engineers' Opposition), Raimundo Aquino (Rural Workers' Union of Serra Talhada), Dílson Peixoto (Telecommunication Workers' Union), Pedro Francisco (Água Preta Rural Workers' Union Opposition), Zildo (Urban Worker), Eraldo (Petrolândia Rural Workers' Union), Israel César de Melo (Watchmen's Association) and Sebastião (Igarassu Rural Workers' Union) (*Folha Sindical*, October 1984).

7. The second congress of the CUT in Pernambuco elected the following directorate: President – João Paulo de Lima e Silva (Metalworkers' Union), Vice-President – Manoel dos Santos Silva (Rural Workers' Union of Serra Talhada), General Secretary – Dílson Peixoto Filho (Telecommunications Workers' Union), Finance Secretaries – Nélson Pecly (Engineers' Union) and José Alves de Siqueira (Metalworkers' Union), Rural Secretary – Eraldo Souza (Rural Workers' Union of 'Petrolândia', Press Secretary – Jorge César Bezerra dos Santos (Metalworkers' Union), Political Formation Secretary – Vera Gomes (Private Schools Teachers' Union) and Political Organisation Secretary – João Ricardo (building industry opposition group).

8. The Coca-Cola plant in the state does not allow any of its employees to become members of the union. Any attempt to join the union is promptly punished with dismissal.

9. The Commerce Employees' Union in 1995 had no shop stewards, enterprise committee, or other ways of membership involvement. The single exception is the fourteen-member 'collective bargaining commission' created to take part in the 1994 negotiations with the employers' association. According to clause 17 of that agreement, members of the commission were awarded one-year job stability.

10. 'Cut Pela Base' is a current strongly influenced by 'Trotskyist' and 'Leninist' militants whose orthodoxy impels them to see the 'central' mainly as a movement. Opposing the main current within the CUT, they disagree with the process of 'institutionalisation' of the entity and its participation in broad negotiations with the government and employers in tripartite 'forums' and national commissions.

5 The Survey: Measuring the Attitude of Active Citizenship

1. By citizenship indicators we understand the level of rights or entitlements enjoyed by citizens so as to enable them to become full members of their societies.

2. In the research setting of our survey, the city of Recife, the social

groups met by individuals in their neighbourhoods have a paramount importance to the shaping of their values and perceptions. Working-class and popular houses are precarious and their small dimensions cause them to pile up one on another. From these conditions together with the tropical weather prevalent almost during the whole year, one can easily infer the intensity of personal contacts of those inhabitants, the street, the pavement, the local bars and the rudimentary shops becoming privileged spaces for social interaction.

3. Such an assumption is much in line with recent studies which came across 'persistent attitudinal structures' of survey respondents which draw on the concept of 'core beliefs and values', according to which individuals hold fundamental and enduring attitudes towards general moral and political principles – like equality. Our investigation on workers' attitudes also assumes they hold some 'core beliefs' on the matter under scrutiny.

4. For a similar procedure, see Ranis (1992: 11).

5. An attitude scale is employed on the grounds that we are not interested in merely gathering data on percentages of a population sample espousing certain opinions, as usually done in the so-called 'opinion-polls'. The employment of a scale seeks to depict differences of intensity or degree instead of mere differences in kind. At this point, it should be added that the degrees of presence of a certain respondent's attitude was measured through an ordinal scale. As it is generally agreed (see, for example, Moser, 1958: 236–7), this type differs from the nominal and cardinal scales. While the nominal scale fails to rank individuals according to the measurement, the ordinal scale which we have used actually ranks them in several steps. It is distinguished from the cardinal scale in that the ranked steps have no implication of distance (step from position 1 to 2 may be greater than from position 2 to 3). The latter type obviously yields more accurate measures in that it permits inference not only on the order of the scores, but also on the distances between them. In our scale we could go no further than the ranking of the order of the scores (that is the using of the ordinal scale) for it is impossible to specify the difference of intensity of identified attitudes accordingly to each step.

6. A further advantage to ensure the measurement of the dimension focused on by this survey derives from the use of a broad range of items (sixty-seven). In the previous paragraph we noticed that multiple-items cancel out other dimensions (different from active-citizen attitudes) possibly embedded in a given item. The same neutralisation is valid for the possible objection that the ordinal scale fails to allow for differences of intensity in the scores attained in each item. So if an interviewee scores five, in, say, item 1, the same score in item 2 does not imply that the measured dimension is present in the same intensity. But such differences in the weight of the indicators are expected to be randomly distributed and, therefore, cancelled out.

7. The whole questionnaire schedule is presented in Appendix 2.
8. Following Judd *et al.*'s recommendations (1991), a balanced number of items worded both in positive and negative directions was included and thereby the presence of the measured dimension was displayed both by agreement and disagreement approximately half the time each. That is the reason why some items score from 1 to 5 in the agreement answers while other ones score from 5 to 1 in the same type of answers. The schedule presented in Appendix 2 indicates the positive and the negative items. The following sections introduce the modules referred to above.
9. The idea of an 'apathetic' group identified in every society is borrowed from Neuman's 'theory of three publics'. According to Neuman (1986), complex societies are made up of three basic social groups: an active, informed and articulate minority élite; a majoritarian intermediate group moderately equipped to take part in politics, and a third extractum of inactive, uninformed and uninterested people. Although Neuman advances the idea that the third section is likely to represent roughly 20 per cent of the population, one should remember that in a society like the Brazilian, such a percentage is likely to be higher because of the widespread lack of educational and material resources.
10. Such 'municípios' are the following: Abreu e Lima, Cabo, Camaragibe, Igarassu, Itamaracá, Itapissuma, Jaboatão dos Guararapes, Moreno, Olinda, Paulista and São Lourenço da Mata.
11. The firms that refused to allow their workers to be interviewed were the 'Coperbo', a rubber factory, and 'Gerdau', a metallurgical company. The former gathered virtually all the workers of an occupational category (rubber industry workers) which initially we wanted to include in our sample. Denied access to them we replaced that category by the metalworkers, who had similar characteristics: industrial private sector and union's affiliation to the CUT. As for 'Gerdau' the refusal was more a matter of practical feasibility in that it promised to authorise the interviews several months later. Because the envisaged date would fall well after the period we had set for the interviews, we preferred to replace it.
12. The conception, development and explanation of the statistical test employed in the analysis of the survey findings was made possible thanks to the patience and expertise of Dr Alexandre Rands Barros, a professor of the Economics Department of the 'Universidade Federal de Pernambuco'.
13. For more details on the consistence and unbiasedness of this estimator, see White (1980).

6 Survey Findings: New Unionism Fostering the Attitude of Active Citizenship

1. For the questions wording, see the interview schedule in Appendix 2.
2. The source of this table and all the subsequent ones comes from the author's data collected in the field research carried out in 1993 and 1994.

3. Theorising on the 'new social movements' has singled out the issue of forging new identities as one of the main elements characterising those movements (Touraine, 1988; Melucci, 1988, 1989; Foweraker, 1995). The challenge of forging new identities has also been regarded as a precondition for workers' collective action (Offe, 1985). This latter point is further developed in the Conclusion.

4. He returned to the field in 1990 and replicated part of the interviews.

5. By multicollinearity we mean the statistical occurrence where two or more variables are 'entangled' with each other and consequently have their explanatory effect captured by the other. Or, in Wickham-Crowley's words: 'intercorrelations between various independent variables and between them and the dependent variable' (1991: 86).

6. Leadership style and local union structure (that is, arrangements of deliberative bodies) were found by Fosh (1993: 581) to count among the most important factors affecting workers' levels of participation and involvement in union struggles. Both variables are encompassed by our independent variable 'union model' as long as it describes practices (leadership style being one instance) and structure (local union arrangements).

7   Conclusion

1. Seidman has characterised the South African new-unionism organised in COSATU (Congress of South African Trade Unions) in a similar fashion. She quotes one of the COSATU's activists: 'In the repressive climate COSATU became an outlet for the political hopes of far more than its membership. It acted as a political center' (1994: 251).

2. 'Brasilia Teimosa' is a special case of successful communitarian struggle. It is a poor community located between the highly valued city centre of Recife and the beach of 'Boa Viagem', a sophisticated zone at the heart of the city. Initially occupied by squatters, this community was marked by resistance against police attempts at displacing them. Such an enduring resilience gave rise to its name. 'Brasilia' is an allusion to the fact that it is a relatively new settlement as is the case of the capital of the country; 'Teimosa' is the Portuguese word for stubborn. By the time of this writing, 'Brasília Teimosa' had become a visible example of successful popular struggle in that the residents have obtained the title of property to their plots, with the state providing a number of significant facilities and services in response to the communitarian pressure.

3. Paulo Afonso is a city of around 89,501 inhabitants (IBGE, 1994) located in the course of the river 'Sao Francisco', where the 'Cia. Hidroelétrica do São Francisco – Chesf' operates five power stations.

4. Easily accessible accounts of the birth and growth of the Workers' Party may be found in Sader (1991), Keck (1992), Angell (1994), and Branford and Kucinski (1995).

5. The expression 'participatory leadership style' has been employed in the sense glossed by Fosh (1993: 581): '[a] participatory leadership style stresses the importance of communications, consultation

and the involvement of members, both formally and informally, in decision-making'.

6. As Table 4.4 in Chapter 4 shows, most members of this union are in the public sector whose affiliation ratios are high. Nevertheless, the SINTTEL also represents around 870 workers (23.9 per cent of the union's membership) who work for the private building firms that provide services of installation and expansion to the state telecom companies. These workers were also included in the sample.

7. Such an approach follows those of studies which similarly depart from the dominant focus on the elites and institutional actors, as exemplied by the works of Maranhão (1979) on labour organisation and politics in the immediate post-World War II period, Humphrey (1982) on the motorcar workers of São Paulo in the 1970s, and Wolfe (1993) on the industrial workers of São Paulo in the first half of the century. These works, focusing not only on unions as formal actors, or even on their leaders, displays certain traits of the phenomenological approach advocated by Welch (cf. specially 1993: 158–65) owing to both the emphasis posed on the way the rank-and-file workers interpreted their own story and context, and to his awareness that workers' identities are socially contructed through their common experiences and relationship, especially as processes of reciprocity in relation to the opposed group of industrialists. An interesting account of a recent shift of the researches on labour social history away from the traditional focus on institutional actors towards workers' factory life and behaviour is offered by Colistete (1995).

8. In the light of this further analysis of our survey data, we may argue that the CUT model contributes to extend the workers' citizenship also through the improvement of their wages, although this effect was not the primary concern of the present dissertation.

Sources

1.1 In-depth Interviews: February 1994–February 1995

1. Abigail Soares da Silva, president of the Textile Workers' Union in Pernambuco, since 1994 (20.09.94).
2. Adeildo Vieira ('Dedé'), president of the Metalworkers Union of Pernambuco since 1990 (25.02.94).
3. Aldeir José da Silva ('Véio do Peixe'), member of the executive board of the CUT/PE since 1990 (13.04.94).
4. Carlos Eduardo de Souza, general secretary of the Pharmaceutical Industry Workers' Union (22.03.95).
5. Carlos Padilha, president of the CUT in the state of Pernambuco from 1994 (01.12.95).
6. Carlos Roberto Aguiar de Brito, president of the Engineers Union of Pernambuco since 1988 and president of the National Federation of Engineers since 1992 (27.03.94).
7. Claudio Ferreira, president of the Data Processing Workers' Union in PE (1989/91), financial director of the CUT/PE (1990/91) and General Secretary of the Workers' Party in Pernambuco (1990/91) (07.09.94).
8. Daísa Amador, former president of the Brazilian Amnesty Committee in Pernambuco, former educational aide of Fetape and actual aide of the CUT/PE (10.11.94).
9. Enílson Simães de Moura (Alemão), general secretary of the national executive board of Força Sindical (02.12.96).
10. Evaldo Costa, member of the executive board of the Journalists Union since 1986 and its president in the period 1992/94 (13.08.94).
11. Fernando Antônio da Silva, former member of the opposition group of the Commerce Employees' Union in Recife (19.11.94).
12. Florindo Morais de Lima ('Rui'), former activist in the communitarian associations of 'Morro da Conceição' (from 1978 onwards) and 'Terras de Ninguém' (1982/83), in Recife, and a staff of Sinttel from 1985 (18.12.95).
13. Francisco Fragoso, lawyer of eight unions affiliated to the Força Sindical in Pernambuco (11.04.95).
14. Gentil Mendonça Filho, head of the Regional Office of the Labour Ministry (DRT/PE) in the period 1980/90 (28.08.94).
15. Geraldo Freire, president of the Radio Operators Union of Pernambuco in 1985/88 (28.08.94).
16. Ivanildo da Cunha Andrade, judge at the labour court and president of the National Association of Labour Court Judges – 'Anamatra' (1993–95) (06.05.95).
17. Izaías Bastos da Silva, member of the factory commission of the COSINOR in 1981/83 and currently an aide of the Banking Employees' Union in Pernambuco (29.03.94).

18. Jair Meneguelli, first president of the National Executive Board of the CUT (1983–93), and currently a member of the federal parliament (07.05.95).
19. Jairo Cabral, former president of the Data Processing Workers' Union (1985/88), president of the National Federation of Data Processing Workers (1988/89), president of the CUT in PE (1990/94) and currently member of the national executive committee of the CUT (06.03.95).
20. Joaquim Ferreira Filho, former lawyer of the 'peasant leagues' (10.11.95).
21. João Batista Filho, former secretary-general of the Neighbourhood Association of Rio Doce, in Olinda-PE (1983–85), member of the directorate of SINTEL since 1984, of the National Federation of the Telecommunications Workers – FITTEL (1992/93), and of the directorate of the Workers' Party in Olinda.
22. Joao Batista Pinheiro de Freitas, former lawyer of the ONG 'Centro Luís Freire' and currently a lawyer of a score of CUT-affiliated unions in Pernambuco (10.12.95).
23. João Paulo Lima e Silva, former president of the Metalworkers' Union (1984–87), president of the state branch of the CUT (1983–89), member of the national directorate of the CUT (1983–89), first councillor elected in the Workers' Party in Recife (1989–90), and currently a member of the state parliament for the Workers' Party (21.01.96).
24. José Carlos Neves de Andrade, president of the 'Confederação Geral dos Trabalhadores' – CGT in Pernambuco, since 1989 (21.09.94).
25. José Francisco da Silva, former president of 'Confederação Nacional dos Trabalhadores na Agricultura – CONTAG' and Minister in the Highest Level Labour Court ('Tribunal Superior do Trabalho – TST') since 1989 (02.12.95).
26. José Inácio Cassiano de Souza, president of the Watchmen's Union in Pernambuco since 1990 (11.04.95).
27. Marcelo Beltrão Correira, member of the directive board of the Telecommunications Workers' Union in Pernambuco since 1988 (15.12.94).
28. Morse Lyra Neto, legal aide of a score of urban and rural unions in Pernambuco, FETAPE inclusive, in the period 1979/93 (10.03.94).
29. Ricardo Estêvão de Oliveira, legal aid of a score of urban unions in Pernambuco since 1980 and also of the CUT's branch in the state (03.03.94).
30. Paulo Valença, president of the State School Teachers' Union in 1985/89 and president of the CUT in Pernambuco in 1988/89 (06.09.94).
31. Ricardo Queiroz Fonseca, member of the directive board of the Telecommunications Workers' Union since 1984 and its general coordinator since 1993 (15.12.94).
32. Samuel Costa Filho, president of the Engineers Union of Pernambuco in the period 1985–88 and member of the executive board of the Urban Workers' Union in 1981–85 (21.09.94).

33. Severino Antônio de Lima ('Biu'), member of the directive board of the Metalworkers Union of Pernambuco since 1981 (09.07.94).
34. Tereza Alves, head of the human resources department of GERDAU Metalindustry in Pernambuco (30.03.94).
35. Vicente Paulo da Silva ('Vincentinho'), president of the national executive board of the CUT from 1994 (02.12.95).
36. José Roberto Leandro, former president of the Bank Employees of Pernambuco (1991–94) and currently a member of its directive board (15.12.95).

Other Sources

Akerlof, G. and Yellen, J. (1990) 'The Fair Wage-Effort Hypothesis and Unemployment', *Quarterly Journal of Economics*, 105(2), pp. 255–83.

Almeida, José Maria (1992) 'A Organização nos Locais de Trabalho (OLT), Situação Atual, Propostas e Tarefas da CUT', *Cadernos da CUT – Jurídico e Relações Sindicais*, no. 7.

Almeida, Maria Hermínia Tavares de (1975) 'O Sindicalismo no Brasil: Novos Problemas, Velhas Estruturas', *Debate e Crítica*, July, pp. 49–74.

Almeida, Maria Hermínia Tavares de (1980) 'Os limites entre a arbitragem e a arbitrariedade', in Folhetim, *Folha de São Paulo*, issue of 22 June.

Almeida, Maria Hermínia Tavares de (1988) 'Difícil Caminhoa: Sindicatos e Política na Construção da Democracia', in Reis, Fábio Wanderley and O'Donnell, G. (eds), *A Democracia no Brasil – Dilemas e Perspectivas*.

Almond, Gabriel A. and James S. Coleman (eds) (1960) *The Politics of Developing Areas*. Princeton, NJ: Princeton University Press.

Almond, Gabriel and Verba, Sidney (1963) *The Civic Culture: Political Attitudes and Democracy in Five Nations*. Princeton: Princeton University Press.

Almond, Gabriel and Verba, Sidney (1965) *The Civic Culture: Political Attitudes and Democracy in Five Nations*, 2nd edn. Boston: Little, Brown.

Almond, Gabriel and Verba, Sidney (eds) [1980] (1980a) *The Civic Culture Revisited*. Newbury Park, London and New Delhi: Sage Publications.

Almond, Gabriel and Verba, Sidney (eds) [1980] (1980b) 'The Intellectual History of the Civic Culture Concept', in *The Civic Culture Revisited*.

Alves, Francisco (1994) 'Balanço das Lutas Sociais no Campo na Década de 80', in Ministério do Trabalho e Centro de Estudos Sindicais e de Economia do Trabalho da Unicamp, *O Mundo Do Trabalho: Crise E Mudança No Final Do Século*. São Paulo: Scritta, Editora Página Aberta.

Andrade, Everaldo Gaspar Lopes de (1994) *Direito Do Trabalho – Itinerários Da Dominação*. São Paulo: Editora Ltr.

Andrade, Everaldo Gaspar Lopes de (1995) *Direito Do Trabalho – Ensaios Filosóficos*. São Paulo: Editora Ltr.

Angell, Alan (1994) 'The Left in Latin America since c. 1920', in Bethell, Leslie (ed.), *The Cambridge History of Latin America*, Volume VI, Part 2 – 1930 to the Present.

Antunes, Ricardo (1991) *O Novo Sindicalismo*. São Paulo: Editora Brasil Urgente.

Araújo, José Prata de (1993) *A Construção Do Sindicalismo Livre No Brasil*. Belo Horizonte: Editora Lê S.A.

Avineri, S. and de-Shalit, A. (1992) *Communitarianism and Individualism*. Oxford: Oxford University Press.

Baglioni, Guido (1990) 'Industrial Relations in Europe in the 1980s', in Baglioni and Crouch (eds), *European Industrial Relations – The Challenge of Flexibility*. London: Sage Publications.

Baglioni, Guido and Crouch, Collin (eds) (1990) *European Industrial Relations – The Challenge of Flexibility*. London: Sage Publications.

Bailey, Rachel (1994) 'Annual Review Article 1993: British Public Sector Industrial Relations', *British Journal of Industrial Relations*, 32(1) (March).

Barbalet, J.M. (1988). *Citizenship*. Milton Keynes: Open University Press.

Barbosa, Cloves and Silva, Vera Lúcia Moraes da (1993) 'O Perfil Dos Trabalhadores Telefonicos Do Estado De Pernambuco', Recife, mimeo.

Barelli, Walter (1993) 'Brasil: Hay que Liberar las Relaciones Laborales', *Trabajo*, no. 4.

Barreto, Túlio Velho (1994) *Algumas Notas (Preliminares) Sobre O Debate Recente Acerca Da Representação Classista Na Justiça Do Trabalho*. Recife: Fundação Joaquim Nabuco Instituto de Pesquisas Sociais, work paper.

Barros, Alexandre Rands (1991) 'A Marxian Theory of Real Wages Determination', in ANPEC (ed.), *Anais do XIX Encontro Nacional de Economistas*, vol. 1. Curitiba: ANPEC.

Barros, Alexandre Rands (1993) 'Some Implications of New Growth Theory for Economic Development', *Journal of International Development*, 5(5), pp. 531–58.

Barros, Alexandre Rands and Barros, Maurício Rands (1995) 'Fatores Determinantes dos Salários Relativos: Um Estudo Empírico com Dados Primários', in ANPEC (ed.), *Anais do XXIII Encontro Nacional de Economistas*, vol. 1. Salvador: ANPEC.

Barros, Maurício Rands (1992) 'Brazilian Industrial Relations: Alternative Proposals by the New Unionism', M.Sc. dissertation, Oxford: University of Oxford.

Barros, Maurício Rands (1994) 'Contrato Coletivo de Trabalho – Alguns Mitos e Falácias', *Revista LTR*, vol. 58, no. 3 (March).

Barros, Maurício Rands (1995a) 'A Flexibilização o Direito do Trabalho', *Revista da Anamatra*, ano VII, no. 23 (April/May/June), pp. 43–50.

Barros, Maurício Rands (1995b) 'Direito do Trabalho na Grã-Bretanha e no Brasil: Pontos de Partida Distintos, Similaridade de Alternativas', paper presented in the 'XVIII Jornada de Derecho Social', Bilbao, Vizcaya, Universidad de Deusto, July 14th.

Barry, B.M. (1970) *Sociologists, Economists and Democracy*. London: Collier-Macmillan.

Becker, Howard S. (1933) *Métodos De Pesquisa Em Ciências Sociais*. São Paulo: Editora Hucitec.

Bendix, R. (1969) *Nation-Building And Citizenship*. Garden City, New York: Doubleday & Company.

Bendix, R. [1956] (1974) *Work and Authority in Industry*. Berkeley: University of California Press.

Benites Filho, Flávio (1991) 'A Representação dos Trabalhadores na Empresa e a Negociação Coletiva', *Cadernos da CUT – Jurídico e Relaçes Sindicais*, no. 5, São Paulo.

298 *Sources*

Bethell, Leslie (ed.) (1994) *The Cambridge History of Latin America*, Volume VI, Part 2 – 1930 to the Present. Cambridge: Cambridge University Press.

Boito Jr., Armando (1991a) *O Sindicalismo De Estado No Brasil*. Campinas: Editora da Universidade Estadual de Campinas – UNICAMP.

Boito Jr., Armando (1991b) *O Sindicalismo Brasileiro Nos Anos 80* (ed). Rio de Janeiro: Paz e Terra.

Boletins do Departamento Intersindical de Estudos Econômicos e Estatísticos – DIEESE, issues of April 1986, May 1986, June 1986, February 1987, April 1989 (separata), April 1990, July 1990, April 1991.

Boletins Informacut, nos 205, 206, 211, 250.

Braga, Douglas Gerson (1991) 'Democracia, Distribuição de Renda e Estratégias Sindicais no Brasil', *Cadernos da CUT – Jurídico e Relações Sindicais*, no. 6, São Paulo.

Braga, Douglas Gerson and Miranda, José Olívio (1991) 'Sem organização não há contratação'. in *Negociação e Contrato Coletivo de Trabalho*, Rainho, L. Flávio and Ferreira, Soraya (eds), São Paulo: Editora Brasil Urgente.

Brandão, Cláudio Mascarenhas (1994) 'A Representação Classista da Justiça do Trabalho – Aspectos Relativos Á Aposentadoria', *Revista da Anamatra*, Ano 6, no. 19 (Mar–April).

Brandão, Juarez Lopes (1994) 'Cultura Política do Mando: Subserviência e Nossas Populações Pobres', *Revista Brasileira de Ciências Sociais*, no. 25 (June), pp. 38–41.

Branford, Sue and Kucinski, Bernardo (1995) *Brazil Carnival of the Oppressed*. London: Latin America Bureau (Research and Action).

Broughton, David (1995) *Public Opinion Polling and Politics in Britain*. London: Prentice Hall/Harvester Wheatsheaf.

Buchanan, Paul G. (1989) 'Plus ça Change? A Administração Nacional do Trabalho e a Democracia no Brasil, 1985–1987', *Dados – Revista De Ciências Sociais*, vol. 32, no. 1, pp. 75–123.

Burawoy, M. (1985) *The Politics of Production: Factory Regimes Under Capitalism and Socialism*. London: Verso.

Camargo, J.M. (1995) Interview with Ubaros Lé Correre, *Revista VEJA*, 21 June 1995.

Cammack, Paul (1991) 'Brazil: Old Politics, New Forces', *New Left Review*, no. 190, pp. 5–58.

Castro, Maria Sílvia Portella de (1991) 'Sistema de Relações Trabalhistas e Democracia', *Cadernos da CUT – Jurídico e Relações Sindicais*, no. 5, São Paulo.

Centro de Estudos e Ação Social (CEAS) and Fundação Joaquim Nabuco (FUNDAJ) (1989) *O Perfil do Movimento Sindical Urbano De Pernambuco*. Recife.

Centro Josué de Castro (1988) *Até Chegar No Zé – Contribuição Á Historia Dos Metalúrgicos*, Recife.

CGT – *Central Geral Dos Trabalhadores*, Ano I, no. 1, Abril.

CGT (1989) *CGT – Confederaçao Geral Dos Trabalhadores*.

CGT (1986) Ano IV, no. 1, Maio.

CIDAS – Centro De Informaçoes, Documentacao E Analise Sindical (1980) *I Conclat*, São Paulo: Edições Loyola.

Clegg, H.A. (1975) 'Pluralism in Industrial Relations', *British Journal of Industrial Relations*, Nov., p. 309.

Clegg, H.A. (1979) *The Changing System of Industrial Relations in Great Britain*. Oxford: Basil Blackwell.

Colistete, Renato Perim (1995) 'Industrialisation and Labour Relations in Brazil, 1945–1960: Comments on Classic and Recent Approaches', St. Antony's College, University of Oxford, mimeo.

Collier, R, and Collier, D. (1991) *Reshaping the Political Arena – Critical Junctures, the Labour Movement, and Regime Dynamics in Latin America*. Princeton, New Jersey: Princeton University Press.

Comin, Álvaro A. (1992) 'Contra a Maré', *Novos Estudos Cebrap*, no. 33 (July), pp. 129–46.

Comin, Álvaro Augusto (1994) 'A Experiência de Organização das Centrais Sindicais no Brasil', in Ministério do Trabalho e Centro de Estudos Sindiciais e de Economia do Trabalho da Unicamp, *O Mundo Do Trabalho: Crise e Mudança no Final do Século*.

Costa, Tarcísio Lima (1992) 'Brazilian Liberals and the Question of Democracy: a Possible Reading', University of Cambridge, mimeo.

Crivelli, Ericson (1991) 'Reordenação da legislação laboral, código de trabalho e contratação coletiva de trabalho apontamentos para compreensão de um dilema', *Cadernos da CUT – Jurídicos e Relações Sindicais*, no. 5, São Paulo.

Crouch, Collin (1993) *Industrial Relations and European State Traditions*. Oxford: Clarendon Press.

CUT (1984) *Cut – 1o. Congresso Nacional Da Classe Trabalhadora*, Rio de Janeiro: Tempo e Presença Editora Ltda.

CUT – PE (October 1985) *Boletim*.

CUT – PE (April/May 1986) Ano II, no. 4, Recife.

CUT (1991a) '4o. Congresso da Central Única dos Trabalhadores – Teses'.

CUT (1991b) *Resoluções do 4o. Congresso da CUT*, September.

CUT (1991c) *Retrato Da Cut*, São Paulo.

CUT (1993a) *Boletim Informacut*, no. 211.

CUT (1993b) *Boletim Informacut*, no. 215 (26/04–06.05.93).

CUT (1993c) *6a. Plenária Nacional – Textos*.

CUT (1994a) *Propostas para Debate – Contrato Coletivo e Liberdade de Organização Sindical*, 21.02.94.

CUT (1994b) *Resoluções do 5o. Congresso da CUT*, June.

CUT (1995a) *Boletim Informacut*, no. 250, janeiro.

CUT (1995b) *Boletim Informacut*, no. 25, setembro.

Pró-Cut (1983) *Boletim, Edição Especial*.

Folha Sindical (October 1984) Recife, special edition.

Negro, Antônio Luigi (1991) 'De Olho no Futuro: O Novo Sindicalismo na Hora da Transição (Democrática?)', *Cadernos da CUT – Jurídico e Relações Sindicais*, no. 5, São Paulo.

Oliveira, José Olívio Miranda (1989) 'Organização, Greve E Contrato Coletivo', *Cadernos da CUT*, no. 2, São Paulo.

Oliveira, José Olívio Miranda (1992) 'Estrutura Vertical: Transição para a Estrutura da CUT', *Cadernos Da Cut – Jurídico E Relações Sindicais*, no. 7.

PT (1991) 'Resoluções do 1o. Congresso', December, mimeo.

Sindicato dos Empregados no Comércio do Recife (1994) *Os Caminhos Da Luta*, mimeo.
Siqueira Neto, José Francisco (1988) 'O Estado de Fora', *Boletim Nacional da CUT*, no. 19.
Jornal do Commércio, issues of 10.11.94, 06.05.95, 31.05.95, 04.07.95.
Folha de São Paulo, issues of 27.11.93, 23.05.94, 04.05.95, 06.05.95, 07.05.95, 12.05.95, 13.05.95, 30.05.95.
Revista Veja, issues of 22.03.89, 25.05.94, 31.05.95, 21.06.95.
O Estado de São Paulo, issues of 15.03.89 and 24.04.91.
Revista IstoÉ, issue of 25.05.94.
The Economist, issue of 27.05.95.
Financial Times, issue of 28.12.95.
Dahrendorf, R. [1959] (1965) *Class and Class Conflict in Industrial Society*. London: Weidenfeld & Nicolson.
Dahrendorf, R. [1965] (1968) *Society and Democracy in Germany*. London: Weidenfeld & Nicolson.
Dahrendorf, R. (1988) *The Modern Social Conflict*. London: Weidenfeld & Nicolson.
Davies, Paul and Freedland, Mark (1993) *Labour Legislation and Public Policy*. Oxford: Clarendon Press.
Dickens, Linda and Hall, Mark (1995) 'The State: Labour Law and Industrial Relations', in Edwards, Paul (1995a), *Industrial Relations – Theory and Practice in Britain*.
Edwards, Paul (1986) *Conflict At Work*. Oxford: Basil Blackwell.
Edwards, Paul (1995a) *Industrial Relations – Theory and Practice in Britain*. Oxford: Blackwell.
Edwards, Paul (1995b) 'The Employment Relationship', in Edwards, P. (1995a) *Industrial Relations*.
Elkins, David J. and Simeon, Richard E.B. (1979) 'A Cause in Search of its Effect, or What Does Political Culture Explain?', *Comparative Politics*, 11, pp. 127–45.
Epstein, J. and J. McPartland (1975) *The Concept and Measurement of the Quality of School Life*. Baltimore: Johns Hopkins University Press.
Erickson, Kenneth Paul (1977) *The Brazilian Corporative State and Working-Class Politics*. Berkeley and Los Angeles: University of California Press.
Ewing, Keith (1988) 'Rights and Immunities in British Labour Law', *Comparative Labour Law Journal*, 1.
Fantasia, R. (1989) *Cultures of Solidarity*. Berkeley, Los Angeles, and London: University of California Press.
Farnham, D. and Pimlot, J. (1979) *Understanding Industrial Relations*. London: Cassell.
Ferner, A. and Hyman, R. (eds) (1992) *Industrial Relations in the New Europe*. Oxford: Blackwell.
Força Sindical (1993) *Um Projeto Para O Brasil: A Proposta Da Força Sindical*. São Paulo: Geração Editorial.
Fosh, P. (1981) *The Active Trade Unionist. A Study of Motivation and Participation at Branch Level*. Cambridge: Cambridge University Press.
Fosh, P. and Heery, E. (eds) (1990) *Trade Unions and Their Members*. Basingstoke: Macmillan.

Fosh, Patricia (1993) 'Membership Participation in Workplace Unionism: The Possibility of Union Renewal', *British Journal of Industrial Relations*, 31(4) (December) 1993.

Foweraker, J. (1995) *Theorizing Social Movements*. London; Boulder, Colorado: Pluto Press.

Franco, Gustavo H.B. (1993) 'A Volta do Modelo Concentrador', *Folha De São Paulo*, 20 May, p. 2.2.

French, John (1992) *The Brazilian Workers' ABC: Class Conflict and Alliances in Modern São Paulo*. London: University of North Carolina Press.

Gacek, Stanley Arthur (1994) *Sistemas De Relações De Trabalho – Exame Dos Modelos Brasil-Estados Unidos*. S ão Paulo: Editora LTr.

Ghera, Edoardo (1990) *Diritto Del Lavoro – Il Rapporto di Lavoro*. Bari: Cacucci Editore.

Giannotti, Vito and Neto Sebasti ão (1990) *Cut Por Dentro E Por Fora*. Petrópolis: Editora Vozes.

Gibbins, J.R. (ed.) (1989) *Contemporary Political Culture*. London: Sage.

Giddens, Anthony (1982) *Profiles and Critiques in Social Theory*. London and Basingstoke: Macmillan Press.

Ginsberg, M. (1959) *Law and Opinion in England in the 20th Century*. London: Steven & Sons Limited.

Giugni, Gino (ed.) (1994) *Codice Di Diritto Del Lavoro*. Bari: Cacucci Editore.

Giugni, Gino (1991) *Diritto Sindacale*. Bari: Cacucci Editore.

Goldthorpe, J.H., Lockwood, D., Bechhofer, F. and Platt, Jennifer (1969) *The Affluent Worker in the Class Structure*. Cambridge: Cambridge University Press.

Goldthorpe, J.H., Lockwood, D., Bechhofer, F. and Platt, Jennifer (1970) *The Affluent Worker: Industrial Attitudes and Behaviour*. Cambridge: Cambridge University Press.

Goldthorpe, J.H., Lockwood, D., Bechhofer, F. and Platt, Jennifer (1971) *The Affluent Worker: Political Attitudes and Behaviour*. Cambridge: Cambridge University Press.

Gomes, Angela de Castro (1988) *A Invenção Do Trabalhismo*. São Paulo: Editora Revista dos Tribunais – Edicões Vértice.

Guimarães, Ivan Gonçalves Ribeiro (1994) 'A Experiência das Câmaras Setoriais', in Ministério do Trabalho e Centro de Estudos Sindicais e de Economia do Trabalho da Unicamp, *O Mundo Do Trabalho: Crise E Mudança No Final Do Século*.

Heery, Ed. and Kelly, John (1994) 'Professional, Participative and Managerial Unionism: An Interpretation of Change in Trade Unions', *Work, Employment and Society*, vol. 8, no. 1, pp. 1–22.

Heycock, Stephen (1993) 'With Every Pair of Hands You Get a Free Brain', in Leisink, Peter and Coenen, Harry (eds) (1993a), *Work and Citizenship in the New Europe*.

Hill, Stephen (1981) *Competition and Control at Work*. Aldershot, Hampshire: Gower Publishing Company Limited.

Hirschman, Albert (1984) *Getting Ahead Collectively: Grassroots Experiences in Latin America*. New York: Pergamon Press.

Hirschman, Albert (1991) *The Rhetoric of Reaction*. Cambridge: The Belknap Press of Harvard University Press.

302 *Sources*

Hobsbawm, Eric (1995) 'Guessing About Global Change', *International Labor and Working-Class History*, no. 47 (Spring), pp. 39–44.

Humphrey, John (1982) *Capitalist Control and Workers' Struggle in the Brazilian Auto Industry*. Princeton: Princeton University Press.

Humphrey, John (1987) *Gender and Work in the Third World – Sexual Divisions in Brazilian Industry*. London: Tavistock Publications.

Hyman, Richard (1989) *The Political Economy of Industrial Relations*. Basingstoke: Macmillan Press.

Hyman, Richard (1994) 'Changing Trade Union Identities and Strategies', in Hyman and Ferner (eds) *New Frontiers in European Industrial Relations*.

Hyman, Richard and Ferner, Anthony (eds) (1994) *New Frontiers in European Industrial Relations*. Oxford: Blackwell.

IBGE (1994) *Anuário Estatístico Do Brasil*.

Inglehart, Ronald (1990) *Culture Shift in Advanced Industrial Society*. Princeton, NJ: Princeton University Press.

IPEA/IBAM (1995) *Subsídios Para A Reforma Do Estado, Vol. 1: O Novo Pacto Federativo*.

Jackson, Michael P. (1985) *Industrial Relations – A Textbook*. London: Routledge.

Judd, C., Smith, E. and Kidder, L. 1991) *Research Methods in Social Relations*. Fort Worth: Holt, Rinehart & Winston.

Kadt, Emanuel (1970) *Catholic Radicals in Brazil*. Oxford: Oxford University Press.

Kahneman, D., Knetsch, J.L. and Thaler, R. (1986) 'Fairness as a Constraint on Profit Seeking Entitlements in the Market', *American Economic Review*, 76(4), pp. 728–41.

Kahn-Freund, Otto (1959) 'Labour Law', in Ginsberg, M., *Law and Opinion in England in the 20th Century*.

Kahn-Freund, Otto (1968) *Labour Law: Old Traditions and New Developments*. Toronto/Vancouver: Clarke, Irwin & Company Limited.

Keck, Margaret E. (1989) 'The New Unionism in the Brazilian Transition', in *Democratizing Brazil*, Stepan, Alfred, ed. New York: Oxford University Press.

Keck, Margaret E. (1992) *The Workers' Party and Democratization in Brazil*. New Haven and London: Yale University Press.

Keller, Wilma (1986) 'As Comissões de Fábrica no Setor Metalmecânico Paulista', Paper presented before AMPOCS, mimeo.

King, D. and Waldron, J. (1988) 'Citizenship, Social Citizenship and the Defense of Welfare Provision', *British Journal of Political Science*, 18 (4) (October).

Kinzo, M.D. (1993) *Brazil. The Challenges of the 1990s*. London: The Institute of Latin American Studies, University of London, and British Academic Press.

Klandermans, Bert, Kriesi, Hanspeter and Tarrow, Sidney (eds) (1988) *From Structure to Action: Comparing Movements Across Cultures*, International Social Movements Research, vol. 1. Greenwich, CT: JAI Press.

Korpi, Walter (1978) *The Working Class in Welfare Capitalism – Work, Unions and Politics in Sweden*. London: Routledge & Kegan Paul.

Lamounier, Bolívar (ed.) (1992) *Ouvindo O Brasil: Uma Análise Da Opinião*

Pública Brasileira Hoje. São Paulo: Editora Sumaré/Instituto Roberto Simonsen.

Lehmann, David (1990) *Democracy and Development in Latin America: Economics, Politics and Religion in the Post-War Period*. Philadelphia: Temple University Press.

Leisink, Peter and Coenen, Harry (eds) (1993a) *Work and Citizenship in the New Europe*. Aldershot, Hants: Edward Elgar.

Leisink, Peter and Coenen, Harry (1993b) 'Work and Citizenship in the New Europe', in Leisink, Peter and Coenen, Harry (eds) (1993a), *Work and Citizenship in the New Europe*.

Levine, Ross and Renelt, David (1992) 'A Sensitivity Analysis of Cross-Country Growth Regressions', *American Economic Review*, 82 (4) (September), pp. 942–63.

Lijphart, A. (1980) 'The Structure of Inference', in Almond and Verba (1980), *The Civic Culture Revisited*.

Lockwood, David [1958] (1989) *The Blackcoated Worker – A Study in Class Consciousness*. Oxford: Clarendon Press.

Magano, Octávio Bueno (1992) 'Contrato Coletivo de Trabalho', *Folha De São Paulo*, 18 September, p. 13.

Malloy, James (ed.) (1977) *Authoritarianism and Corporatism in Latin America*. Pittsburgh: University of Pittsburgh Press.

Mangabeira, Wilma (1993) *Dilemas do Novo Sindicalismo: Democracia e Política em Volta Redonda*. Rio de Janeiro: Relume-Dumará: ANPOCS.

Mann, Michael (1973) *Consciousness and Action Among the Western Working Class*. London: Macmillan Press.

Mann, Michael (1987) 'Ruling Class Strategies and Citizenship', *Sociology*, 21, pp. 339–54.

Maranhão, Ricardo (1979) *Sindicato e Democratização: Brazil, 1945–1950*. São Paulo: Brasiliense.

Marginson, Paul (1984) 'The Distinctive Effects of Plant and Company Size on Workplace Industrial Relations', *British Journal of Industrial Relations*, vol. xxii, no. 1 (March).

Marshall, T.H. [1950] (1964) 'Citizenship and Social Class', in *Class, Citizenship and Social Development*. New York: Doubleday & Company.

Martinez-Lara, Javier (1994) 'Building Democracy in Brazil: The Politics of Constitutional Change, 1985–1993', doctoral dissertation, Oxford: University of Oxford.

Martins, Luciano (1986) 'The "Liberalisation" of Authoritarian Rule in Brazil', in O'Donnel, Schimitter and Whitehead *Transitions from Authoritarian Rule – Latin America*.

Martins, Milton (1991) *Sindicalismo e Relações Trabalhistas*, São Paulo: Editora LTr.

Maybury-Lewis, Biorn (1994) *The Politics of the Possible: The Brazilian Rural Workers' Trade Union Movement, 1964–1985*. Philadelphia: Temple University Press.

Medeiros, Carlos Aguiar (1994) 'Contrato Coletivo e Mercado de Trabalho no Brasil', in Ministério do Trabalho e Centro de Estudos Sindiciais e de Economia do Trabalho da Unicamp, *O Mundo Do Trabalho: Crise E Mudança No Final Do Século*.

Medeiros, Mário (1994) *Concepção De Sindicato E Mobilização Da Classe Trabalhadora*. Recife: Comunicarte.

Medeiros, Rejane Pinto de (1992) 'Cotidiano Sindical: Entraves E Bandeiras', Thesis presented to the Master of Sociology at the Universidade Federal de Pernambuco.

Melucci, Alberto (1988) 'Getting Involved: Identity and Mobilisation in Social Movements', in Klandermans, Bert, Kriesi, Hanspeter and Tarrow, Sidney (eds), *From Structure To Action: Comparing Movements Across Cultures*, International Social Movements Research, vol. 1. Greenwich, CT: JAI Press.

Melucci, Alberto (1989) *Nomads of the Present: Social Movements and Individual Needs in Contemporary Society*. Philadelphia: Temple University Press.

Mendes, Chico (1989) *Fight for the Forest – Chico Mendes in His Own Words*. London: Latin America Bureau (Research and Action) Ltd.

Mericle, Kenneth (1977) 'Corporatist Control of the Working Class: Authoritarian Brazil Since 1964', in Malloy, James (1977) (ed.), *Authoritarianism and Corporatism in Latin America*.

Ministério do Trabalho (1994a) *Forum Nacional Sobre Contrato Coletivo e Relações do Trabalho no Brasil*. Brasília: Ministério do Trabalho/PW Gráficos e Editores Associados.

Ministério do Trabalho e Centro de Estudos Sindicais e de Economia do Trabalho da Unicamp (1994b) *O Mundo Do Trabalho: Crise E Mudança No Final Do Século*. São Paulo: Scritta, Editora Página Aberta.

Moisés, José Alvaro (1978) *Greve De Massa E Crise Política: Estudo Da Greve Dos 300 Mil Em São Paulo – 1953–1954*. São Paulo: Polis.

Moisés, José Alvaro (1982) *Lições de Liberdade e Opressão*. Rio de Janeiro: Paz e Terra.

Moisés, José Alvaro (1993) 'Democratization and Political Culture in Brazil', in Kinzo (ed.), *Brazil. The Challenges of the 1990s*.

Moisés, José Álvaro (1994) 'Entre a incerteza e a tradiçao política', *Novos Estudos Cebrap*, 40 (Nov.).

Moore, Barrigton (1966) *Social Origins of Dictatorship and Democracy*. Harmondsworth: Penguin Books.

Morais, J.V. (1992) 'New Unionism and Union Politics in Pernambuco (Brazil) in the 1980s', doctoral thesis, London School of Economics.

Morais, Jorge Ventura de (1993) 'Assistencialismo, "Burocracia" e Novo Sindicalismo: 1978–1989', *Caderno CRH*, 19, Salvador, pp. 58–78.

Moser, C.A. (1958) *Survey Methods in Social Investigation*. London: Heinemann.

Mouffe, Chantal (ed.) (1992a) *Dimensions of Radical Democracy*. London: Verso.

Mouffe, Chantal (1992b) 'Democratic Politics Today', in Mouffe (ed.), *Dimensions of Radical Democracy*.

Neuman, R.W. (1986) *The Paradox of Mass Politics*. Cambridge, MA: Harvard University Press.

Noronha, Eduardo Garuti (1994) 'Greves e Estratégias Sindicais no Brasil', in Ministério do Trabalho e Centro de Estudos Sindiciais e de Economia do Trabalho da Unicamp, *O Mundo Do Trabalho: Crise E Mudança No Final Do Século*.

O'Donnel, Guillermo (1977) 'Corporatism and the Question of the State', in Malloy, James (ed.), *Authoritarianism and Corporatism in Latin America.*

O'Donnel, Guillermo (1986) 'Introduction to the Latin American Cases', in O'Donnel, Schimitter and Whitehead (eds), *Transitions from Authoritarian Rule – Latin America.*

O'Donnel, Guillermo (1988) 'Transições, Constinuidades e Alguns Paradoxos', in Reis, F. Wanderley, and O'Donnel, Guillermo (eds), *A Democracia no Brasil – Dilemas e Perspctivas.*

O'Donnel, Guillermo, Schmitter, Philippe and Whitehead, Laurence (1986) *Transitions from Authoritarian Rule – Latin America.* Baltimore and London: The Johns Hopkins University Press.

Offe, Claus (1985) *Disorganised Capitalism.* Oxford: Polity Press.

Offe, Claus and Wiesenthal, Helmut (1985) 'Two Logics of Collective Action', in Offe, Claus (ed.), *Disorganized Capitalism.*

Oliveira, Marco Antônio (1994) 'Avanços e Limites do Sindicalismo Brasileiro Recente', in Ministério do Trabalho e Centro de Estudos Sindiciais e de Economia do Trabalho da Unicamp, *O Mundo Do Trabalho: Crise E Mudança No Final Do Século.*

Olson, Mancur (1971) [1965] *The Logic of Collective Action – Public Goods and the Theory of Groups.* Cambridge, MA: Harvard University Press.

Omaji, Paul Omojo (1993) 'The State and Industrial Relations: Background to the Adoption of Compulsory Arbitration Law in Australia and Nigeria', *British Journal of Industrial Relations,* 31 (1), (March).

Oppenheim, A.N. [1966] (1992) *Questionnaire Design, Interviewing and Attitude Measurement.* London and New York: Pinter Publishers.

Pastore, J. (1992) 'O Contrato Coletivo no Brasil – Que tipo? Em que condições?', São Paulo, mimeo.

Pastore, J. (1993) 'A flexibilização como estratégia de competição. A trajetória da contratação coletiva do trabalho', Brasília, Confederação Nacional do Trabalho/USP, mimeo.

Pastore, José (1993) 'Contrato Coletivo por via Democrática', *Folha De São Paulo,* 9 Dec.

Pateman, C. (1970) *Participation and Democratic Theory.* Cambridge: Cambridge University Press.

Peled, Yoav (1992) 'Ethnic Democracy and the Legal Construction of Citizenship: Arab Citizens of the Jewish State', *American Political Science Review,* 86 (2) (June).

Pocock, J.G.A. (1971) *Politics, Language and Time.* London: Methuen.

Poole, Michael (1981) *Theories of Trade Unionism: A Sociology of Industrial Relations.* London: Routledge & Kegan Paul.

Poole, Michael (1986) *Industrial Relations. Origins and Patterns of National Diversity.* London: Routledge.

Price, R. and Bain, G.S. (1983) 'Union Growth in Britain: Retrospect and Prospect', *British Journal of Industrial Relations,* vol. XXI, no. 1, p. 51.

Przeworski, Adam (1991) *Democracy and the Market – Political and Economic Reforms in Eastern Europe and Latin America.* Cambridge: Cambridge University Press.

Putnam, Robert D. (1993) *Making Democracy Work. Civic Traditions in Modern Italy.* Princeton, New Jersey: Princeton University Press.

Pye, Lucian W. and Sidney Verba (eds) (1965) *Political Culture and Political Development*. Princeton, NJ: Princeton University Press.

Rainho, L. Flávio and Ferreira, Soraya (eds) (1991) *Negociação E Contrato Coletivo De Trabalho*. São Paulo: Editora Brasil Urgente.

Ramos Filho, Wílson (1991) 'A Superação do Modelo Corporativo, a Construção da Autonomia Sindical e o Contrato Coletivo', *Cadernos da CUT – Jurídico e Relações Sindicais*, no. 5. São Paulo: CUT publication.

Ranis, Peter (1992) *Argentine Workers – Peronism and Contemporary Class Consciousness*. Pittsburgh: University of Pittsburgh Press.

Rawls, J. (1972) *A Theory of Justice*. Oxford: Oxford University Press.

Reis, Fábio Wanderley and O'Donnell (eds) (1988) *A Democracia no Brasil – Dilemas e Perspectivas*. São Paulo: Editora Vértice.

Richardson, Bradley M. (1974) *The Political Culture of Japan*. Berkeley: University of California Press.

Richardson, Robert Jerry and Wanderley, José Carlos Vieira (1985) *Medindo Atitudes*. João Pessoa: Editora Universitária/UFPB.

Rodrigues, Leôncio Martins (1980) 'Os Limites entre a Arbitragem e a Arbitrariedade', *Folha de São Paulo*, 22 June 1980, p. 3.

Rodrigues, Leôncio Martins (1990a), *CUT: Os Militantes e a Ideologia*. São Paulo: Paz e Terra.

Rodrigues, Leôncio Martins (1990b) *Partidos E Sindicatos*. São Paulo: Editora Ática.

Rodrigues, Leôncio Martins (1991) *Retrato da CUT: Delegados do 3° Congresso, Representação nas Categorias*. São Paulo: Edição da Central Única dos Trabalhadores.

Rodrigues, Leóncio Martins and Cardoso, Adalberto Moreira (1993) *Força Sindical – Uma Análise Sócio-Política*. São Paulo: Paz e Terra.

Rorty, Schneewind and Skinner (eds) (1984) *Philosophy of History*. Cambridge: Cambridge University Press.

Rubery, Jill and Fagan, Colette (1995) 'Comparative Industrial Relations Research: Towards Reversing the Gender Bias', *British Journal of Industrial Relations*, 33 (2), (June).

Sader, Emir S. (1988) *Quandos Novos Personagens Entram Em Cena*. Rio de Janeiro: Paz e Terra.

Sader, Emir S. (1991) *Without Fear of Being Happy – Lula, the Workers Party and Brazil*. London: Verso.

Salgado, Lúcia H. (1993) *Política De Concorrência E Estratégias Empresariais: Um Estudo Da Indústria Automobilística*. Rio de Janeiro, IPEA, Junho, Série Seminários 10/93.

Sales, Teresa (1994) 'Raízes da Desigualdade Social na Cultura Política Brasileira', *Revista Brasileira De Ciências Sociais*, 25, ano #9 (June).

Sandel, Michael [1984] (1992) 'The Procedural Republic and the Unencumbered Self', in Avineri, S. and de-Shalit, A. (eds), *Communitarianism and Individualism*.

Sandoval, Salvador (1994) *Os Trabalhadores Param – Greves E Mudança Social No Brasil 1945–1990*. São Paulo: Editora Ática.

Santos, Wanderley Guilherme dos (1979) *Cidadania E Justiça*. Rio de Janeiro: Editora Campus.

Schmmiter, Philippe C. (1971) *Interest Conflict and Political Change in Brazil*. Stanford, California: Stanford University Press.

Seidman, Gay, W. (1994) *Manufacturing Militance – Workers' Movements in Brazil and South Africa, 1970–1985*. Berkeley, Los Angeles, London: University of California Press.

Simão, Azis (1981). *Sindicato E Estado*. São Paulo, Ãtica.

Sinclair, Diane M. (1995). 'The Importance of Sex for the Propensity to Unionize', *British Journal of Industrial Relations*, 33 (2), (June).

Siqueira Neto, J. Francisco (1991) *Contrato Coletivo De Trabalho*. São Paulo: Editora LTR.

Siqueira Neto, J. Francisco (1994a) 'Contrato Coletivo de Trabalho', in Ministério do Trabalho e Centro de Estudos Sindiciais e de Economia do Trabalho da Unicamp, *O Mundo Do Trabalho: Crise E Mudança No Final Do Século*.

Siqueira Neto, J. Francisco (1994b) 'Contrato Coletivo de Trabalho no Brasil – Diferentes Propostas, Objetivos e Finalidades', in Ministério do Trabalho e Centro de Estudos Sindiciais e de Economia do Trabalho da Unicamp, *O Mundo Do Trabalho: Crise E Mudança No Final Do Século*.

Skidmore, Thomas (1988) *The Politics of Military Rule in Brazil, 1964–1985*. Oxford: Oxford University Press.

Skinner, Q. (1984) 'The Idea of Negative Liberty: Philosophical and Historical Perspectives', in Rorty, Schneewind and Skinner (eds), *Philosophy of History*.

Soares, José Arlindo (1982) *A Frente Do Recife E O Governo Do Arraes – Nacionalismo Em Crise: 1955–1964*. Rio de Janeiro: Paz e Terra.

Souza, Amaury de (1990) 'Do Corporativismo ao (Neo)Corporativismo: Dilemas da Reforma Sindical no Brasil', in *Modernização Política E Desenvolvimento*, Velloso, João Paulo dos Reis (ed.). Rio de Janeiro: José Olympio Editora.

Souza, Amaury de (1992a) 'Relações de Trabalho e Reforma Constitucional', mimeo, Instituto de Estudos Econômicos e Políticos de São Paulo – IDESP.

Souza, Amaury de (1992b) 'Sindicatos e Greves: A Visão do Público', in Lamounier, Bolívar (ed.), *Ouvindo O Brasil: Uma Análise Da Opinião Pública Hoje*. São Paulo: Editora Sumaré/Instituto Roberto Simonsen.

Steenbergen, Bart Van (1994a) *The Condition of Citizenship*. London: Sage Publications.

Steenbergen, Bart Van (1994b) 'The Condition of Citizenship: An Introduction', in Steenbergen, *The Condition of Citizenship*.

Stepan, Alfred (ed.) (1989) *Democratizing Brazil*. New York and Oxford: Oxford University Press.

Street, John (1994) 'Review Article: Political Culture – from Civic Culture to Mass Culture', *British Journal of Political Science*, vol. 24, pp. 95–114, Part 1, Janeiro.

Tilly, Charles (1995) 'Globalization Threatens Labor's Rights', *International Labor and Working-Class History*, no. 47 (Spring), pp. 1–23.

Topf, Richard (1989) 'Political Change and Political Culture in Britain, 1959–87, in Gibbins (ed.), *Contemporary Political Culture*.

308 *Sources*

Touraine, Alain (1988) *The Return of the Actor: Social Theory in post-Industrial Society*. Minneapolis: University of Minnesota Press.

Touraine, Alain (1989) *America Latina Politica Y Sociedad*. Madrid: Espasa-Calpe.

Townley, B. (1987) 'Union Recognition: A Comparative Analysis of the Pros and Cons of a Legal Procedure', *British Journal of Industrial Relations*, 25 (2), pp. 177–99.

Turner, B. (1992) 'Outline of a Theory of Citizenship', in Mouffe, C. (ed.) (1992), *Dimensions of Radical Democracy*.

Ubeku, A.K. (1983) *Industrial Relations in Developing Countries – The Case of Nigeria*. London: Macmillan Press.

Vianna, Luís Werneck (1986) 'A Cidadania do Trabalhador Urbano', in *A Construção Da Cidadania*, org. by Teixeira, J.G.L.C. Brasília: Editora Universidade de Brasília.

Vianna, Luís Werneck (1976) *Liberalismo e Sindicato no Brasil*. Rio de Janeiro: Paz e Terra.

Vianna, Oliveira (1987) *Populações Meridionais do Brasil*. Niterói: Editora da Universidade Federal Fluminense.

Velloso, João Paulo dos Reis (ed.) (1990) *Modernização Política e Desenvolvimento*. Rio de Janeiro: José Olympio Editora.

Wallington, P. (1993) *Butterworths Employment Law Handbook*. London: Butterworths.

Webb, Sidney and Beatrice [1894] *History of Trade Unionism*.

Wedderburn, Lord (ed.) (1983) *Labour Law and Industrial Relations: Building on Kahn Freund*. Oxford: Clarendon Press.

Wedderburn, Lord (1991) *Employment Rights in Britain and Europe*. London: Lawrence & Wishart.

Wedderburn, Lord (1995) *Labour Law and Freedom – Further Essays in Labour Law*. London: Lawrence & Wishart.

Weffort, Francisco (1973) 'Origens do Sindicalismo Populista no Brasil: A Conjuntura do Após-Guerra', *Estudos Cebrap*, 4, pp. 65–104.

Weffort, Francisco (1981) 'A Cidadania dos Trabalhadores', in Lamounier, Bolívar, Weffort, Francisco and Benevides, Maria Vitória (eds), *Direito, Cidadania e Participação*. São Paulo: TA Queiroz Editor.

Weffort, Francisco [1978] (1986) *O Populismo na Política Brasileira*. São Paulo: Paz e Terra.

Welch, Stephen (1993) *The Concept of Political Culture*. London: St. Martin's Press.

White, H. (1980) 'A Heteroskedasticity-Consistent Covariance Matrix Estimator and Direct Test for Heteroskedasticity', *Econometrica*, 48, pp. 817–38.

Wickham-Crowley, Timothy (1991) 'Approach to Latin American Revolutions', *International Journal of Comparative Sociology*, vol. XXXII.

Wolfe, Joel (1993) *Working Women, Working Men – São Paulo and the Rise of Brazil's Industrial Working Class, 1900–1955*. Durham: Duke University Press.

World Bank (1995) *World Development Report – Workers in an Integrating World*. Oxford: Oxford University Press.

Zald, Mayer Nathan and MacCarthy, John (eds) (1979) *The Dynamics of Social Movements: Resource Mobilization, Social Control, and Tactics.* Cambridge, Mass.: Winthrop Publishers.

Zapata, Francisco (1986) *El Conflicto Sindical En America Latina.* México: El Colegio de Mexico.

Zylberstajn, Helio (1993) 'Contrato Coletivo e Aprimoramento das Relações de Trabalho: para onde vamos?', *Estudos Econômicos*, São Paulo, IPE/USP, vol. 22, número especial.

Index